Indigenous
Confluences

Charlotte Coté and Coll Thrush

Series Editors

CHINOOK RESILIENCE

Heritage and Cultural Revitalization on the Lower Columbia River

JON D. DAEHNKE

Foreword by Tony A. Johnson

A Capell Family Book

UNIVERSITY OF WASHINGTON PRESS

Seattle and London

ILLUSTRATIONS

FOREWORD

A vibrant blue camas flower peeks out from under the low branches of a Douglas fir tree just across a ditch along a gravel road not frequently traveled.

Camas, a formerly abundant root food, doesn't go unnoticed in our families. Once it filled meadows edge to edge. Not so long ago, it flourished. Now it is relegated to a ditch, to some out of the way place. Away from the light its predecessors once enjoyed. Away from its former prominence. Eking out an existence in some undesired location.

The painful metaphor hidden under those branches doesn't go unnoticed either. When we, members of the Chinook Indian Nation, see that flower we see ourselves. We have been relegated to out of the way places. We have been uprooted from where we once flourished. We have been driven to the very edge of extinction.

"Look, kids, it's just like us." We have said it many times to our children. We have said it to the point that they are bored with it, but still we say it. This metaphor that we live alongside of, and that our children take for granted, matters. It is a reminder of a wealthy past. It is a reminder to not forget the struggles of our ancestors. It is a rallying cry to fight. The fight for our inheritance. The fight for something better than being relegated to out of the way places and away from our former prominence.

It is ironic that the territory of the five ancestral tribes of the Chinook Indian Nation is home today to tens of thousands of acres of preserved lands, refuges, set aside for the benefit and revitalization of those plants and animals in need of protection from the encroachment of "civilization." It is even more ironic that Chinook families were once removed to make way for this idealized "natural" environment.

So what about us, the human beings who have been here since time immemorial, since the last ice age and beyond? Surely we are as much a part of the environment that these refuges and lands seek to protect. Where is our protection? Where are our lands? Where is our refuge?

The minuscule amount of land that the Chinook Indian Nation does own today has been donated to us by our membership. Not a single acre has been set aside by the federal government for us within our aboriginal territory. The total is significantly less than five acres.

Rather than benevolent governmental efforts focused on our survival, we have had our lands taken without compensation, been denied access to our resources and forced to attend Indian boarding schools, schools with the stated intention of "kill the Indian, save the child." More recently it has simply been neglect and processes so thick with bureaucracy that we can't even know if our stated concerns have been heard, even when those concerns were sent daily for months on end (see "A Letter a Day," www.chinooknation.org).

Why is this? What have we done to deserve this fate? We have been the friends of the newcomers from the beginning. We have shown them how and where to access resources and live in this beautiful territory. We have stepped aside as more came. We have married them, loved them, and fought for them in every war and conflict since the nineteenth century. We still work alongside them, celebrate their successes, and mourn their losses.

Have we not lived up to their expectations? Have we abandoned too many of our villages? Do not enough of us speak our own languages? Do we not look exactly as they expect? Well, who we are today is wholly a product of their policies and desires. It is not of our making. We say unequivocally that they haven't lived up to our expectations.

Despite all of this, we survive. Some of us do speak our own languages. We invest countless hours volunteering to protect the lifeways and knowledge of our ancestors. We practice our culture in private, with our tribal neighbors and relatives and occasionally for public consumption. We live up to our obligations with the natural world. We acknowledge our *t'amanawas* (spirits), the gifts of the plant people, and we welcome the first salmon, even while we are denied the right to take a single fish from the waterways of our ancestors.

For us to step out of the shadows we must have access to resources, a land base, and unambiguous federal acknowledgment.

Our current unrecognized status never ceases to amaze. The presumption of people to judge us from thousands of miles away proves their astounding cultural ignorance and bias. All three thousand members of our community are undeniably descendants of the Lower Chinook, Clatsop, Kathlamet, Wahkiakum and Willapa Chinookans. The Bureau of Indian Affairs (BIA) has clearly acknowledged that fact. The non-Native residents of our territory know we are here and continue to express their dismay at our situation. Every local, state, and federal government agency, including the BIA, interacts with us regularly. Regional Indian agents, treaty parties, Congress, and the Supreme Court have acknowledged us.

Unlike the federal government, this book sees us for who we are. We didn't commission it. The author came to us out of his own interests and without the expectation of writing a book. We are profoundly grateful that he came (and continues to come) to our community and that he has witnessed us in our place. Without the blinders of government policy or the influence of others, he has seen us for who we are. What a gift it would be if the federal government would come to us in the same way.

Our children are the descendants of chiefs, canoe makers, weavers, tool-makers, orators, doctors, hunters, and fishermen. Descendants of a community pushed to the brink of extinction—pushed to the shadows of a great tree, alongside a road seldom traveled.

The true value of a book like this is a glimmer of sunlight—of hope that we may well one day be welcomed out of the shadows and once again given the chance to flourish openly where we have lived since time immemorial.

With sincere gratitude and a heartfelt thank-you to Jon, his wife Amy, and the readers.

TONY A. JOHNSON
Chair, Chinook Indian Nation

ACKNOWLEDGMENTS

Writing a book is always a collaborative process, and this may be even more true when the book itself, at its heart, is about collaborations. Over the course of the long and incredible journey that has led to the production of *Chinook Resilience,* I have been supported, guided, and inspired by friends, family, and professional colleagues. The truth is that this book would not exist without their many and varied forms of generosity. And while that generosity can never be fully repaid, I am thankful for the opportunity to acknowledge all that they have meant to me and to recognize their role in the completion of this project.

First I must express my deepest gratitude to the citizens of the Chinook Indian Nation. It truly has been an honor to have had the opportunity to work with them on this story and to get to know so many wonderful people in the process. There have been three chairs of the Chinook Indian Nation during the course of this project: Gary Johnson, Ray Gardner (now deceased), and Tony Johnson. All three of them were incredibly gracious with their time and knowledge. Given the strength and resilience demonstrated by each of them, it is no surprise that the Chinook as a nation are so strong and resilient. I also wish to thank Sam Robinson (current vice-chair), who spent many enjoyable hours with me talking about the history and culture of the Chinook, and Charles Funk, who in many ways served as the starting point for this collaborative project. Greg Robinson, Kate Elliott, and Jeremy Wekell also graciously offered their insights, and for this I am very appreciative. The Chinook could have been skeptical of this project given the dubious relationship between anthropologists and Indigenous communities historically. Instead they graciously welcomed me with kindness and friendship, and for this I am extremely grateful and humbled. I hope this book does their story justice.

My two primary mentors in the world of archaeology and anthropology are Ken Ames, emeritus professor of Portland State University, and Anan Raymond, regional archaeologist for the US Fish and Wildlife Service. Nearly everything I know about the anthropology of the Pacific Northwest, and much of what I know about anthropology in general, comes from Ken. He was an anchor for me in an academic career that has been a bit circuitous in its path, and for all of this I am eternally grateful. While Ken taught me about the anthropology of the Pacific Northwest, Anan taught me most of what I know about cultural resource management and applied anthropology. My internship with the US Fish and Wildlife Service changed the course of my career, and I owe this positive change in direction to all that Anan has taught me. Both Ken and Anan also established the collaborative groundwork with the Chinook Indian Nation that made my entry into this story possible in the first place. Although they never tout themselves as such, they are models for an ethical approach to the practice of anthropology. I'm thankful for their example and also proud to call both of them my friends.

While at the US Fish and Wildlife Service I had the good fortune to work with excellent colleagues. Alex Bourdeau taught me about the floodplain of the Columbia River and the joys of scientific curiosity, Virginia Parks served as a source of inspiration as she tirelessly worked to promote the cultural history of the Columbia River, Nick Valentine modeled the best in dedication to ethical public service, and Jorie Clark demonstrated boundless energy and optimism in the face of navigating bureaucratic mazes. Finally, they all offered many hours of laughter and friendship both while in the office and out in the field. I look at my years with the US Fish and Wildlife Service with great fondness.

Mike Iyall of the Cowlitz Indian Tribe graciously offered his time to share with me his thoughts on the history of the Columbia River and the Cowlitz Indian Tribe's place in that history, and Scott Aikin, national Native American liaison for the US Fish and Wildlife Service, offered excellent insights into the politics of heritage along the Columbia River. I am very grateful to both of them. I've had numerous conversations about the history of the river and the politics of heritage with Nathan Reynolds, an ethno-ecologist who is employed in the Natural Resources Department of the Cowlitz Indian Tribe. These conversations had a central impact on this book, and in fact it was Nathan who first directed me to the connections between Hale and Boas and the history of mapping in the Pacific Northwest. Jane Nelson and Johana Pintado (and now little Henry), provided a home away from home on my many research trips to Portland, and their kindness and friendship made an already enjoyable project even more worthwhile.

Numerous academic colleagues played a central role in the development of this book. Sonya Atalay, a friend and colleague, provided a model for collaboration that I have tried my best to emulate. Lynn Meskell provided an avenue for my first publication resulting from this project, and her recognition that this work had value to the field provided a boost of confidence at an early stage in the process. The initial seeds of this work as a book-length project were planted when I was a graduate student at Berkeley, and I'm thankful to my fellow classmates there, including David Cohen, Donna Gillette, Esteban Gómez, Sara Gonzalez, Doris Maldanado, Ora Marek-Martinez, Mark McCoy, Shanti Morell-Hart, Lee Panich, Andy Roddick, Liz Soluri, Burcu Tung, and Sven Ouzman, for their help in the process.

From the fall of 2007 to the spring of 2011 I was fortunate to hold a fellowship in the Introduction to the Humanities (IHUM) program at Stanford University. This fellowship provided stable employment, financial resources, and some time to write at a stage when this project was moving from a loose collection of ideas to a more formalized framework. I thank Ellen Woods for giving me the opportunity in IHUM, and I thank Stacey Caro, Galen Davis, Justin Higinbotham Lind, and Laura Rossi for the administrative support. While with IHUM I worked with numerous inspirational Stanford faculty, including Scott Bukatman, Ian Hodder, Henry Lowood, and Barb Voss. I also was surrounded with brilliant fellow colleagues, whose intellects and example helped to shape the direction of this book. For that I thank Lalaie Ameeriar, Jenny Barker, Maggie Barrera, Renu Capelli, William Carter, Kathleen Coll, Dan Contreras, John Corbally, Gary DeVore, Michael Feola, Melissa Ganz, Phil Horky, Ulrike Krotscheck, Kathryn Lafrenz Samuels, Kathryn Mathers, Zena Meadowsong, Alice Petty, Christy Pichichero, Uzma Rizvi, Matt Sayre, Melissa Colleen Stevenson, Bulbul Tiwari, Hsuan Tsen, Candace West, Josh Wright, and Gabe Wolfenstein.

Portions of this book were written while I was a visiting research associate at the School for Advanced Research (SAR) during the first two-thirds of the 2013–14 academic year. This position not only offered some much-needed time to write in beautiful Santa Fe but also gave me the benefit of being part of a cohort of scholars that I will never forget. Patricia Baudino, Abigail Bigham, Kent Blansett, Debbie Boehm, Philippe Bourgois, Jason De León, Laurie Hart, Islah Jad, George Karandinos, He Li, Amy Lonetree, Máijá Tailfeathers, and Jordan Wilson were not only my cohorts at SAR, they are all also world-class scholars and intellectuals who constantly challenged and sharpened my thinking. They are also some of the most kind, thoughtful, and fun folks I've ever met. I still miss all of them tremendously and often think of our gatherings in the SAR Billiards Room, our trips to Pueblo feast days, and our adventure at an alien-themed roller-skating rink. I also thank former SAR president James Brooks and the administrative staff at SAR for putting the class of 2013–14 together. That class truly is one of a kind.

The University of California, Santa Cruz, has been my academic home since the fall of 2011 and is a constant source of inspiration, resources, and stability. During my first two years at UCSC I was a visiting assistant professor in American Studies, where I worked with a wonderful set of students and fellow faculty. I thank Kimberly Lau, Eric Porter, and Catherine Ramírez for their support during my enjoyable time in that department. Beginning in the fall of 2013 I joined the Anthropology Department at UCSC. My colleagues there have been a source of inspiration and encouragement, even before I officially joined the department. Danilyn Rutherford was the chair when I was hired, and her optimism, professionalism, and unbounded energy helped to move my hiring forward, even when it looked like the position might disappear into the ether. For this I am eternally grateful. Mark Anderson, Chelsea Blackmore, Don Brenneis, Lissa Caldwell, Nancy Chen, Shelly Errington, Lars Fehren-Schmitz, Mayanthi Fernando, Diane Gifford-Gonzalez, Judith Habicht Mauche, Susan Harding, Andrew Mathews, J. Cameron Monroe, Megan Moodie, Olga Najera-Ramirez, Vicky Oelze, Triloki Pandey, Renya Ramirez, Lisa Rofel, Tsim Schneider, Anna Tsing, and Jerry Zee have all been inspirational in their own ways and have helped to shape this book. I also thank Fred Deakin, Taylor Ainslie, Molly Segale, and Richard Baldwin, who are without a doubt the best departmental staff at UCSC. It's a wonderful thing to work in a department that is collegial, that is made up of brilliant minds, and whose members not only tolerate my hybridity within the field of anthropology but actually celebrate it. Those of you who know the nature of anthropology departments across the academy know that this is not always the case, and the project I'm presenting in this book might not have been as strongly supported everywhere. I am very grateful that I work in a department where it is.

I'm thankful that this book has found a perfect home at the University of Washington Press. I've worked with three editors during this process: Marianne Keddington-Lang at an early stage of this project, Ranjit Arab as the book took a more solid form, and Larin McLaughlin as it was ushered to its conclusion. All three were very helpful, and I am thankful for their assistance and support. I'm also grateful to the series editors of Indigenous Confluences, Coll Thrush and Charlotte Coté, who offered their support to the book from the beginning. Niccole Coggins (assistant editor) and the marketing and design teams handled the nitty-gritty details that I often overlooked and have made the book look far better than I imagined it could. I am also thankful to the two anonymous reviewers who offered excellent suggestions and improved the book overall.

I would like to thank my family, most notably my parents, Harold and Dede Daehnke. Not only have they supported me throughout my life—financially, emotionally, and in any number of additional ways—but they both have also provided excellent examples of how to live a good life. My father loved history and was curious about other people and other cultures. Given this, it is probably no surprise that I eventually ended up in anthropology and doing this type of project. He is no longer with us, but I think that he would have enjoyed this book, and that means the world to me. My mother is perhaps the strongest and most steadfast person that I know. She approaches the challenges of life with a sense of optimism and resilience, and whenever I faced challenges while writing this book it was her example that helped me to move forward. My gratitude and love to both; this book would not have been possible without them.

My final note of thanks goes to my partner, Amy Lonetree. Without question the completion of this book owes the most to her. I would not have been able to finish this project without Amy's unwavering support from the very beginning, her help in clarifying conceptual paths during those points when I was at a crossroads, and her patience with me as this book occasionally tested my own patience. Her confidence in the book, her own brilliance, and her love always helped me through. Perhaps most significantly, she provided for me an example of the importance of relevant and grounded scholarship and a continual reminder that the best work has service as its goal. I can't imagine having taken this journey without her, and I am grateful every day that she is in my life. This book is dedicated to her.

CHINOOK RESILIENCE

fully in chapter 1, a tribe's "identity"—as demonstrated by such things as continuity, cohesiveness, and distinctiveness—is used to determine if a tribe should be recognized. Within the context of federal recognition, however, these standards of identity are strongly steeped in anthropological (rather than tribal) assumptions, and anthropologists quite often play a role in recognition determinations. Anthropologist Les Field has written extensively on the role that anthropologists and anthropological assumptions play in the process of federal acknowledgment. He notes that "indigenous groups in the United States that are not federally recognized tribes must undertake the unforgiving and Byzantine acknowledgment process if they want to obtain the minimal rights that such status conveys. This process is, of course, based on some of the most egregious and rigid essentialist discourse anthropology has ever produced."[6] While the arena of the Federal Acknowledgment Process is certainly not the only place where the legacies of colonialism are made manifest on questions of tribal identity and "authenticity" (including the role of anthropology in that process), it is certainly a centrally important one for the non-recognized Chinook Indian Nation.[7]

It is important to note, however, that although anthropology is widely recognized as one of the disciplines most directly implicated with a colonial and imperial history it is by no means the only one. As Linda Tuhiwai Smith points out, the legacies of colonialism are present in any number of Western disciplines: "Although many indigenous writers would nominate anthropology as representative of all that is truly bad about research, it is not my intention to single out one discipline over another as representative of what research has done to indigenous peoples. I argue that, in their foundations, Western disciplines are as much implicated in each other as they are in imperialism. Some, such as anthropology, made the study of us into 'their' science, others were employed in the practices of imperialism in less direct but far more devastating ways."[8]

As a trained anthropologist myself, I am certainly aware of and recognize the problematic and colonial history of my chosen discipline. But as I will demonstrate throughout this book, historians, geographers, explorers, politicians, and priests and ministers—just to name a few—are all involved in the legacies of colonialism, typically in ways that are intertwined and mutually reinforcing. Furthermore, the central point here is that the effects of these legacies are not relics of the past but rather continue to shape the world of Indigenous communities in the present. As Gary Johnson, current Chinook Tribal Council member and former chair of the Chinook Indian Nation has stated, "We're not talking about ancient history, we're talking about things that are still happening today."[9]

HERITAGE, RECIPROCITY, AND PROTOCOL

My aim in this section is to offer a brief introduction of the concept of heritage and a short description of what I have come to view as its most important aspects, namely the centrality of reciprocity and protocol to the practice of heritage. My intent here is not to offer an exhaustive discussion of the topic of heritage or to give a history of its development as a field of practice and study.[10] Instead, a fuller view of what this all encompasses should further unfold for the reader as the book progresses. For the moment, however, I will start with a definition of heritage as described by Rodney Harrison, an expert in the field of heritage studies. Harrison notes that while *heritage* is a term that is both ambiguous and broad, it is possible to recognize that "heritage is not a 'thing' or a historical or political movement, but refers to a set of attitudes to, and relationships with, the past. These relationships are characterised by a reverence and attachment to select objects, places and practices that are thought to connect with or exemplify the past in some way." Heritage is, therefore, a form of remembering that is centrally entangled with the importance of the past. But although rooted in the past, Harrison also notes, it is fundamentally about the present: "Perhaps most importantly, heritage is formed in the present and reflects inherited and current concerns about the past."[11] In effect, heritage is the way that we, as cultures and societies, meaningfully constitute the past in the present and give it purpose.

To a greater or lesser extent, all cultures and societies place importance on the past. While there are certainly a variety of ways to approach the past in the present, the modern West—at least at the level of the state or nation—has bureaucratized heritage. This has been done through the creation of a series of policies, regulations, and laws designed to protect and organize heritage. (Many of these laws will be addressed in this book.) For instance, in the United States, at the federal level, we have laws such as the Antiquities Act, the National Historic Preservation Act (NHPA), the National Environmental Policy Act (NEPA), the Archaeological Resources Protection Act (ARPA), and the Native American Graves Protection and Repatriation Act (NAGPRA). All of these laws require the federal government to, at a minimum, demonstrate some level of concern and consideration for archaeological and historical sites, as well as historical objects that hold cultural importance. In order to comply with these mandates, federal and state agencies and numerous private firms are staffed with "experts" whose jobs entail ensuring that the appropriate paperwork and procedures for compliance are used. Typically, at least in the United States, the experts are archaeologists, but architectural historians, conservationists, cultural anthropologists, and museum professionals, just to name a few, are also often involved. The process of complying with the various laws, regulations, and policies surrounding the past is often referred to as *cultural resource management*, often shortened to CRM. In the West, "management" of heritage tends to focus on material objects, preservation/conservation, categorization, and recordation, and, as Rodney Harrison explains, the idea of heritage in the Western context cannot be separated from this: "Heritage, at least insofar as those agencies charged with managing it are concerned, cannot exist independently of a process of categorising, ordering, listing and subsequently conserving and/or archiving it."[12] One result of the equation of heritage with a process of categorization is the creation of lists of places designated historically and culturally important, such as the National Register of Historic Places in the United States or UNESCO's World Heritage List at the international level.

The vision of heritage as a managed bureaucracy directed by state-sanctioned experts whose job it is to categorize and archive is referred to as "official heritage" by Harrison and is part of the "authorized heritage discourse" as described by Laurajane Smith.[13] This approach to heritage tends to focus on places associated with important individuals or events or that may hold academic or scientific research value. It also tends to emphasize the tangible (objects that can be held, measured, and recorded) over the intangible (such as cultural practices, expressions, or knowledge).[14] It is not, however, a universally shared approach to the importance of the past in the present, and this can lead to disconnection and tension between official heritage managers and those communities or individuals outside of that sphere. The potential for discord is especially likely in settler colonial nations where heritage officials—predominantly descendants of colonists—are often managing the heritage of those Indigenous cultures that have been displaced by colonial invasion. The problems that can arise in these situations are not just a result of simple differences in perspective but can also reflect a deep-seated need for colonial invaders to erase or minimize the reality of a long history of Indigenous occupation of the landscape prior to the arrival of colonizers. Harrison suggests that "because of their peculiar colonial histories, heritage management in settler societies must work to metaphorically and/or physically erase the traces of prior indigenous occupation as a way of emphasising the roots of contemporary nationhood in colonial settlement."[15] When the traces of Indigenous occupation cannot easily be physically erased or ignored, heritage experts (most often non-Indigenous) minimize this by transferring to themselves the authority over these sites and objects from the Indigenous communities to which they are tied. Furthermore, the importance of these sites and objects tends to rest in their scientific and research value as examples of past lifeways rather than their cultural importance to Indigenous communities in the present.

Deborah Bird Rose and Rodney Harrison, in a set of writings published both separately and collaboratively, argue that rather than the categorization and preservation of objects and places from the past more typical of Western approaches to heritage, Indigenous views of heritage tend to emphasize ongoing relationships and interactions.[16] Furthermore, these relationships and interactions occur not only between humans and other humans, but between humans and nonhumans as well. They refer to this as *dialogical heritage*: "A dialogical concept of heritage suggests that heritage making is interactive—meaningfulness arises out of encounter and dialogue among multiple subjects, some of whom are human. Place (construed interactively) may also be a subject in its own right. . . . Communication runs through living systems, including land and people. The processes and practices of keeping the past alive in the present, like the practices and processes of keeping the future alive in the present, is collaborative. We are not alone (as humans) and while we certainly are meaning-making beings, we are not the only ones."[17] This view of heritage— one based on dialogue and collaborations with a multiplicity of actors and objects—certainly matches my own experiences working alongside the Chinook Indian Nation and their approach to the importance of the past in the present. I, however, tend to refer to this as *reciprocal heritage* in order to emphasize the point that heritage in these cases is not just dialogue and connections but is most importantly made up of reciprocal responsibilities between actors (both human and nonhuman). The terms of these reciprocal responsibilities are defined in protocols, the rules of behavior that come from the past but that must be followed to ensure the future. As Claire Poirier describes, "Acts of protocol [are] intended to reinforce the relational, reciprocal connection between and among human and non-human agents. In acts of protocol, all facets of the wider collective of agents—both human and nonhuman—are engaging in reciprocal exchange. . . . Appropriately carrying out protocol . . . is crucial to maintain and safeguard not only [the] contemporary community and familial network of ceremonial connections but also . . . the intergenerational kinship ties that continually govern through the laws of protocol."[18] As I will demonstrate in the rest of the book, protocols are essential to the Chinook Indian Nation (as well as other Indigenous nations on the Pacific Northwest), and following them is necessary for connecting the past to the present, and the present to the future.

THE IMPORTANCE OF PLACE AND SPACE

The foundational position of place and space to questions of heritage, Indigenous identity, and colonial legacies has become increasingly apparent to me during my years of work on these questions in the Pacific Northwest and is a necessary undercurrent to this book. My thinking on place and space has developed out of direct observation, but it has also been informed by the work of a number of scholars exploring the connections between place, space, and heritage. I will address some of these scholars specifically later.[19] For the moment, however, I will note that I approach questions of place and space in the following ways. First, I view place as central to human experience. As humans we are born in place—place comes first—and it is through our concrete experience of place that we come to make sense of the world. The experience of place is what creates a sense of rootedness and attachment and serves as a container for memory. Heritage, as a form of remembering within the context of attachment, is therefore often tied directly to place. This is especially true for Indigenous communities like the Chinook Indian Nation, communities that have been rooted to particular landscapes for generations and whose identities and claims to sovereignty are directly attached to long-term persistence in place. This long-term rootedness creates a view of place that is very particular and heterogeneous. Each place has its own identity and its own importance.[20]

Second, although place is primary and central to human existence, its role has been undercut by an emphasis on "space." Space is the result of place made abstract. The concrete details and experienced aspects of place are replaced by spaces emptied of attachments. As such, space becomes universal (rather than specific) and can be defined by Cartesian coordinates, easily measured, mapped, and managed. The emphasis on space over place is the consequence of a particularly Western view on spatiality, one that served as advantageous to European imperialism and colonialism. A focus on space over place was— and still is—an important tool that gave imperial and colonial agents the ability to disassociate Indigenous populations from their own long-occupied landscapes, and to transfer those lands into the hands of Euro-American colonizers. Both of these iterations—place as a container of memory, rootedness, and identity; space as abstract, empty, and bureaucratic—are present to varying degrees in the pages that follow and are a central component of the story of the Chinook Indian Nation.

HISTORY OF CONNECTIONS

This book results from a history of chance and interconnections. My personal and professional entanglement with the history and heritage of the Columbia River goes back to the late summer of 1999 when I moved to Portland, Oregon, to begin graduate work in anthropology at Portland State University. My advisor at Portland State, Kenneth Ames, had recently been selected as one of the scholars tasked with compiling a "cultural affiliation" report for the US Department of the Interior regarding the Kennewick Man (Ancient One) case. Two other Portland State graduate students and I assisted Ken with the report, primarily by tracking down and organizing bibliographic sources and compiling lists of radiocarbon dates and other archaeological data. Although I did not have a direct hand in drafting the text, the case and the cultural affiliation report immediately and directly introduced me to the contentious question of Native American identity along the river. I learned the strong connection that present-day Native Americans feel with ancestral remains—regardless of the depth of age of those remains. The experience also provided me with a bit of a behind-the-scenes view of the ways that the federal government and the legal system (rather than Native Americans themselves) hold the power to determine who is or is not an "authentic" Native American, as well as the roles that archaeology and anthropology often play in that process. My experience with this case altered my career trajectory.

A few months afterward, in the spring of 2000, I was offered employment with the US Fish and Wildlife Service (USFWS). Specifically, I was given the opportunity to work as an archaeologist for the USFWS Cultural Resources Team headquartered in Sherwood, Oregon, and under the supervision of Anan Raymond, a regional archaeologist for the USFWS. The Cultural Resources Team was responsible for managing and overseeing archaeological and historic sites located within the boundaries of federal national wildlife refuges—as well as any sites that might be located on the property of private landowners who were receiving funds from the USFWS—in the states of Washington,

Oregon, Idaho, Nevada, California, and Hawaii. This was my first extended experience with the world of cultural resource management (CRM), especially within the context of federal government management of archaeological sites and other aspects of cultural heritage. It was also my introduction to the process of compliance with federal cultural resource laws, most notably the NHPA. I learned a great deal about "managing" cultural heritage from Anan and my colleagues during my tenure at the USFWS. For instance, I learned that the successful "management" of cultural heritage is really more about establishing relationships, collaborating, and negotiating differences with all of those communities and stakeholders who are interested in the past than it is about archaeological excavation and research. It also became apparent to me during my work at the USFWS that the mandates of federal policy and law, the value and purpose that is attached to the past, and the government's definition of what constitutes heritage often do not reflect or completely coincide with the views of the communities whose ancestry is connected to these sites—thus making the role of relationships, collaboration, and negotiation all the more important.

My work at the USFWS was also interconnected with my graduate studies and academic life at Portland State. One of the archaeological sites that Anan and his USFWS team are in charge of overseeing is Cathlapotle, a Native American village within the boundaries of the Ridgefield National Wildlife Refuge near Ridgefield, Washington. Just off of the Columbia River, Cathlapotle was occupied from roughly A D 1450 into the 1830s or 1840s, well into the period of contact with Euro-Americans. It was also one of the Native American villages visited by Lewis and Clark. Archaeological work at the site began in the early 1990s and was conducted under the umbrella of the Cathlapotle Archaeological Project, a partnership between the USFWS, Portland State, and the Chinook Indian Nation. Ken Ames from Portland State served as the principal investigator for the archaeological research. Therefore, as part of Raymond's team and one of Ames's students, I had a double connection with the site.

Although excavations at the site had ended a few years before my arrival at Portland State, research and interpretation of the excavated material was ongoing, and a number of my fellow graduate students were writing master's theses related to the archaeology of the site. My own graduate research at Portland State was a bit more broad-based and addressed the role that archaeological methods could positively play in models of education, as well as the importance of including discussions of research methods in all of our archaeological public outreach.[21] As a component of this work, however, I created a public outreach booklet on the archaeology and history of Cathlapotle, and this was eventually published by the USFWS.[22] The bicentennial of Lewis and Clark's Corps of Discovery was looming on the horizon, and the memory and celebration of their brief voyage along the Columbia River was rapidly overshadowing the much longer history of Indigenous peoples in the region. Therefore, part of the purpose of the booklet was to shift focus back to the people of Cathlapotle and their generations of occupation on that landscape.

The booklet was created in collaboration with Charles Funk, an artist who illustrated it. A citizen of the Chinook Indian Nation, Charlie has served as a member of both the Chinook Tribal Council and the Culture Committee. His beautiful illustrations profoundly enhanced the booklet, but they also helped to shape my understanding of Cathlapotle and Chinookan culture. My partnership with Charlie on this project was just the first in a series of dialogues on the history and heritage of the Columbia River that I would have with citizens of the Chinook Indian Nation over the years. Other Chinook citizens—Gary and Tony Johnson, Sam Robinson, Katherine Elliott, Ray Gardner, and Greg Robinson, to name just a few—have shared with me their knowledge about and direct experience of Chinookan history and heritage. It is important to note, however, that I was fortunate to have been introduced to the heritage of the Columbia River in an environment where collaboration and trust had already been established. Building respectful and effective collaborations can be difficult and time-consuming, but citizens of the Chinook Indian Nation, Anan Raymond and his team at the USFWS, and Ken Ames had spent years developing mutually respectful and positive relationships. While others in the field of archaeology were perhaps garnering more attention and building careers based on their collaborative efforts, Anan and Ken were more quietly, but just as completely, producing groundbreaking collaborative work. This preexisting framework of collaboration between Anan, Ken, and the Chinook Indian Nation greatly facilitated—and in fact made possible—my entry into the conversation, and my part in these conversations has now continued for more than a decade and a half.

METHODS AND COLLABORATIONS

I have arrived at *Chinook Resilience* by navigating the overlaps and interstices of a few closely related methodologies and after wading through a diverse range of data and sources. Certainly a good portion of this book is owed to the types of conversations I mentioned in the previous paragraph. Some of these conversations were conducted formally with tribal members, government officials, and archaeologists—all individuals who are or were directly involved with cultural heritage concerns along the Columbia River. These include Scott Aikin (USFWS), Kenneth Ames (Portland State University), Kate Elliott (Chinook Indian Nation), Mike Iyall (Cowlitz Indian Tribe), Gary Johnson (Chinook Indian Nation), Tony Johnson (Chinook Indian Nation), Anan Raymond (USFWS), and Sam Robinson (Chinook Indian Nation). There were also, however, hundreds of conversations that were much less formal and that occurred over cups of coffee, while riding in vans driving out to archaeological sites, in office meetings, while paddling in canoes, and at tribal ceremonies and feasts. Many occurred while I was observing or directly participating in a range of both public and private cultural heritage events. In several ways these sustained series of participations and conversations, both formal and informal, served as the emotional driver of my research, and they form the heart of the book.

Chinook Resilience is also, however, the result of explorations and considerations of a range of historical documents, archival materials, and archaeological work. During the course of the development of this book I have analyzed letters of correspondence between Franz Boas and Horatio Hale, the text of treaties drawn between tribal nations in the Pacific Northwest and the US government, legal documents from Indian Claims Commission (ICC) cases, governmental decisions regarding tribal recognition, internal memos and correspondence from government bureaucracies, and a host of historical maps. These primary documents—in conjunction with a rich suite of available secondary material from fields like anthropology, history, Native American studies, and cultural heritage studies—have, I hope, led to a book that is both comprehensive and critically well informed. Additionally, I am trained as an archaeologist, and many of my earliest introductions to the history and heritage of the Columbia River stem from archaeological research and understandings. I have worked on a number of archaeological projects in the region in the past, and I am part of an ongoing project that focuses on long-term use of landscape in the river's floodplain. In its earliest conceptual iterations, I envisioned that this book would be primarily tethered to archaeological sites, especially those sites located within the Ridgefield National Wildlife Refuge. Although the scope of this book dramatically expanded beyond those sites and boundaries—in both a geographic and conceptual sense—that early archaeological influence is still strongly present. Archaeological sites still play a central role in the discussions of this book, and a concern with the interplay between material and culture (a hallmark of an archaeological mind-set) underlies much of what follows.

Given this background, my research for this book could be situated under the umbrella of what Lynn Meskell calls *archaeological ethnography*, a form of hybrid practice that combines standard ethnographic approaches with archaeological insight.[23] Archaeological ethnography therefore includes much of what you would expect: interviews with descendant communities, participation in and observation of heritage events, analyses of public representations of the past, and archival research. But it does so within the anchoring context of the role archaeology and archaeologists play in the production of heritage. The application of ethnographic approaches to the study of archaeologically related practices has certainly increased over the years. This includes efforts by both cultural anthropologists (who do not necessarily have direct training in archaeology), as well as those by anthropologists who are trained as archaeologists (as is the case with this book).[24] But in either case, although archaeology provides the research framework, the focus of archaeological ethnography is not on the past. Rather, the goal is to understand how archaeology gets used and incorporated into meaningful constructions of the past in the present. As Meskell notes, archaeological ethnography ultimately attempts to help us "know the ways in which archaeology works in the world."[25]

In her book *The Nature of Heritage in South Africa*, Meskell notes that although her project began by focusing on the role played by archaeology in shaping stories about the past, it quickly and necessarily moved beyond this focus and included analysis of such things as the complex relationship between nature and culture, questions about biodiversity and conservation, and issues of race and identity. Her work on heritage therefore came "to embrace a much larger framing" as she realized that "an archaeology of archaeology alone would not suffice."[26] My experience while conducting the research that has ultimately led to this book is similar. In the many conversations that I've had during the years of research, discussions nearly always moved beyond the realm of archaeology. Even when the starting point for discussion was based in questions surrounding the practice of archaeology and the role of archaeology in shaping the past, the conversation quickly moved to other topics: public interpretation of history, cultural memory, fishing rights, federal recognition, canoe gatherings, language revitalization, food and diet, tribal sovereignty, and protocol, just to name a few. While archaeology remains one of the ways for making claims on the past in the present, it is only one (and often not even the centrally important one). For this reason I instead prefer to think of this project as *heritage ethnography,* a term used by Charlotte Andrews.[27] The use of *heritage ethnography* emphasizes that the focus of study is on the concept of heritage and all of the varied aspects that fit underneath that umbrella (e.g., identity, law, language, historical interpretation, land, and archaeology), rather than either a more traditional ethnography, where the focus of study is on a particular culture, or one that is more specifically focused on and driven by archaeology.

The methods that led to this book can also be considered as a form of *collaborative ethnography.* The project was developed in direct communication and collaboration with citizens of the Chinook Indian Nation, and it was initially presented to and approved by both the Tribal Council and the Culture Committee. My dialogue with Chinook citizens continued throughout the research and writing process, and they offered analysis and also initiated discussions on the representations of their own histories and culture. Drafts of all of the chapters were shared with members of the Tribal Council and the Culture Committee, and together we discussed any suggested additions, subtractions, or modifications of emphasis. Although I discussed the work with a number of tribal members, the most detailed and concentrated discussions were with Tony Johnson, who was the chair of the Culture Committee when the project started and was elected tribal chair as the drafting of the book neared completion. While the final wording and form was ultimately up to me, the overall goal of this sustained collaborative effort was to create a book that in the end is, at least in part, a co-creation of the Chinook Indian Nation and myself.

By working in close conjunction with the Chinook Indian Nation on this book I am attempting to emulate the work of a body of scholars who have increasingly moved toward collaborative methods. One of these scholars, Les Field, has engaged with and written extensively on the benefits, challenges, and motivations surrounding collaborative ethnographic work, especially within the context of collaborations between anthropologists and Indigenous communities.[28] Field notes that collaborative ethnographies shift the locus of authority away from exclusively resting with anthropologists and toward one that is shared. Indigenous citizens become co-creators of scholarship, and their role in the process of ethnography changes from what it had been historically: "The production of such ethnographies . . . hinges on profound relations of collaboration between anthropologists and individuals who were called 'informants' in the past, but who some now call 'interlocutors' or 'collaborators,' among other terms."[29] The desired result of this shared authority is a narrative that is more inclusive and multivocal, as well as more relevant to those communities whose stories are actually being told.[30]

It is important to note, however, that although Indigenous voices are now more often directly present in anthropological research than they were in the past, this should not be taken as an indication of enlightenment on the part of anthropologists. The greater inclusion of Native American voice in both ethnographic and archaeological work is more the result of a history of Indigenous activism than it is a sudden rapprochement generated within the halls of anthropology departments. Indigenous communities have long demanded greater control over the telling of their own stories and the representations of their own cultures, and in recent decades those calls for a more meaningful participation in the process of knowledge production have been increasingly recognized both as a matter of policy and law and as part of a changing body of ethics among academics (although there certainly remain those who actively and stubbornly oppose this change). As Les Field notes, "Collaborative research and writing are important not because anthropologists have suddenly decided to make them so but, rather, because they are obliged to work and write in this way by new relationships with the world in which they work."[31] In effect, tribal activism has shifted the landscape of anthropology, creating those "new relationships," and it has done so in a positive direction. The result is a "world in which we work" where collaborative projects—which one hopes are more inclusive and relevant to tribal communities—are no longer anomalous.

Working collaboratively with Indigenous nations in the United States is also typically very different than working collaboratively with other types of stakeholder communities. This difference stems from the unique position that tribes hold both in terms of legal status and a long and damaging entanglement with colonial histories. Historian Katrine Barber, who also works collaboratively with the Chinook Indian Nation, notes that, "simply put, Indigenous partners are not like other partners with whom we engage. Indigenous partners have unique, legally defined, ongoing relationships with a colonizing United States and individual states."[32] At the heart of this uniqueness is recognition that tribal communities are sovereign and self-determining entities, and as collaborative partners they should be treated as such. As academic researchers, one way to respect this sovereignty and self-determination is to work directly with collaborators and collaborative bodies that tribal members deem appropriate, rather than work with individuals who may be speaking only for themselves or who lie outside or at the peripheries of the community. As Barber points out, "although many communities have 'gatekeepers' whose approval and collaboration are integral to the success of projects, those individuals do not represent separate sovereign nations. But cultural committees and councils do. A decolonized practice requires collaborative processes grounded in and respectful of Indigenous sovereignty and self-determination."[33]

This does not mean, of course, that the community is united in a single voice or that there are not a multitude of perspectives on issues. Of course there are disagreements and dissenting viewpoints, as well as individuals who are better informed, more interested, or more willing to speak about certain topics than other members of the community. This is certainly the case with the Chinook Indian Nation, and it is not my intent in the following pages to suggest that the Chinook are unified in their beliefs or their approaches to the value of the past in the present. What it does mean, however, is that respecting sovereignty requires us as researchers to follow the protocols as established by the community, to adhere to community government structures and hierarchies, and to work with experts as identified by the community itself. The authority for knowledge production, therefore, lies with the community at an official level, rather than at the level of a set of self-interested individuals. This is why it was important for me to work directly with the Tribal Council and Culture Committee of the Chinook Indian Nation on the creation of this book.

Finally, I should note that the story of colonial legacies and entanglements that I am presenting in this book necessarily includes other tribal nations in the greater Columbia River and Pacific Northwest regions. Most notably, this includes the Cowlitz Indian Tribe and the Quinault Indian Nation, but also the Shoalwater Bay Tribe, the Confederated Tribes of Grand Ronde, the Chehalis Tribe, and many others. While each of these nations has its own unique history, they were all dramatically affected by colonialism. Furthermore, they all have histories that intertwine, in dynamic and complex ways, with Chinook histories both before and after colonial invasion. This book, however, is principally about the challenges that the Chinook Indian Nation faces in its efforts to control its own history, its experiences with places of heritage, and its ability to remain culturally resilient in the face of colonial legacies. These issues are viewed through a Chinook lens. Therefore, while the involvement and interconnections of other tribal nations is noted in this book, and their voice is occasionally included, the voice of the Chinook Indian Nation is given prominence. This should not be taken as an assertion that the viewpoints of the

Chinook Indian Nation outweigh all others but rather as a result of the scope and purpose of the book.

LAYOUT OF THE BOOK

In addition to this introduction, the book contains five chapters and a conclusion. The five chapters do two primary things: they provide the reader with the necessary history and background to make the arguments throughout the book understandable, and they offer a series of episodes of heritage encounters. Although it was not my initial intent to settle on five central chapters—the layout of the book developed somewhat organically—the number of chapters seems apropos since five is the central number in Chinookan culture. Chapter 1 offers a focused history, and it does so through addressing that history by means of a set of nested geographies, starting with the Pacific Northwest Coast as a region. My emphasis in this first section is on the Indigenous cultures that made this region their home for millennia, as well as the central role that the Pacific Northwest played in the development of anthropology as a discipline and the long history of entanglement between Indigenous people and anthropologists. The next section of the chapter focuses on the lower Columbia River, that portion of the river that stretches from The Dalles in present-day Oregon to the river's mouth at the Pacific Ocean. This area was historically densely populated by Indigenous groups, but it was also dramatically impacted by Euro-American invasion beginning in the eighteenth-century. The impacts of disease, white settlement, and the treaty process shaped and imposed conceptions of Native identity and fundamentally and forever altered the lives of Indigenous people living on the river. The final section of the chapter focuses on the Chinook Indian Nation, a present-day tribal organization that represents the five westernmost Chinookan tribes. Of central importance is the Chinook Indian Nation's status as a federally non-recognized tribe, their continuing struggle for recognition, and their cultural resilience despite the lack of recognition.

The focus of chapter 2 is on the archaeological excavations of Cathlapotle, a Native American village located on the Columbia River that was inhabited at the time of first contact between Indigenous populations and Euro-Americans and that is located within the current boundaries of a federal national wildlife refuge. The excavation of Cathlapotle was undertaken jointly by the US Fish and Wildlife Service and Portland State University, in direct consultation with the Chinook Indian Nation. The site's cultural connection to the Chinook

diseases like smallpox, measles, malaria, and influenza that had devastating effects on the people who had lived on the land for generations. The epidemics didn't stop, nor did the invasion of waves of new settlers who brought with them colonial attitudes and government policies that further served to separate the original inhabitants from their own land. The combined effects of disease, invasive settlement, and colonial policies left the people of the river on the brink of extinction.

But they did not go extinct. The descendants of these people still live on the river and coast today, and their lives continue to be shaped by the legacies of this long history. A central argument of this book is that present-day conflicts over Indigenous heritage spaces can only be understood through a historical lens that includes the reality and consequences of colonial entanglements. The goal of this chapter is to provide that necessary long-term view. It is neither my intent nor is it within the scope of this chapter to provide an exhaustive account of the history of the Pacific Northwest, the Columbia River, or the Chinook Indian Nation.[1] Instead the goal is to provide sufficient historical background to address the questions that serve as the foundation for the rest of the book. As such, the chapter is written with some of the following questions in mind: How did Indigenous populations of the region and the river organize their societies? What were the immediate effects of contact with Euro-American populations? How did colonial attitudes and policies shape the actions of government agents and scholars? What is the long-term effect of these attitudes and policies, and how does the Chinook Indian Nation address these effects in the present?

I approach the history of the region through a series of nested geographies. The first and most expansive of these geographies is that of the Pacific Northwest Coast of North America. The Pacific Northwest is an area that is iconic in terms of the Indigenous cultures that made and still make the area their home and for the central role that the region played in the development of American anthropology. The second geography is that of the lower Columbia River, the portion of the river that stretches from its mouth at the Pacific Ocean to roughly the present-day location of The Dalles, Oregon. Prior to the invasion of Euro-Americans this portion of the river was heavily populated by Chinookan-speaking people who inhabited both shores. The lower Columbia was also a major trade highway and the setting for cultural contact and politics both before and after colonial invasion. The final geography focuses on the landscape of the Chinook Indian Nation, the modern-day political entity that unites the descendants of the five westernmost groups of Chinookan-speaking populations. Each of these nested geographies is important for the purposes of this book at its own specific level. But the levels are all interconnected. It is difficult, therefore, to understand the challenges that the Chinook Indian Nation face today without also understanding the broader history of both the Pacific Northwest and the lower Columbia River, and for that reason all of these geographies will be touched on in the following pages.

THE PACIFIC NORTHWEST COAST

The Pacific Northwest is a region known for its high mountain ranges, dense coniferous forests, ocean shorelines, and wet climate. It is also the home to some of the most iconic Native American cultures on the continent, whose totem poles, wood carvings, large cedar plankhouses, and potlatches captured the attention of anthropologists, art collectors, explorers, and photographers for decades. While there is no consensus regarding the exact geographic extent of the Pacific Northwest Coast, a widely accepted definition—at least within the circles of anthropology—places the northern boundary near Yakutat Bay in the Alaskan panhandle and the southern boundary near Cape Mendocino in California. This represents a straight-line distance of roughly twelve hundred miles.[2] Given this vast distance, it should be unsurprising that the region holds considerable environmental diversity and numerous microclimates. Despite this diversity, however, the environment and landscape of the Pacific Northwest can be divided into two primary patterns: (1) the classic Northwest Coast of southeastern Alaska and British Columbia, which contains numerous islands, bays, fjords, sheltered coves, and deep hidden passages, and (2) the straight coasts of Washington, Oregon, and Northern California, which are only occasionally broken by bays and estuaries.[3]

Although there are differences between the northern and southern shorelines, some broad-scale environmental commonalities exist across the region. First, the climate is typically moderate with cool and dry summers and mild and wet winters, especially when compared to winters in the adjacent inland areas. Annual precipitation along the entire stretch of the shoreline is high, exceeding one thousand millimeters—a meter—in most areas of the region, including even the typically drier southern end. The region is also dominated by vegetation—most notably conifers—that is adapted to abundant rain and moderate temperatures.[4] The coastal coniferous forests consist primarily of Sitka spruce (*Picea sitchensis*), western hemlock (*Tsuga heterophylla*), and

Douglas fir (*Pseudotsuga menziesii*). Western red cedar (*Thuja plicata*), while less abundant than spruce, fir, and hemlock, plays a prominent role in the Indigenous material culture and ideology of the region. Numerous berries, acorns, hazelnuts, ferns, and bulbs are also available in abundance throughout the region, although the importance of these plants tends to diminish as one moves northward.[5]

Perhaps the most important environmental constant in the region is the wide-scale availability of marine and riverine resources, especially anadromous fish like salmon. At least six species of salmon (*Onchorynchus* sp.), each with its own geographic range, as well as smelt such as eulachon (*Thaleichthys pacificus*), spawn in the streams and rivers of the Northwest. Shellfish and numerous other neritic resources are also widely available. While marine and riverine resources are abundant regionally, there can be dramatic variations in resource availability locally. Resource variation also occurs from season to season or year to year, as the number of fish in a run can be staggering one year and nearly zero the next. Historically, this type of variation has resulted in periods of scarcity and even occasional starvation for Indigenous populations.[6] Of these marine and riverine resources, salmon is typically considered the most abundant and important. Early anthropologists like Alfred Kroeber and F. Clark Wissler placed so much emphasis on the role of salmon in the economy of Northwest Coast Indigenous cultures that they viewed salmon as almost defining the region itself.[7] Gregory Monks, however, has coined the word "salmonopia" to suggest that researchers like Wissler and Kroeber overlooked the other abundant resources in the area.[8] For instance, a wide variety of freshwater and saltwater fish were caught and processed by a large number of methods. Marine mammals such as seal were a prominent resource, while many coastal groups opportunistically scavenged whales and some, like the Nuu-chah-nulth, Ditidaht, and Makah, actively hunted them. Shellfish were also a valuable resource, and their importance has often been overlooked in ethnographic accounts.[9] Northwest Coast peoples also took advantage of terrestrial fauna like deer (*Ocdocoelious* sp.) and elk (*Cervus elephas*), as well as a wide variety of plants. Still, maritime resources were the staple of Northwest subsistence, and, of these, salmon were the most important.

As is the case across all of North America, there is considerable diversity of Indigenous cultures throughout the Pacific Northwest Coast: there is no single "Pacific Northwest Coast Culture." At least in part, this cultural diversity can be connected to differences in local environments, both the differences between the northern and southern portions of the coast, for instance, as well as differences between the coast itself and the more riverine environments as one moves inland. But despite these local variations (and at the risk of homogenizing culture) it is still possible to generalize a "Northwest Coast Pattern" that encompasses most of the Indigenous cultures in the region and distinguishes them from the rest of Indigenous North America. Anthropologists have noted the uniqueness of this Northwest Coast Pattern for some time, and a number of versions of this pattern—each with its own slight variations—have been attempted over the years.[10] Leland Donald, however, provides perhaps the best summary of the Northwest Coast culture pattern. Donald provides nine characteristics that define the Northwest Coast: (1) a marine and/or riverine orientation that directly shapes subsistence practices, ideology, and cultural outlook; (2) a highly evolved and sophisticated technology adapted for exploiting marine and riverine resources; (3) a highly developed woodworking technology for the creation of plankhouses, canoes, artworks, watertight storage boxes, and basketry; (4) some of the densest human populations in Indigenous North America, in many areas even higher than densities found in agricultural societies; (5) an emphasis on wealth and property, both tangible and intangible (such as the ownership of songs and dances), with control of wealth a central component of social success; (6) a tripartite system of social stratification, including a nobility, free commoners, and slaves; (7) true slavery, including in some cases owners' having control over whether or not a slave lives or dies; (8) no form of intercommunity political organization, with the village typically being the largest political unit; and (9) no formal political offices.[11] Kenneth Ames adds a tenth characteristic to this list: (10) large, coresidential households as the basic unit for economic production, food processing and storage, and social and ceremonial life.[12]

Another component of Pacific Northwest culture is the centrality of and reliance on trade. Subsistence resources were gathered not just for consumption but also as trade items that were moved along extensive trade networks. As much as the cultures of the Northwest can be called fishers and hunters, they can also be called traders. For instance, the Makah on the northwestern corner of Washington traded surplus halibut, whale blubber, and whale oil for quality cedar (which was not readily available in their immediate location), from which they made house planks and canoes.[13] Dentalium shells, which come from a deep-water mollusk and were highly prized as objects of decoration and a central medium of exchange, were traded from the coast to well into the North American interior as early as 4400 BC.[14] Eulachon grease, the oil rendered from eulachon and used extensively in cooking, was widely traded along interior trails that were guarded at spots and required tariffs for passage.[15] Copper from Alaska has been found all along the coast, and there is even evidence of pre-contact iron. Most often, the presence of iron is explained as a result of scavenging from Japanese ships that helplessly drifted across the North Pacific.[16] A few researchers, however, have suggested that iron could have arrived via a Siberia–Alaska trade network.[17] Slaves were also a very important trade item along the coast and were important not only for their labor value but for their exchange value as well.[18] The primary point is that trade was an extremely important activity throughout the region, both pre-contact and post-contact. In fact, a common trade language—Chinook Jargon or Chinuk Wawa—was developed by Chinooks living near the mouth of the Columbia and spoken throughout the region in order to facilitate trading activities.[19] The centrality of trade was also tied to and reflected in the omnipresence of canoes in Northwest cultures, which allowed traders to carry large loads over long distances in relatively short periods of time.

ANTHROPOLOGY AND THE PACIFIC NORTHWEST COAST

Few Indigenous people have been more heavily "anthropologized" than the Native American cultures of the Pacific Northwest Coast. For more than 125 years anthropologists have made the Pacific Northwest a center of scholarly attention, so much so that the practice of American anthropology itself owes much of its development to the region.[20] No one is more central to the connections between anthropology and the Pacific Northwest than Franz Boas, typically considered the foundational figure in the development of professional anthropology in America. Boas made twelve trips to the region to conduct ethnographic fieldwork with Indigenous people between 1886 and 1930, including trips to Chinookan territory in the summers of 1890 and 1891 and the winter of 1894.[21] In total Boas spent nearly two and a half years in the field at various places in the Pacific Northwest, and many of the ethnographic accounts we have of the region are directly attributable to his work. Boas also helped to organize and fund numerous other ethnographic expeditions, and many of his students, such as Edward Sapir (who served as the first director of the Anthropological Division of the Geological Survey of Canada), made the Northwest Coast an important component of their research.[22] The professionalization of anthropology in the United States and Canada during the late nineteenth and early twentieth century cannot be separated from its connections to the Pacific Northwest and the field's fascination with Pacific Northwest Indigenous culture.

Paige Raibmon notes that American anthropology as practiced during these early days was focused on the preservation and collection of what anthropologists viewed as the remnants of dying Indigenous cultures. High levels of disease, encroachment by white settlers, and policies of assimilation led anthropologists to conclude that Indigenous people—along with their material culture—would soon disappear. In the midst of these demographic and cultural upheavals, researchers initiated "salvage anthropology" projects designed to document and collect the last vestiges of these cultures before they disappeared forever. They saw themselves in a race against time and inevitability. Their primary interest lay in collecting those items considered to be the most "authentically" Indigenous: those least contaminated by contact with whites and most characteristic of Native culture. Because of the iconic nature of Pacific Northwest material culture and the belief that these objects retained high levels of "authenticity," the region became a hub for collecting. As a result, thousands of totem poles, masks, bentwood boxes, carved spoons, and bowls were taken from the Pacific Northwest and sent to museums, labs, and private collectors in the United States and across the globe.[23]

In addition to collecting material culture, anthropologists were also collecting Native American human remains. Boas, during his period of research on the Northwest Coast, collected roughly one hundred complete skeletons and two hundred skulls belonging to ancestors of the communities he was working with. He did so in secret and at night, as he knew this was a violation of Indigenous beliefs and that he did not have their permission. While conducting ethnographic work and collecting oral traditions with the Kwakwaka'wakw by day, Boas dug up graves at night. He noted, "It is most unpleasant work to steal bones from a grave, but what is the use, someone has to do it."[24] Boas mostly sold these human remains to the Field Museum in Chicago, although some were sold to parties in Berlin.[25] Numerous other celebrated figures of anthropology, such as anthropological luminaries Aleš Hrdlička and George Dorsey, were also voraciously collecting Native American human remains during this time.

It eventually became clear that Native Americans of the Pacific Northwest were not going extinct, despite the devastating upheavals that they had faced. As a result of Native resilience and survival, the type of salvage anthropology that researchers in the region had initially conducted was no longer viewed as imperative. This did not, however, result in a reduction of anthropological interest in the Pacific Northwest. Instead, the uniqueness of the social and political organization of Pacific Northwest societies helped to fuel the next round of anthropological research in the region. Culturally, anthropologists viewed the Pacific Northwest Coast as distinctive, a place where stereotypical patterns of what it meant to be an Indian seemed not to hold. Northwest Coast populations made their livings by hunting, fishing, and foraging, not agriculture. But unlike most other hunter-gatherers, they were relatively sedentary, had distinct social classes (including slaves), built large and permanent structures, had strongly developed notions of private property, lacked a strong sense of "tribe," and could trade and conduct business as well as (and usually better than) any Euro-American settler. They did not fit neatly into anthropological expectations about non-agrarian societies or Native Americans. Because of these distinctive characteristics the cultures of the Northwest Coast were considered excellent examples of "complex hunter-gatherers."[26]

Due to their status as complex hunter-gatherers, the cultures of the Northwest Coast came to play an important role in the development of general anthropological theory, especially theory directed toward explaining the rise of social complexity, the development of social inequality, and the development of "middle-range" societies. Anthropological studies on complex hunter-gatherers have appeared with regularity over the last three decades.[27] The anthropological focus on complex hunter-gatherers grew out of ethnographic research in the 1960s and 1970s that explored the extent of sociopolitical complexity present in hunter-gatherers and identified the Northwest Coast as an ideal area for research.[28] Interest in complex hunter-gatherers continued to grow in the 1980s and 1990s as a series of articles and edited volumes appeared in the anthropological literature and as the research shifted from purely ethnographic to archaeological.[29] The goals of these studies were to define hunter-gatherer complexity, compare the various complex hunter-gatherer cultures spread geographically and temporally, explore the causes and necessary conditions relating to the emergence of complexity, and analyze what complex hunter-gatherers can tell us about the development of social inequality in general. Northwest Coast cultures, as unquestioned examples of complex hunter-gatherers (and, perhaps more importantly, hunter-gatherers with ethnographic records), served as ideal case studies for anthropologists interested in these questions.

The central point to all of this is that entanglements between Indigenous cultures of the Pacific Northwest and anthropologists have occurred since the

beginnings of American anthropology. And carried within these entanglements are a multitude of assumptions and tensions that reflect the legacies of
colonialism and are still felt today. Salvage anthropology and the desire for
authenticity "erased the historical specificity" of Northwest cultures, Raibmon
writes, and "transformed the most traumatic and turbulent period in the history of western North American Aboriginal people into the benchmark of time-
less aboriginal culture."[30] Additionally, the assertion that Indigenous
populations were disappearing, if not already extinct—combined with the role
that anthropologists played as official and scientific collectors of those dying
cultures—effectively transferred cultural authority from Indigenous communities to anthropologists. Indigenous communities were viewed as too frac-
tured, too transformed, or maybe even no longer present to serve as experts
on their own cultures; that role was left to anthropologists.[31] The interest in
Northwest Indigenous cultures as complex hunter-gatherer analytical arche-
types only served to generalize them further, and studies with this mind-set
were effectively meaningless to contemporary living Indigenous groups. In the
midst of all of this, vast amounts of Indigenous material culture—artifacts and
human remains—were transferred out of Indigenous communities to museum
and anthropological laboratory shelves, where many remain to this day.

THE LOWER COLUMBIA RIVER

One component of the greater Pacific Northwest—and one that is central to
this book—is that of the lower Columbia River. As denoted in the name, the
defining feature of this region is the Columbia River itself, one of the largest
rivers in North America and the largest of the western United States. Only the
Mississippi, Saint Lawrence, and Mackenzie Rivers exceed the Columbia in
total water volume. The source of the Columbia River lies on the western slope
of the Canadian Rockies of British Columbia, and from these headwaters it
charts a course to the Pacific Ocean that flows through four mountain ranges
for a distance of roughly 1,250 miles. In total, the Columbia drains an area
of approximately 260,000 square miles. The river is culturally and historically
significant for a number of reasons, but two are especially important. First, it
supported more salmon than almost any other North American river, and
second, due to a drop of roughly twenty-seven hundred feet in elevation from
its headwaters to its mouth at the Pacific, it was identified shortly after World
War I as an excellent source for hydroelectric power. (It currently generates
more hydroelectric power than any other river in North America.)[32]

The Columbia River can be roughly divided into two stretches: the upper Columbia and the lower Columbia. The upper Columbia generally flows south from its headwaters in Canada through Washington until turning westward and forming part of the modern boundary of Washington and Oregon. The lower Columbia—which is the focus of the remainder of this section—refers to the portion of the river that generally flows westward from the edge of the Columbia Plateau to the river's mouth at the Pacific Ocean. This portion of the river begins at The Dalles in Oregon and flows for a distance of roughly two hundred miles till it reaches the ocean.[33]

Where it enters the ocean, the Columbia is nearly four miles wide and appears more as a bay than the mouth of a major river. This expanse, combined with extremely heavy and nearly ever-present fog, probably explains why early European maritime explorers so often overlooked the mouth. It wasn't until 1792, seventeen years after European and American maritime expeditions first passed through the region, that explorers realized this was the mouth of a river, not a bay.[34] Moving upstream (eastward) from the mouth, the river varies from four to ten miles wide for roughly thirty miles until it narrows considerably. For the next thirty-five miles it is less than a mile wide and characterized by many low-lying, swampy islands. At sixty-five miles from the mouth the river makes a sharp southern bend into the Portland Basin (located between the Cowlitz and Willamette drainages), an area of meandering waterways and numerous islands. Richard Pettigrew argues that in the Portland Basin the Columbia should still be viewed as an extension of the Pacific Ocean, as tide fluctuations can be as high as two feet.[35] Not far beyond the Portland Basin the river moves through the Columbia River Gorge, a beautifully scenic region of high basalt cliffs and waterfalls. About 30 miles upstream from the beginning of the gorge (and roughly 130 miles from the mouth), the river cuts through the Cascade Mountain Range, where, prior to the installation of dams, a 2.5-mile stretch of rapids, falls, and whirlpools served as a major impediment to water travel. Roughly forty miles farther upstream a nine-mile stretch of falls and narrows, known today as The Dalles (also called the Long Narrows), served as an additional obstacle. These rapids and falls—along with Celilo Falls immediately upriver—served as excellent Native American fishing sites. Due to twentieth-century dam construction these rapids and falls are now all submerged.[36] This eastern portion of the lower Columbia lies at the western boundary of the Columbia Plateau and was an area where Sahaptin-speaking peoples lived as neighbors with Chinookan-speaking populations from downriver. The region also was the site for a large trade fair at The Dalles that brought together Native populations from miles away and through which tons of trade goods flowed on an annual basis. The trade fair at The Dalles was considered "one of the most important trade centers in Aboriginal America."[37]

Chinookans of the Lower Columbia

As noted, both shores of the lower Columbia River, from The Dalles, Oregon to its mouth at the Pacific Ocean, were heavily populated with Chinookan villages. The Chinookan population of the lower Columbia River prior to white invasion was at least fifteen thousand, and the region had a greater population density than nearly anywhere else in Indigenous North America north of Mexico.[38] Chinookan peoples all spoke Chinookan, a branch of the Penutian phylum of languages. Based on differences in dialect, Chinookans have historically been grouped into "Lower" and "Upper" divisions. Lower Chinookans, including the Lower Chinook, the Willapa Chinook, and the Clatsop, lived along the Columbia River from its mouth to Grays Bay on the northern shore and approximately Tongue Point on the southern shore. The territory of the Lower Chinook also extended north and south along the Pacific coast from the river's mouth. Upper Chinookans established villages on both shores of the Columbia River from Grays Bay and Tongue Point to The Dalles, including the shores of the Willamette River upstream to Willamette Falls. Upper Chinookan dialects included Kathlamet, Multnomah, and Kiksht.[39]

It is important to note that these dialect groupings—and the boundaries between them—were very fluid. Different dialects were understood by all Chinookans, and trade, marriage, and visitation between groups was common and extensive.[40] Interaction with non-Chinookan populations, such as Salish- and Sahaptin-speaking populations, was also prevalent, and multilingualism was common. In fact, it was probably the norm in many villages as marriage with non-Chinookan people was frequent (the wife usually joined the husband's household), and slaves were almost always non-Chinookans, leading to the possibility that "in some villages speakers of the 'native' language were in the minority."[41] Lower and Upper Chinookan dialects should not be confused with Chinuk Wawa, the pidgin hybrid that arose from Chinookan roots and served as a lingua franca that at its peak extended south into California and north to southeastern Alaska.[42]

In some instances the term *Middle Chinookan* is used to delineate a third group of Chinookan populations. The Middle Chinookans, as implied by their name, occupy a central portion of the lower Columbia River, with villages located along both sides of the river from roughly the present-day location of Vancouver, Washington, to near Oak Point, Washington. This also includes the Chinookan populations living in the Willamette Valley up to Willamette Falls (near the present-day location of Oregon City, Oregon).[43] The homeland of the Middle Chinookans corresponds closely to the Portland Basin, an area that is defined by three features: the confluence of the Sandy and Columbia Rivers near the western edge of the Columbia River Gorge, Willamette Falls, and the confluence of the Kalama and Columbia Rivers near present-day Kalama, Washington. Lewis and Clark referred to this same stretch of the river as the "Wapato Valley," due to the extensive amount of wapato (*Sagittaria latifolia*), a plant with a potato-like tuber that was a primary staple of trade and that grew in the floodplain lakes and marshes common along the shores of the Columbia in this region. The Chinookans of the Portland Basin or Wapato Valley are a central component of many of the discussions in this book, especially in connection to the village and archaeological site of Cathlapotle and the construction of a Chinookan plankhouse on the grounds of the Ridgefield National Wildlife Refuge (see chapters 2 and 4). For that reason, the term *Middle Chinookan* is occasionally used in this book.

While there was certainly some variation—both in language and cultural practice—between the Chinookan villages located along the river, they shared a number of cultural traits: a heavy reliance on marine and riverine resources (as evident in the First Salmon Ceremony), a focus on hunting and gathering rather than agriculture, a heavy reliance on canoes for transportation and trade, a highly developed tradition of woodworking and carving, a complex system of social stratification that included high-ranking members, commoners, and slaves, and the use of large multifamily cedar plankhouses as a central place of residence. While most of these traits are very similar to other Northwest Coast Indigenous cultures (as described above in this chapter), Lower Columbian Chinookans had some traits that were more specific to the area. This included a particular form of head flattening, which visually separated free members of society from slaves, and a little-known Chinookan art style that is distinctive from the better known Northwest Coast art of the northern Pacific Coast region.[44]

The somewhat unique identity of Lower Columbia populations is also influenced by the fact that the lower Columbia River served as a conduit between the Pacific coast and the Columbia Plateau. Well before Euro-Americans ever arrived on the shores of the Pacific Ocean, Chinookan peoples were part of an established large-scale trade network that stretched between present-day

Canada and California and into the plains and interior plateau. For at least ten thousand years, people of the lower Columbia participated in this network, trading salmon, wapato, elk hides, obsidian, blankets, beads, and countless other goods of both local and exotic origin. Due to their location on the banks of the Columbia, Chinookan populations were situated directly in the middle of this trade network and thus were able to serve as the primary middlemen in trade between the coast and the interior plateau. This position allowed them to greatly influence the terms of trade, and it allowed many to acquire a great deal of wealth. Because of their central place in this extensive network, Chinookans principally became known as traders.[45] In addition to connecting people by trade, the river also served as a conduit for culture, linking coastal cultures with those of the interior. Chinookan peoples were thus affected by influences from both of these larger cultural areas, and, as anthropologist Verne Ray notes, "it appears that the Chinook occupied a distinctly intermediate position between the typical Northwest Coast cultures and those of the Plateau."[46]

While there were certainly close similarities in language, culture, and trade that linked the Chinookan villages on the lower Columbia River, the region was not united by strict boundaries (either geographic or cultural) or formal political ties. As is typically the case with Indigenous cultures of the Pacific Northwest, the village served as the primary economic and political unit. Prior to contact with Euro-Americans, villages were self-governing and autonomous, operating as individual actors in trade and politics. There were often, however, highly ranked villages that had associated satellite villages, and these satellite villages typically consisted of individuals closely related to the hereditary leader of the high-ranked village. Individuals within villages were connected to the wider region through a complex set of relationships based on marriage, kinship, and trade that cut across political entities and language groups.[47] Anthropologist Yvonne Hajda has noted that Chinookans of the lower Columbia were part of what she refers to as the "Greater Lower Columbia network," which included not only the Chinookans but also Indigenous groups from the Quinault to the Alsea who lived along the Pacific coast, and the Cowlitz, Tualatin Kalapuya, and Lower Chehalis who lived along important tributaries of the Columbia. The result of this network was an extensive and highly complex set of interrelationships that existed at both village and individual levels.[48]

Euro-Americans who came into contact with Chinookans were not easily able to conceptualize, or were not necessarily interested in, the complexity and extensiveness of the type of kinship and trade networks present on the Columbia River. As a result, they often attempted to impose more encompassing labels on Indigenous inhabitants, placing them together in categories of shared language and cultural traits that may have made sense to whites but were of little meaning or accuracy to Natives (this will be addressed further in Chapter 3). In effect, white colonists conceptually created unified "tribes" where they did not really exist.[49] This process of redefining Native identity into categories that made more sense to whites only continued as colonial invasion persisted. The dramatic cultural and demographic changes to Indigenous society caused by introduced disease, the power of colonial merchants to influence who was or was not a powerful person within Indigenous societies, and the desire of white government officials to create easily defined and bounded tribal units for purposes of things like the treaty process only exacerbated a fundamental transformation and imposition of Indigenous identity. As I will show, this transformation and imposition of what constitutes Indigenous identity continues to haunt Native people in the present.[50]

Euro-American Invasion of Chinookan Homelands

A certain mythology has grown around the idea that Meriwether Lewis and William Clark were the first non-Natives to visit the mouth of the Columbia River and see the Pacific Coast. This is far from true. Some have suggested that Hwui Shan, a Buddhist monk from China, made it to the Columbia River in the fifth century A D, but neither oral nor written history gives any credence to this. What is historically documented, however, is that Euro-Americans had entered the mouth of the Columbia, and thus the homelands of the Chinooks, by 1792 and traveled upriver as far as the present-day location of Washougal, Washington. This is thirteen years before Lewis and Clark ever saw the river's banks or the Chinookans living there. Euro-American contact with Chinookans living on the river was early and extensive, and given the important location of the river in terms of trade and imperial designs, the region became the scene of intense international politics and boundary disputes. Chinookans were central players in this process but also got caught between shifting politics and alliances, as well as ever-increasing invasion of their lands. Additionally, devastating changes in demographics caused by introduced diseases fundamentally altered their position on the river.[51]

Chinookan contact with non-Native mariners arriving in their lands likely occurred by at least as early as the seventeenth and early eighteenth centuries. There is evidence, from both Native American oral histories and the archaeological record, of wrecked vessels and their contents washing ashore in Chinookan lands. These ships likely came from both Japan and Europe—sometimes drifting across the Pacific after losing masts and rudders—and oral history suggests that at least in some cases the shipwrecks included survivors. In at least one instance the survivors were taken as Chinookan slaves.[52] More extensive and regular contact with non-Natives, however, occurred toward the end of the eighteenth century. On August 17, 1775, at roughly 6:00 P.M., the Spanish explorer Bruno de Hezeta, sailing in his flagship *Santiago*, became the first European to provide a written description of the mouth of the Columbia River. Hezeta described in his log what he saw as a great bay, but based on the currents and motion of the water he speculated that the bay might actually be the mouth of a great river. The lateness of the day, the *Santiago's* inability to make headway against the currents, and his resolve to return to Mexico ultimately kept Hezeta from entering the river's mouth.[53] While Hezeta's failure to enter the Columbia also kept him from making direct contact with Chinookans, it did set the stage for later excursions to the river's mouth and a long series of world-changing entanglements.

Seventeen years after Hezeta, in May 1792, the first non-Native vessel entered the mouth of the Columbia. Robert Gray, an American sea captain and merchant, guided his ship the *Columbia Rediviva*—after which the river is named—across the dangerous bar and into the river. While Gray's appearance at first caused a bit of alarm to the Chinook of the coast, their interest in the new arrivals quickly turned to the possibility of new business ventures. Nearly as soon as the *Columbia* had entered the river's mouth, they sent twenty canoes, full of furs and salmon, out to the ship to trade. Rather than being terrified of the new arrivals, the Chinook were prepared for the opportunity to further enhance their material wealth, and important Chinook leaders like Concomly, Shelathwell, and Taucum quickly initiated trade relationships with Euro-Americans. The Chinook had already been part of an extensive trade network that had thrived for perhaps thousands of years, and the arrival of Euro-Americans added to the range of goods available for trade as well as the geographic extent of the trade network. The Chinook were now part of a global economic system. Although trading ventures were occasionally tense and often conducted within the realm of cultural misunderstandings, trade with the newcomers quickly flourished.[54]

While initial contact between Euro-Americans and Chinookans first occurred on the Pacific Coast, direct contact quickly moved upriver. In late October 1792, the British explorer George Vancouver—based on information

The Devastation of Disease

For Chinookans the years following the arrival of Euro-Americans in their homelands were a period of intense change. Relying on their long-standing expertise in trade and commerce, Chinookans were initially able to use the influx of new trading partners as a way to increase their already considerable wealth and maintain their positions of power on the river. But as the new settlers began to make permanent homes on the river, and as imperial battles over territory and colonial designs on the regions increased, the ability of Chinookans to maintain control over their own lands began to dissipate. The most devastating agent of change, however, came in the form of introduced disease. The Columbia River, which had served so well as a highway for trade, unfortunately served equally as well as a highway for disease. The arrival of Europeans and Americans in the Northwest brought devastating diseases for which Native populations had no defense. While Indigenous populations throughout the Americas suffered dramatically from diseases introduced by European invaders, the people of the lower Columbia River were some of the most heavily affected. From a period even before direct contact to the middle of the nineteenth century, Indigenous populations faced an onslaught that nearly destroyed them. And for those who survived, their way of life was forever and tragically altered.[73]

Smallpox may have reached the Pacific Northwest as part of the pandemic that struck the Western Hemisphere in the 1520s, but there is no solid evidence for this. There is, however, more tangible evidence for smallpox epidemics occurring in 1781–82, 1801–2, 1836–38, 1852–53, and 1862.[74] Although smallpox was catastrophic to Indigenous populations throughout the Pacific Northwest, the worst epidemic to hit the Columbia River—in terms of casualties and cultural disruption—began in the summer of 1830. Called "fever and ague" by the Americans and "intermittent fever" by the British, this epidemic—most likely malaria—raged through the lower Columbia and Willamette River valleys for several summers. The epidemic had a destructive effect on Native populations. Both the Hudson's Bay Company and Lewis and Clark estimated a regional Native population of somewhere near 15,500 in the early decades of the nineteenth century. By 1841 this number had been reduced to 1,932, a decline of nearly 90 percent.[75] While the effects of the epidemic were felt throughout the lower Columbia and Willamette valleys, as well as river valleys as far south as the San Joaquin valley in northern California, the greatest devastation was inflicted on the Middle Chinookan populations of the Portland Basin. Sauvie and Deer Islands, large Middle Chinookan population centers in close proximity to present-day Portland, Oregon, were entirely depopulated by 1835, which led John McLoughlin of Fort Vancouver to state that the Natives once living on Sauvie Island had "become as a tribe extinct."[76] Although the rate of mortality was extremely high, Middle Chinookan populations had not gone extinct. Some survived, and those who did joined villages within their kinship networks, moved to the seacoast, or fled into the mountains. Some of the survivors even fled to what they thought would be the safety of Fort Vancouver, located across from the mouth of the Willamette River. But employees of the company felt "obliged to drive the Indians away instead of affording them the assistance they implored of us by our having as many of our people on the sick list as we could possibly attend to," McLoughlin wrote.[77]

By 1850 the overall population of the region had rebounded to pre-1830 levels. Its composition, however, had undergone a radical transformation. English-speaking Americans had almost totally supplanted Native Americans, and many of the Chinookan villages along the banks of the river sat empty.[78] The few Native Americans that remained came under intense pressure and even further competition from white squatters who rapidly moved into areas they considered empty. The settlement of the region by citizens of the United States occurred before title to Native lands had been extinguished, and therefore settlers had no legal rights to these lands, regardless of how empty they thought they were or how entitled they felt to them. But despite this, white settlers took the land as their own and in effect became illegal squatters. Rather than addressing the situation through measures that might have given Natives at least some measure of recompense for these stolen lands, the US Congress instead passed the Donation Land Act in 1850. This act granted land to Americans after four years' "occupancy" and in effect gave official sanction to the formerly illegal activities of white settlers.[79]

The levels of devastation that Indigenous populations of the Columbia River suffered due to diseases brought by Europeans and Americans cannot be overstated. The loss of nearly 90 percent of the Native population brought with it fundamental changes to Native life, as cultural practices, kinship networks, societal roles, and leadership lineages that had all existed for generations were upended. Introduced disease caused not only a demographic collapse, but a cultural upheaval as well. Furthermore, Yvonne Hajda notes, the losses caused by disease, especially the epidemics of 1830–34, fundamentally altered the relative positions of strength between Chinookans and white settlers and mercantile interests along the river (such as the Hudson's Bay Company).[80] Prior to 1830 lower Columbia Chinookans had been able to retain their central role in controlling trade along the river. While the arrival of whites altered some of the networks and products, Chinookans still played a powerful role in determining the terms of the trade. The onslaught of disease effectively broke this position of strength. The shift in power manifested itself not only in the area of trade, but also in Chinookan efforts to retain their homelands in the face of continued invasion by white settlers.

Chinookans and the Treaty Era

The flood of white settlers moving into Chinookan homelands only increased after the devastation of the 1830s epidemics. The US Congress, in legislation that created the Oregon Territory, recognized that Indigenous populations held title—albeit a limited form of title—to their own lands. In order to extinguish that title and acquire those lands for American settlement, government officials technically needed to negotiate and ratify treaties with Native American groups, Chinookans included. In the summer of 1850, Congress organized a department of Indian affairs for the Oregon Territory and established a treaty process that would work to resolve conflicts between Natives and settlers over land and resources. No treaties, however, were negotiated or ratified before the Oregon Donation Land Act was passed in 1850, and as a result numerous white settlers were granted ostensibly legal title to Native land whose title had never officially been extinguished. The rush for rich lands along the Columbia and its tributaries, racist misperceptions about Native use of land, and an overall lack of concern for Indigenous rights resulted in a process that either moved lower Columbia Chinookans from their homelands or left them with no treaties and little recognition.[81]

Middle Chinookans—those groups living in the Portland Basin and who were perhaps most hard hit by the epidemics of the 1830s—were parties to a series of treaties negotiated during the early 1850s. The first round of treaties began in 1851 and was led by Anson Dart, the superintendent of Indian affairs for the Oregon Territory. Dart was directed to negotiate a treaty that would remove Native Americans—who were viewed as failing to utilize the land in ways that Euro-Americans considered productive—from the rich and highly desired Willamette Valley to a single reservation east of the Cascades. The tribes of the Willamette Valley and Portland Basin were determined, however, not to leave their homelands, and ultimately Dart was forced to sign treaties that would allow Middle Chinookans and others to stay. However, under pressure from white settlers who were upset that Natives were not being removed, Congress refused to ratify and implement these treaties.[82]

The treaty process began again in 1853 under the direction of the new superintendent of Indian affairs for the Oregon Territory, Joel Palmer. Palmer also hoped to move all of the Middle Chinookans (as well as numerous other Willamette Valley groups) to a reservation east of the Cascades, but, as in 1851, the tribes refused to sign. Palmer then decided to create a reservation in the Grande Ronde Valley in western Oregon, much closer to the homelands of the Willamette Valley Indians. In January 1855 the Willamette Valley Treaty was signed and ratified: the entire Willamette River drainage was ceded to the United States. Natives in the region were placed on scattered small temporary reserves until the larger reservation at Grand Ronde was ready for occupation. Finally in 1856—and facing intense pressure from white settlers fearful of "Indian raids"—Palmer ordered the remaining Middle Chinookans to be rounded up and sent to the Grand Ronde Reservation to live alongside members of thirty other western Oregon tribes.[83] While many Middle Chinookans relocated to Grand Ronde, some refused to go. Left without a reservation or representative body of their own, they chose instead to disperse throughout the region, often intermarrying with other Native communities like the Yakama, Warm Springs, Cowlitz, and Lower Chinook.

Chinookan peoples living farther downriver also went through a series of treaty negotiations. In August 1851, Superintendent Dart met with representatives of a number of Native American groups at Tansy Point, located near the mouth of the Columbia River in what is now Warrenton, Oregon. Included in these treaty negotiations were seven Lower Chinookan bands: the Clatsop Tribe of Indians, the Nue-que-clah-we-muck Tribe of Indians, the Waukikum Band of Chinook Tribe, the Konnack Band of Chinook, the Kathlamet Band of Chinook, the Wheelappa Band of Chinook, and the Lower Band of Chinook. Over the course of several days tribal leaders were effectively able to negotiate treaties with Dart that reserved land within their traditional homelands, that allowed them to retain their right to harvest and hunt within their traditional territories, that offered them access to goods and services through the federal Office of Indian Affairs (later renamed the Bureau of Indian Affairs) and that secured annuity payments for ten years for any lands they relinquished.[84]

The Tansy Point treaties were brought to the US Congress in November 1851. By late 1852, however, the treaties had been blocked. The two people most directly responsible for obstructing their passage were Oregon territorial delegates Joseph Lane and Samuel Thurston. Lane and Thurston, along with their congressional supporters, blocked the treaties for two primary reasons. First, they objected to the fact that the Tansy Point treaties allowed Native

Americans to stay on reserved lands within their traditional homelands. They preferred instead that Indigenous groups be removed to lands east of the Cascade Range, thereby opening more of the rich and desirable land along the river and coasts to white settlement. Second, opponents of the treaties rejected the tribes' demands that payments for relinquished land be paid over a ten-year period. Due to Lane and Thurston's objections and their support from other congressional delegates, the Tansy Point treaties were never ratified. Left without any ratified treaties, Lower Chinookans faced continued invasion and appropriation of their lands by white settlers. And as non-treaty tribal nations they held very little political or legal power to effectively halt this invasion.[85]

After Congress created the Washington Territory in 1853, treaty negotiations with Indigenous nations in the area began anew. Isaac Stevens was appointed both the territorial governor and its superintendent of Indian affairs. In February 1855, on the Chehalis River near Grays Harbor, Stevens met with a council of 350 Natives, representing the Chinook, Upper and Lower Chehalis, Quinault, Satsop, Queets, and Cowlitz. Stevens planned to place all these groups on one reservation extending from Grays Harbor to Cape Flattery in Washington Territory. After several tense days of treaty negotiations, the tribal representatives decided not to sign. Their refusal to sign was motivated, in part, by their continuing unhappiness with the government's failure to ratify the earlier Tansy Point treaties. But their strongest objection was directed toward the government's requirement that they leave their traditional homelands and all be placed on one reservation.[86] Certainly, for Chinookan representatives at the negotiations, the removal from their homelands was a central cause for objection. Stevens's treaty would move them north off of the Columbia River and Naselle River drainage, and into the homelands of the Quinault, who were historic enemies. Katherine Elliott, former Tribal Council member of the Chinook Indian Nation, notes that an additional concern was that Chinookans did not want to leave the resting sites of their ancestors: "Nobody wanted to go. And over and over again you see in the written documents . . . that we didn't want to leave our ancestors, you know. That's why we didn't want to leave."[87]

Stevens was so angered by the tribes' objections to the treaties and their refusal to concede on removal that he stormed out of negotiations and refused to enter into any further discussions. Later that year, and into the early part of 1856, a number of other treaties were negotiated by Washington territorial officials and ratified by Congress, including the Treaty of Olympia, which established the Quinault Reservation on the Olympic Peninsula. By the end of 1856 most of western Washington had been ceded to the United States via treaty. The Chinook, however, were not a party to any of these ratified treaties and as such they never ceded their lands. But they also remained federally unrecognized, and their status—at least in the eyes of the federal government—was nebulous.[88]

The lack of a ratified treaty continued to impact the Chinook through the remainder of the nineteenth century and through the twentieth as well. As noted by Fisher and Jetté, they continued to experience declines in population levels, invasion and appropriation of their lands, and pressure to assimilate into white society.[89] After the failure of the initial treaty process, the federal government did attempt some modest and sporadic efforts to address the status of the Chinook. For instance, the 640-acre Shoalwater Bay Reservation was created in 1866 to serve as reserved land for some of the Chinook and Lower Chehalis. And in 1873 the benefits of the Treaty of Olympia—which had created the Quinault Reservation—were extended to the "other tribes of fish-eating Indians on the Pacific coast," the Chinook among them.[90] Overall, however, these modest efforts at redress were partial solutions at best: they either affected only a portion of Chinookan populations living in Washington and Oregon, or they forced them to move away from their homelands along the rivers and coasts. Many refused to move, choosing instead to maintain their place on the landscape even in the face of continued pressure for their lands, policies of assimilation, and erratic attention from the federal government.

The intrusion of colonial practices into the Pacific Northwest—like the federal government's treaty process—profoundly affected Indigenous people of the region. Robert Boyd notes that one of the central impacts of this intrusion was the federal government's power to "make tribes." The government defined what constituted a tribal group and appointed their leaders. Additionally, while Indigenous people were sometimes allowed to remain in their homelands, the treaty process more often forced the removal of groups, breaking them apart and reconfiguring them into new confederations. This was certainly the case with many Chinookan peoples along the central and eastern portions of the lower Columbia River, as many were removed and placed into multi-tribal confederations like the Grand Ronde, Yakama, and Warm Springs. In these newly created confederations Chinookans became "minorities within minorities," which occasionally led to further cultural leveling and loss.[91] This reconfiguration and imposition of tribal identity—in response to and as a result of colonial policies—is something that continues to affect Chinooks today, especially in their struggle to be officially recognized by the federal government as a Native American nation and in their ongoing efforts to maintain control over their own cultural heritage.

THE CHINOOK INDIAN NATION TODAY

Today the Chinook Indian Nation has approximately three thousand enrolled citizens who are descendants of the five westernmost Chinookan tribes: the Clatsop and Kathlamet of what is now Oregon, and the Lower Chinook, Wahkiakum, and Willapa of what is now Washington (see figure 1). Its tribal offices are located in Bay Center, Washington. Despite invasion and theft of their lands by outsiders, devastating population decline from introduced disease, and the failure of the federal government to fulfill its responsibilities to the tribe, the Chinook survived and continue to maintain a distinct Indigenous identity. While citizens of the Chinook Indian Nation live throughout the Pacific Northwest and the United States, most still reside near traditional Chinookan lands in Pacific and Wahkiakum Counties in Washington, and Clatsop and Columbia Counties in Oregon. There are many families that tie their ancestry to Chinookan villages, and some of the representative family lines include the Pickernells, Hyasmans, Olivers, and Hawks (Lower Chinook); Salakies, Cultees, and Jacksons (Clatsop); Georges and Charleys (Willapa); Elliotts, Goodells, and Eros (Wahkiakum); and Mallets and Talltriches (Kathlamet).[92] The Chinook Indian Nation has an elected tribal chair and nine council positions, as well as committees that oversee communications, culture, enrollment, fisheries, fund development, heath and social services, lands, and scholarship.[93]

In the decades following the arrival of whites, Chinookans were in a battle to maintain their lands, their traditional fishing spots, their lives and livelihoods, and their Indigenous identities. In addition to suffering societal rupture from losses due to disease, Chinookans also faced challenges from two other colonial agents of cultural genocide: the introduction of alcohol and boarding schools. Tony Johnson notes that before the introduction of alcohol, deaths due to drowning were a very rare occurrence, despite the central place of water to the Chinookan world. After alcohol was introduced a high number of Chinookans died due to alcohol-related drowning, contributing to the already high losses from disease. Furthermore, the fact that Chinookans were a nontreaty tribe and held no reservation lands did not protect their children from being taken to the Chemewa or Cushman Indian boarding schools in Salem,

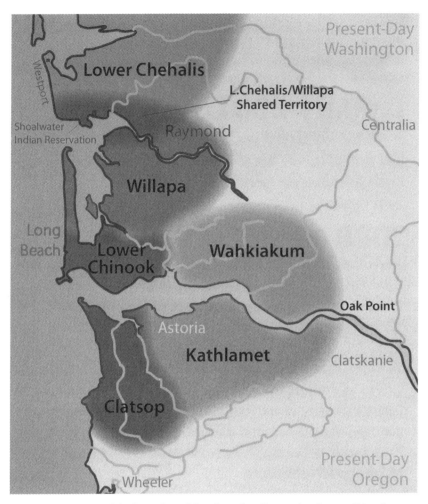

FIGURE 1. Location of the five tribes of the Chinook Indian Nation (Lower Chinook, Clatsop, Kathlamet, Wahkiakum, Willapa). There are close connections with the Lower Chehalis people, both in the past and present. Courtesy of the Chinook Indian Nation.

Oregon, and Tacoma, Washington. The goal of boarding schools was to "kill the Indian [to] save the child" (a policy phrasing attributed to Carlisle Indian School founder Richard Pratt) and so Native children were forbidden from speaking their languages, forced to dress in white clothing, and often prevented from seeing or visiting their families.[94] Boarding schools, therefore, represented an effort to assimilate Indigenous children but also served as an active mechanism for removing children from their families. They were painful places and left a legacy of cultural loss and separation. Former Chinook chair Gary Johnson explains it this way:

> It's also important, too, that the story is told about what happened to the land, how people in my father's generation, my grandmother's generation, were taken and sent to Indian schools and the government policy was clearly stated. You know, kill the Indian, save the child. And it was really tough times for people to live through, and to try to maintain their culture and try to maintain their family connections. Those stories need to be told so people understand. Some of our families have a tough time today, and it's because of what parents and grandparents and great grandparents have gone through.[95]

Removing children from their families had a dramatic and negative impact on the children, but it was also devastating for those who remained behind in villages that were suddenly bereft of the young. The current presence of the Chinook Indian Nation demonstrates, however, that despite all of the colonial pressures to destroy their culture, they were and are resilient: they still exist. They are a visible and well-known tribal community in Oregon, Washington, and the greater Pacific Northwest, and they are active in efforts to maintain culture. And part of their goal as a nation is to do what Gary Johnson suggests: to tell the story about what happened and to preserve and strengthen their culture through family and tribal relationships.

One of the primary areas of concern for members of the present-day Chinook Indian Nation is their continuing battle for federal recognition. The federal government's failure to ratify a treaty with the Chinook—as well as its arbitrary and uneven dealings with the tribe in the years following the failed treaty process—left them formally unrecognized and has created significant challenges for the Chinook Indian Nation, perhaps threatening its very survival. Tony Johnson notes that the lack of formal recognition makes it very difficult for the Chinooks to engage in "economic development, the establishment of a land base, the preservation of our culture, the reinstatement of fishing and hunting rights, the ability to repatriate our ancestors' bones and sacred items from museum collections, and the ability to better care for our community's health and well-being."[96]

Former Chinook Tribal Council member Katherine Elliott notes that the issue of federal recognition is of central importance to current tribal members and a crucial responsibility of the Tribal Council: "Our last climate survey was in 2008, and . . . overwhelmingly, the number one concern of the people is restoring our federal recognition, still today. . . . We're always trying to make sure that we meet that goal."[97] But the pursuit of recognition has been incredibly arduous and draining—emotionally, physically, and financially—and fraught with painful losses and disappointments.

The Chinooks' struggle to have their relationship with the federal government clarified has been nearly continuous. As early as 1899 they hired an attorney to assist them in their efforts. These efforts remained mostly unsuccessful, but with the development of the Federal Acknowledgment Process (FAP) in 1978—which provided an avenue for federal recognition—the tribe had reason for optimism, and the Chinook Indian Nation made a concerted effort for recognition at this time. After decades of working with attorneys and government officials, compiling thousands of pages of historical documentation, and demonstrating monumental levels of patience, the Chinook Indian Nation was formally recognized by the federal government through the FAP. On January 3, 2001, US assistant secretary of the interior Kevin Gover signed documents granting the Chinook formal recognition. It was one of Gover's last acts as a member of the outgoing Clinton administration and a day of celebration and relief for the Chinooks. On that very day, however, a Bureau of Indian Affairs (BIA) official wrote a memo questioning whether the Chinooks had adequately made their case for recognition, and in July 2002, under the Bush administration, the agency reversed itself and denied formal recognition to the Chinooks.[98]

Groups petitioning the government for recognition via the FAP must meet all seven criteria described in the US Code of Federal Regulations (25 C.F.R. 83.7). Further, they must do this to the satisfaction of scholars and BIA officials who may never have visited their territories. The seven mandatory criteria for federal acknowledgment are:

a. The petitioner has been identified as an American Indian entity on a substantially continuous basis since 1900.

b. A predominant portion of the petitioning group comprises a distinct community and has existed as a community from historical times until the present.

c. The petitioner has maintained political influence or authority over its members as an autonomous entity from historical times until the present.

    d. A copy of the group's present governing document including its member-
ship criteria [must be provided]. In the absence of a written document,
the petitioner must provide a statement describing in full its membership criteria and current governing procedures.

    e. The petitioner's membership consists of individuals who descend from
a historical Indian tribe or from historical Indian tribes which combined
and functioned as a single autonomous political entity.

    f. The membership of the petitioning group is composed principally of
persons who are not members of any acknowledged North American
Indian Tribe.

    g. Neither the petitioner nor its members are the subject of congressional
legislation that has expressly terminated or forbidden the Federal
relationship.

These regulations for tribal acknowledgment were created in 1978 by the
BIA and were intended to "make tribal acknowledgment more expeditious
and more objective than in the past."[99] The criteria place strong emphasis on
demonstration of continued tribal unity and identity. They can, however, be
difficult to meet. This is especially true for Indigenous groups of the Northwest, where the drastic effects of disease and high levels of intermarriage—in
combination with long-standing policies of assimilation—had taken a devastating toll.

    After the final determination to acknowledge the Chinook Indian Nation
was issued in January 2001, and on the eighty-ninth day of an allowed ninety-
day comment period, the Quinault Indian Nation sent a letter to the Interior
Board of Indian Appeals (IBIA) arguing that the Chinooks had not met the
standards of the FAP requirements and asking them to reconsider recognition.
On August 1, 2001, the IBIA affirmed the determination of recognition as
handed down by Kevin Gover, arguing that the Quinault Indian Nation had
not proven its allegations by a preponderance of the evidence. The IBIA, however, also determined that there were additional allegations by the Quinault
Nation that fell outside of the jurisdiction of the IBIA.[100] These allegations were
referred to the secretary of the interior, who then sent them to the new assistant secretary for Indian affairs in the Bush administration, Neal A. McCaleb.
McCaleb took the Quinault arguments into consideration, and in a document
dated July 5, 2002, he concluded that the Chinook had failed to satisfactorily

meet three of the seven mandatory criteria: "The petitioner failed to meet criteria (a), (b), and (c) of the acknowledgment regulations—failing to demonstrate that it has maintained political influence over its members from historical times to the present [criterion (c)], that a predominant portion of its members comprise a distinct social community at present, or since 1950 [criterion (b)], or that it has been identified historically as an Indian entity by outside observers on a substantially continuous basis [criterion (a)]."[101]

The Chinooks' status as a recognized tribe was rescinded only a year and a half after it had been granted. Gary Johnson, the tribal chair of the Chinook Indian Nation at the time, heard the devastating news while he was in Washington DC, only two days after he had dined with President George W. Bush during an event honoring tribal nations that had offered aid to Lewis and Clark.[102]

The irony of the Chinooks' non-recognition and the claim that they lack continuity as a tribal body lies in the historical reality of years of policies of assimilation, theft of land, and the disruption of social networks after disease-driven population declines. As Johnson notes, "Government policy for probably a couple of hundred years tried to take our land, or did take our land, our culture, our language, our songs, everything away from us. . . . The government worked against Chinook all of these years and how can you expect us to have this perfect—and I guess I would use the term 'white man's government'—with paper trails over all this period of time." Johnson says, "It ends up that people that are three thousand miles away are making decisions about us without even spending much time with us. . . . [The Federal Acknowledgment Process] was a long and frustrating journey." He suggests, however, that despite years of assimilation and attempts at cultural genocide, the Chinook Indian Nation holds in its tribal office nearly nineteen thousand pages of documents that demonstrate its continuity, a paper trail that Johnson notes is as extensive as those of most of the tribes that have received recognition and more extensive than many.[103] It is this arbitrariness of the recognition process— added to the necessity of having to prove an "authentically" Indian identity— that leads to so much frustration and results in a reality where "the majority of acknowledgment determinations are cloaked in shades of gray."[104]

The Chinook Indian Nation was shell-shocked by the government's reversal and understandably in disbelief, and the decision had repercussions felt throughout the tribe and is something that they have not fully gotten over. But despite this, citizens of the Chinook Indian Nation did not simply acquiesce to the government's decision about their status. They have kept up their fight for formal recognition. Initially there was some disagreement within the nation regarding the appropriate response and course of action. Some members thought the best approach was to sue the federal government and challenge the decision in court. They felt that the reconsideration under the Bush administration was clearly flawed and would not withstand legal scrutiny. Navigating the byzantine Federal Acknowledgment Process, however, is only one avenue to recognition. Tribes can also be formally recognized through an act of Congress. Many members of the tribe—skeptical of the likelihood of success in the courts and worried about the costs of litigation—felt that recognition via the legislative process would more likely be effective.

The Chinook Indian Nation found an ally for this route in Brian Baird, who was the US Representative for Washington State's Third Congressional District and had been present at the initial signing of the Chinook recognition paperwork in 2001. Baird agreed to sponsor the Chinooks' bid for recognition, and after months of meetings and negotiations with the Chinook Nation he introduced H.R. 6689, "A Bill to Restore Federal Recognition to the Chinook Nation, and for Other Purposes" in the second session of the 110th Congress, on July 31, 2008. The bill was referred to the Committee on Natural Resources. The text of the bill noted the contributions that the Chinook Indian Nation made to Lewis and Clark, pointed out that the Chinook were recognized as an Indian tribe in the Tansy Point and Chehalis treaties, and asserted that the failure of the United States to ratify those treaties resulted in serious harm to the Chinook and the loss of their lands on the Columbia River. The bill also noted that four of the five tribes of the present-day Chinook Indian Nation—the Lower Chinook, the Clatsop, the Wahkiakum, and the Kathlamet—were named in the Western Oregon Termination Act of 1954, and it said that this act was the only basis for termination of the formal relationship between the tribe and the federal government. Therefore, "It is time for Congress to restore the Chinook Nation to Federal tribal status."[105]

The bill, however, never made it out of the Committee for Natural Resources. Baird reintroduced it—with some slight changes—as H.R. 2576 in May 2009, in the first session of the 111th Congress. The bill was again slightly modified and reintroduced in the 111th Congress as H.R. 3084 on June 26, 2009. On July 15, 2009, Chinook Indian Nation chair Ray Gardner, vice-chair Sam Robinson, and Tribal Council member Phil Hawks traveled to Washington DC to testify on Chinook recognition before the Committee on Natural Resources. Congressman Baird also testified during this hearing, offering his strong support for federal recognition. Members of the Chinook Indian Nation again had reasons to feel optimistic. Unfortunately, the bill got enveloped in national debates about the federal recognition process, and the specifics of the injustice of the Chinook situation were lost.[106] Once again, the bill never moved beyond the Committee for Natural Resources, and the bill for recognition was effectively dead.

The Chinook did not give up hope for the eventual passing of the bill, but the retirement of Brian Baird in early January 2011 required renegotiation and the search for a new sponsor. While Baird has continued to help the tribe in efforts toward restoration, the Chinook still needed a member of Congress to officially reintroduce a restoration bill. Members of the Tribal Council met with Jaime Herrera Beutler (Baird's replacement), as well as Maria Cantwell (junior senator from Washington State) and Doc Hastings (representative from Washington's Fourth District and the chair of the Natural Resources Committee). While all said they supported Chinook recognition, the general tone from these politicians—especially Hastings and Cantwell—was that the Chinook Indian Nation should wait. Their suggestion was based on the fact that the BIA was working to make its recognition process more fair, efficient, and transparent. They hoped that forthcoming FAP revisions would allow the Chinook Indian Nation to eventually resubmit paperwork in a climate that was much more conducive to recognition.[107] The Chinook worried, however, that the process for drafting, approving, and then implementing revisions might take years, if revisions were made at all. Additionally, there was no guarantee that the result would be any more equitable or logical than the previous system. As I noted at the end of the introduction, their concerns proved prescient.

The lack of federal recognition creates a number of economic and political challenges to the Chinook Indian Nation. Their right to hunt and fish, the guarantee that they be consulted on archaeological and cultural resource projects, and financial backing to develop programs for community health and well-being are only fully assured with recognition. Presently all Tribal Council and committee members work for the nation entirely on a volunteer basis, and most continue to work full-time jobs in addition. The nation barely has sufficient income to pay for a skeleton crew for its tribal office in Bay Center, Washington. And in November 2011, right before the holiday season, the tribe had to cut their food bank due to insufficient funding.[108]

In the face of these economic and political challenges, the Chinook Indian Nation demonstrates tremendous cultural resilience and strength. They remain a close-knit and active community and are well known and respected

Smith had been right about the location of Cathlapotle. As a result of the controversy and confusion, the National Register designation was withdrawn, and the location of Cathlapotle would remain unconfirmed for a few more years.[6]

While there was no agreement on which of these two archaeological sites represented the remains of Cathlapotle, there was no controversy over who owned the sites: both were under the control of the federal government. The US Fish and Wildlife Service had purchased the land from the Cartys in 1965, and the land was then incorporated into the Ridgefield National Wildlife Refuge. In 1989 Anan Raymond was hired as regional archaeologist (Region 1) for the US Fish and Wildlife Service. Since the archaeological remains of Cathlapotle are located on federal property, stewardship of the remains are mandated and guided by a number of US cultural resource laws, most notably sections 106 and 110 of the National Historic Preservation Act (NHPA).[7] As regional archaeologist, this stewardship responsibility fell to Raymond. He knew that Cathlapotle was located within the boundaries of the Ridgefield National Wildlife Refuge and had no doubt that it was a historically important site. Operating under his responsibilities to comply with federal law—in this case Section 110 of the NHPA was especially pertinent—Raymond knew that he would need a plan to conclusively identify the remains of Cathlapotle and to establish a program for long-term stewardship.[8]

In the years after the controversy erupted, additional archaeological work was conducted under the auspices of the US Fish and Wildlife Service on the Ridgefield National Wildlife Refuge. High levels of erosion near the upriver site—the one Starkey and Ross believed to be Cathlapotle—required the initiation of archaeological work there in 1984. Kathryn Anne Toepel and Rick Minor of Heritage Research Associates, a local cultural resources firm, led that work. Based on their observations, they concluded that the upriver site was actually a series of small camps and not a more permanent village. Therefore, they felt it unlikely that this was the site of Cathlapotle and that Hudziak and Smith's initial designation of which site was Cathlapotle was likely correct.[9] Anan Raymond felt confident in the accuracy of Minor and Toepel's assessment about the upriver site, but he still needed to determine conclusively that Hudziak and Smith's site near the confluence of the Lewis and Lake Rivers was indeed the remnants of the Cathlapotle village. This would require a substantial amount of subsurface testing and perhaps even multiyear work. And while Raymond was responsible for stewarding this potentially large archaeological site, he did not have a large staff to work with. He knew he would need help.

In 1990 Raymond approached Kenneth Ames about the possibility of help-
ing him with the work at Cathlapotle. Ames had been a faculty member in the
Department of Anthropology at Portland State University since 1984. While
at Portland State Ames had initiated and led the Wapato Valley Archaeology
Project (WVAP) with the goal of increasing the understanding of the history
of the Portland Basin, especially through archaeological excavation. When
Raymond contacted Ames about the possibility of conducting archaeological
work at Cathlapotle, Ames and his students were nearing the end of archaeological excavations at the Meier Site (35CO5) located on private land near
Scappoose, Oregon. Over the course of five field seasons Ames and his students
had excavated and exposed large portions of this site, most notably the remains
of a 14-by-35-meter (45-by-115-foot) cedar plankhouse, including archaeological
evidence for walls, house posts, storage cellars, and hearths. The plankhouse
had been occupied continuously from roughly A D 1400 to 1810, and, based on
analysis of these features as well as the thousands of artifacts recovered from
the site, Ames and his students were able to virtually reconstruct the plankhouse, assess the amount of material and labor that had gone into its construction, and examine what the differential spatial and numerical distribution of
artifacts within the house might have to say about status distinctions.[10]

Ames welcomed Raymond's offer to work at Cathlapotle. While leading an
archaeological project at the Cathlapotle village had not been in Ames's plans
when he initially was hired at Portland State, he was nearing the end of the
Meier project and was ready for a new opportunity. Cathlapotle offered the
chance to research a historically well-known village site, one that fit well
within the parameters of the already established Wapato Valley Archaeology
Project. Furthermore, due to high levels of urban expansion in the Portland/
Vancouver metropolitan region, few Native American village sites along the
Columbia River in this area remained. Due in part to its location within the
boundaries of a federally protected refuge, the area surrounding Cathlapotle
had been remarkably well protected from this type of encroachment, and
therefore the site represented a potentially valuable—and, most importantly,
intact—storehouse of archaeological information. Finally, the location of the
site on federal land, as well as its connection to the Lewis and Clark story,
brought the possibility of more dependable sources of funding for research
and archaeological field schools. For all of these reasons Ames happily accepted
Raymond's offer.[11]

The partnership between the US Fish and Wildlife Service and Portland
State University effectively began in December of 1991 when students from

FIGURE 2. Kenneth Ames (*center*), now professor emeritus, Department of Anthropology, Portland Sate University, was the principal investigator for the archaeological excavations at Cathlapotle. Courtesy of the Wapato Valley Archaeology Project.

Portland State, working under the guidance of Ames and Raymond, instituted a series of subsurface tests at the site believed to be Cathlapotle. Based on the positive results of these initial tests the team returned to the site for more extensive testing in February 1992. This more extensive testing uncovered numerous artifacts, evidence for cultural deposits that were both deep and dense, and the outline of an archaeological site that extended, at a minimum, for two hundred meters.[12] These results provided sufficient evidence to both Raymond and Ames that this was the likely location of Cathlapotle, and they moved forward with plans for larger-scale archaeological excavations at the site. Excavations began in the summer of 1993 and continued every summer through 1996. Over the course of the fieldwork conducted between 1991 and 1996 the remains of six plankhouses, as well as thousands of artifacts, were recovered and catalogued. Through their work archaeologists had located a town that had been in existence from roughly AD 1450 to the 1830s or 1840s. They had relocated Cathlapotle.[13]

The NHPA mandates that federal agencies consult with Indian tribes that attach religious or cultural significance to sites that will be impacted by federal activities—in this case the archaeological excavations at Cathlapotle.

Additionally, both Ames and Raymond had histories of working positively with Native American communities on archaeological projects. For both of these reasons, outreach to Native American communities that might be interested in the work at Cathlapotle was written into the research plans for the site. One of these communities was the Chinook Indian Nation, and Ames and Raymond traveled to the coast to officially present the plans for the Cathlapotle project to them. The Chinook Indian Nation expressed their strong interest in the work at Cathlapotle and soon became a full partner in the project. A memorandum of agreement (MOA) in 1995 formally codified the terms of the partnership between the US Fish and Wildlife Service, Portland State University, and the Chinook Indian Nation, and with that the Cathlapotle Archaeological Project (CAP) was born. In addition to the archaeological excavations at the site, the goals of the CAP included the development of public outreach materials to promote understanding of Chinookan culture and the natural history of the Ridgefield National Wildlife Refuge, public tours of the excavation site, and public presentations by both archaeologists and citizens of the Chinook Indian Nation. Additionally, plans were initiated for the development of a museum and interpretive center to exhibit and store the artifacts recovered from Cathlapotle during excavations and for the reconstruction of a Chinookan plankhouse on the grounds of the refuge.[14]

DETERMINING VOICES: "EMPTY" SPACES

The Chinook Indian Nation became the federal government's primary consulting party and partner on all work conducted within the boundaries of the Ridgefield National Wildlife Refuge. They were not, however, the only tribal body in the region potentially interested in the work at Cathlapotle. The site of Cathlapotle lies in a region that has no official or single modern tribal representative body. The ambiguity of modern representation for this area is the result of a number of interrelated factors: the devastation—in both demographic and cultural terms—wrought by the extremely high levels of disease that swept though the region as a result of contact with Euro-Americans, the consequent invasion of the region by settlers, and the complexity and ambiguity of the treaty-making process. As noted in chapter 1, diseases introduced to the region by Euro-Americans shattered Indigenous populations of the Pacific Northwest. Villages along the Columbia River were certainly not immune to this onslaught, and in fact the ease of transport that made the river such an effective route for trade made it an equally effective vector for carrying disease.

Additionally, villages like Cathlapotle that were located along the Columbia River were often densely populated and their residents relatively sedentary, characteristics that made the transmission of disease more likely and more rapid. Disease along the Columbia River quickly followed first contact—and in fact likely even preceded it. Smallpox affected the region immediately surrounding Cathlapotle by 1776 and perhaps earlier, as evidenced by the smallpox scars Lewis and Clark noted on some of the Natives along the river, and a series of smallpox outbreaks continued well into the nineteenth century. This was followed by the devastation of malaria epidemics that hit the immediate area around Cathlapotle particularly hard during the 1830s.[15]

The few Native Americans who survived the ravages of disease came under intense pressure and competition from white settlers. The arrival of white settlers into the region began shortly after the establishment in 1811 of Fort Astoria on the Columbia River near the coast. Additional settlement in the region followed the establishment of the Hudson's Bay Company's Fort Vancouver (located in present-day Vancouver, Washington) in 1824. White settlement of lands near Cathlapotle began as a trickle but expanded exponentially in the early 1840s just as Native populations had experienced the worst ravages of disease and many Native villages had been abandoned. While some of the early settlers into the region had intermarried with Native populations and had relatively workable relationships with local tribes, many of the settlers arriving in the 1840s held much more rigid and hostile views on Native Americans. Historian Gray Whaley writes, "The overriding problem that Indian people faced was the near absolute colonial conviction of racial exclusivity: the Western lands were for 'whites,' and Indians were to be removed and confined."[16] The conviction that these lands were meant for whites only resulted in little concern by whites regarding the rights of surviving Native Americans in the region.

After having lost most of their lands to white settlers, Chinookans of the region around Cathlapotle were parties to a series of treaties negotiated during the early years of the 1850s, all of which would have removed them from their homelands. As noted in chapter 1, however, none of these treaties were successfully implemented or ratified. In 1856, under pressure from white settlers fearful of "Indian raids," the few remaining Chinookans of the region were rounded up and sent to the Grand Ronde Reservation.[17] Left without a specifically Chinookan reservation or representative body of their own, many of those who remained refused to go and instead dispersed throughout the region, intermarrying with other Native communities.

Based on this history of disease and displacement, federal archaeologists knew that Chinookan peoples of the Cathlapotle area had been absorbed into a number of other tribal groups throughout the Northwest. Furthermore, additional historical evidence suggested that after the devastation of disease other nearby Native groups, such as the Klikitat and Cowlitz, moved into the regions formerly inhabited by Chinookans. For these reasons Anan Raymond sent letters of consultation to four tribal organizations in the region that he thought would have connections to the village of Cathlapotle and that might be interested in the archaeological research planned for the refuge. Two federally recognized tribes (the Confederated Tribes of Grand Ronde and the Yakama Nation), and two non-federally recognized tribes (the Chinook Indian Nation and the Cowlitz Indian Tribe) were sent research proposals and a request for comment and consultation.[18]

All four groups responded to the request. The Yakama Nation asserted that it had usual and accustomed fishing rights in the region but otherwise showed no interest in participation in the project. Grand Ronde responded by saying that it had a strong interest in the region but that it would be more appropriate to defer to the Chinook Indian Nation on this project. The Cowlitz Indian Tribe chose not to get involved because, in the minds of many Cowlitz at the time, the village of Cathlapotle was outside of their area of interest. Furthermore, they were enmeshed in a struggle for federal recognition and felt that involvement with the work at Cathlapotle would be a distraction.[19] Of these four tribal bodies, only the Chinook Indian Nation, headquartered near the mouth of the Columbia River roughly eighty miles away from Cathlapotle, requested an active voice in the project and a partnership status in the research.[20]

As noted, the Chinook Indian Nation represents the five westernmost tribes of Chinookan-speaking peoples, and the home territories of all five tribes historically were located downriver from the village of Cathlapotle. The eastern border of the modern Chinook Indian Nation on the north side of the Columbia River is located roughly at Oak Point, Washington, approximately fifty miles from Cathlapotle. But, despite the distance from the site, citizens of the Chinook Indian Nation felt strongly connected to Cathlapotle. Gary Johnson, who served for six years as chair of the Chinook Indian Nation Tribal Council, explains, "We feel the responsibility, and we are tied by blood to the tribes further on up the river. And we feel it is very much our responsibility to oversee our ancestors' territories. . . . There are blood connections of our family members marrying people from those villages . . . that's Chinookan territory. We see that as an area that is really important for us to protect and to be sure that things there are done properly."[21] In addition to the history of intermarriage with villages upriver, the Chinook felt that they had inherited the responsibility to care for the heritage of an area where there was now a vacuum of tribal presence and influence. While tribal groups like the Yakama Nation were responsible for heritage sites farther to the east on the north shore of the Columbia River, and the Grand Ronde community was responsible for sites on the south shore of the river (as well as on the shores of the Willamette River), the northern shore of the river in the area of Cathlapotle was not clearly defined. The Chinook felt that this was their responsibility. Additionally, the Chinook Indian Nation was fighting for federal recognition during this time, and Cathlapotle served as an important place for cultural memory and legitimization of the legacy of Chinookan-speaking peoples along the length of the lower Columbia.

Both Anan Raymond and Ken Ames felt that in terms of cultural continuity the Chinook Indian Nation was certainly an appropriate party for consultation. This was based primarily on generally accepted historical and ethnographic documents that placed Chinookan-speaking peoples on both sides of the Columbia River from its mouth to the present-day location of The Dalles, Oregon. But they also understood that due to high levels of precontact intermarriage and the dispersal of surviving Native populations from the region to a number of intertribal bodies, any of the other modern tribal organizations could assert a cultural connection to the site of Cathlapotle. What made the difference for Raymond, however, was the Chinook Indian Nation's active request for participation:

> The ones that speak up the loudest and exert their will and their interest and want to participate, that plays a huge role. . . . The Chinook in the 1990s had no greater capacity—financial or human—than the Cowlitz or any other organization. Yet they said "you know what, we connect to this place. Sure it's a hundred miles away, sure we all live here at the mouth of the river. But that is Chinook, it's a Chinookan site. We're the representatives. . . . We're going to make it a priority." To me that was very impressive because they didn't have the capacity or resources to get involved, yet they did it anyway.[22]

The 1995 memorandum of agreement between the Chinook Indian Nation, the US Fish and Wildlife Service, and Portland State was followed by years of productive research and analysis of Cathlapotle, as well as collaborations on other archaeological work within the refuge and public education materials concerning the history of the site. Over the course of time, strong friendships and a sense of trust developed between the partners. The strength of this partnership, however, would soon be challenged by an emerging voice.

CONTESTING CATHLAPOTLE

In December 2003, the newly federally recognized Cowlitz Indian Tribe, headquartered in Longview, Washington, contacted US Fish and Wildlife Service archaeologists with a number of concerns about the cultural affiliation of Cathlapotle.[23] In a series of meetings with Fish and Wildlife employees, members of the Cowlitz Tribal Council expressed their claims. The possibility that Cathlapotle was a Cowlitz village, rather than a Chinookan village, was brought up by the Cowlitz representatives during these meetings, but their more common claim centered around the ambiguity of identity at Cathlapotle. While it could not be conclusively stated that Cathlapotle was a Cowlitz village, the true identity of the Cathlapotle people was never historically recorded. Additionally, the Cowlitz representatives noted that the people of Cathlapotle had nearly been eliminated by the plagues that had devastated the Columbia River and that some of the surviving citizens of Cathlapotle certainly moved to nearby Cowlitz villages and intermarried with Cowlitz people. Therefore, some present-day members of the Cowlitz Indian Tribe are direct descendants of the Cathlapotle people. Furthermore, they argued that while it is possible that people who spoke Chinookan dialects once resided in the area of Cathlapotle, the Lewis River Cowlitz had most recently lived there. They stated that the last chief of Cathlapotle was Cowlitz and not Chinookan and that the US Fish and Wildlife Service even listed this chief—Tyee Umtuch—in one of its publications for the site.[24] Finally, the Cowlitz argued that even if the Cathlapotle people were Chinookans, they were Upper or Middle Chinookans and not directly associated with any of the five tribes that make up the modern-day Chinook Indian Nation, headquartered at that time more than eighty miles downstream in Chinook, Washington. Therefore, they said, federal government consultation with the Chinook Indian Nation aided an inappropriate extension of historic Lower Chinookan territory into upriver areas of the Columbia River. Based on these points, the Cowlitz representatives argued that the Cowlitz Indian Tribe was an appropriate consulting tribe for the project, and since they were now federally recognized they called for the immediate initiation of government-to-government consultation with the US Fish and Wildlife Service concerning the cultural resources of the refuge.

Defining boundaries and territories lay at the heart of Cowlitz claims. They strongly asserted that the traditional boundaries of the Cowlitz world encompassed the site of Cathlapotle and that their cultural connection to that land had been lost during years of colonization and assimilation. Furthermore, they argued that other federally recognized tribes had encroached on Cowlitz territories for years, but lack of federally recognized status during this time had prevented the Cowlitz from legally challenging this encroachment. Mike Iyall, director of natural and cultural resources for the Cowitz Indian Tribe at the time, noted this connection between federal recognition and the protection of territory: "One of the challenges that recognition brings is that it brings you sovereignty. Well, I believe that the most important dimension of sovereignty is what is your true footprint, because your sovereignty exists only within your footprint. Now we've had neighbors that are long-time recognized tribes with big feet that have gotten their claims in our world."[25] With the realization of federal recognition in 2002, the Cowlitz Indian Tribe have had a stronger institutional authority to claim areas they feel are their own and to which they believe they have a cultural connection.

It is important to note that the Chinook Indian Nation and the Cowlitz Indian Tribe have a long, close, mutually respectful relationship. Their communities have been positively intertwined both before and after colonial contact, trade and intermarriage between the two have been common, and the two are culturally very similar. There is a history of close friendships between the two nations, including former tribal chairs who grew up together as friends and who worked together as tribal leaders. And as non-recognized tribal nations they traveled similar paths in their struggles for justice and restoration. In fact, they shared the same historian (Stephen Dow Beckham) and attorney (Dennis Whittlesey) in their fights for federal recognition. Despite this history of positive connections, the claims to Cathlapotle resulted in tensions between the two nations. Cowlitz claims regarding Cathlapotle did not go unchallenged, and citizens of the Chinook Indian Nation disputed the assertion that the area now encompassed within the boundaries of the Ridgefield National Wildlife refuge was or is Cowlitz territory. Former chair Gary Johnson understands that the devastation of disease created havoc in the region, destroying social systems and altering kinship networks, allowing other tribal groups to move into the area during the post-contact period. But he stresses that, through the depth of time, occupation at Cathlapotle was Chinookan, and that at the moment of contact Cathlapotle was still a Chinookan village: "All historical evidence tells us that Cathlapotle was a Chinookan village. The people were Chinookan. After contact and after considerable devastation, with so many people dying, there were movements among some of the surviving people. For instance, a number of Chehalis came into Southwest Washington and lived with Chinooks. Chinooks went to different reservations and places where they could live their lives the way that they wanted to. There was some movement, and there are one or two records of Cowlitz people perhaps fishing and trading in that area, but it clearly was not their historical area." Johnson accepts that residents of Cathlapotle may have included people from Cowlitz villages, mostly because intermarriage was such a common occurrence throughout the Pacific Northwest and because there were Cowlitz villages located a few miles off of the Columbia River but still in proximity to Cathlapotle. But he also noted that intermarriage occurred with numerous tribes, not just the Cowlitz, and furthermore that the presence of non-Chinookan people in a village should not lead to the designation of that village as non-Chinookan.[26]

The motives behind the Cowlitz Indian Tribe's claims of cultural connection to the Ridgefield area were also questioned more broadly. As is often the case today in tribal recognition and territory matters, the specter of potential gaming revenues was offered as the primary cause for the controversy. Critics of the Cowlitz Indian Tribe suggested that its newfound interest in the site of Cathlapotle was merely a ploy to establish ties to the region so that a 152-acre parcel of land (located on the heavily traveled Interstate 5 corridor and mere miles from the Portland-Vancouver Metropolitan Area) could be placed in "fee-to-trust" status and qualify as a center for gaming operations and the development of a casino.[27]

Scott Aikin, who served at the time as a Native American liaison for the US Fish and Wildlife Service and who was involved in mediating the dispute, did not believe that the Cowlitz Indian Tribe was primarily motivated by casino revenues or were trying to expand into the territories of other tribes: "I think the perception is that they were trying to build a broader homeland. . . . I don't think, in all my years of working with them now, . . . that is what drives them. I think that they see it as a fairness issue, and I think that they believe that [Cathlapotle] is not a place that the Chinook Nation really has as strong a stake, as strong of a foothold as is being portrayed, and that it was institutionalization, it was the nine years of [the Chinook Nation] working with [the USFWS] that they kind of became the personified tribe."[28]

Regardless of motives, the claims of the Cowlitz Indian Tribe resulted in a difficult and often emotional struggle for control of the cultural resources of

Cathlapotle. The Chinook Indian Nation, which had been the consulting tribe on the project since its inception, threatened to pull out if the Cowlitz Indian Tribe were included in any meaningful way. Meanwhile, the Cowlitz Indian Tribe temporarily blocked a $220,000 US Department of Transportation grant that was earmarked for the reconstruction of a cedar plankhouse near the Cathlapotle site (about which I write in chapter 4).[29] To add to the mounting tensions, individuals descended from Chinookan-speaking Clatsops, and who were former members of the Chinook Indian Nation, formed an entirely separate body called the Clatsop-Nehalem Confederated Tribes, and they promised to begin their own quest for recognition. There was also speculation that these disagreements were not just about stewardship of cultural heritage but also about control of substantial dollars set aside for upcoming Lewis and Clark Bicentennial festivities as well.[30]

The struggle was also difficult for the archaeologists who worked at Cathlapotle. In the course of fulfilling stewardship obligations attached to the site, partnerships and friendships had been made during the nearly fifteen years of collaboration. As Anan Raymond noted,

> Things were initially tough because we had this fourteen-year relationship with the Chinook tribe and the Cowlitz tribe came in and told us that we were all wrong. And, you know, on the one hand we have our understanding of the history and archaeology, but on the other hand, I'll be perfectly honest, we have this longstanding relationship with the Chinook tribe that is very difficult to deny or to turn off just because some new information shows up. . . . Even if the information were right it would have been very difficult to turn off a longstanding, productive, professional, and personal relationship with several members of the Chinook tribe.[31]

In a series of meetings with representatives of the Cowlitz Indian Tribe, Raymond recognized their interest in the Cathlapotle site. He refused, however, to concede—based on his understanding of the ethnography, history, and archaeology—that Cathlapotle was a Cowlitz village. The Cowlitz representatives saw this refusal as an abrogation of Cowlitz rights as a sovereign nation. Furthermore, they contended that the relationship between the US Fish and Wildlife Service and the Chinook Indian Nation was the result of the institutionalization of an arbitrary partnership rather than based on an accurate assessment of history. The fact that it was a longstanding partnership was irrelevant to whether or not it was an appropriate one.

The meetings at times turned acrimonious, as participants lost their patience and tempers flared. Scott Aikin, tribal liaison for the US Fish and Wildlife Service, was brought in to mediate and, according to Raymond, "serve as a temper to my temper."[32] Aikin served as a calming influence and provided a measure of stability, but his involvement was not sufficient to address the concerns of the Cowlitz Indian Tribe. On January 5, 2004, the Cowlitz Indian Tribe sent a letter to the manager of the Ridgefield National Wildlife Refuge and a copy was also sent to Washington congressman Brian Baird. It expressed their dissatisfaction with the progress of the meetings, questioned the objectivity of federal employees, and suggested that the Fish and Wildlife Service had failed in its good-faith effort to establish a government-to-government relationship. Therefore, "after lengthy attempts to resolve our differences we are seeking outside help."[33]

At this point David Nicandri of the Washington State Historical Society was brought in as a neutral third party to help mediate the dispute. Raymond believes that while there were both positives and negatives involved with this mediation process—in his opinion, one of the problems was the failure to directly involve the Chinook Indian Nation as an active party in the dispute— the mediation was effective in pushing a stalled process forward: "It moved us to a written agreement with the Cowlitz, and it also provided a relatively neutral forum for the Cowlitz to make their claims and for the US Fish and Wildlife Service to explain its position. . . . It's always good to have a third party when there is strong disagreement."[34] The principle result of the mediation was a memorandum of understanding (MOU) between the US Fish and Wildlife Service and the Cowlitz Indian Tribe. This document codified the relationship between the two parties and created a protocol for future cooperation. Further details about this MOU are discussed in chapter 4. Meanwhile an MOU between the Fish and Wildlife Service and the Chinook Indian Nation was instituted at the same time, and this noted that other tribal bodies had the right to be involved with interpretive and educational materials associated with the cultural resources of the refuge. Both the Chinook Indian Nation and the Cowlitz Indian Tribe were notified, however, that the Chinook Indian Nation "is the principal organization that exclusively embodies and perpetuates the traditional and modern culture of the Chinookans of the greater lower Columbia River, including the Cathlapotle Chinookans who historically lived on what is now the Refuge."[35] For Anan Raymond it was important that this statement be clear and directed to both tribal organizations: "We stated this in a letter to both tribes, the Chinook and Cowlitz, that we consider the Chinook tribe to be the principle organization that represents Chinookan culture and history and therefore they represent the best organization for us to consult with on issues concerning Chinookan culture. That does not mean we would not consult with the Cowlitz tribe, but the upshot is that if you were to sort of prioritize where would we go first, or who has most authority in that sense, the Chinook tribe does."[36] Although no one was entirely satisfied with the terms of the MOUs, and there was certainly concern that they left some long-term issues unresolved, they were "enough to Band-aid the situation" and allowed for a stalled process to move forward.[37]

RECOGNIZED AND NON-RECOGNIZED VOICES

The legitimacy of the Cowlitz Indian Tribe's claim to Cathlapotle was strengthened by its status as a federally recognized tribal entity, a status that the Chinook Indian Nation did not have at the time and still does not have to this day. But why does federal recognition matter, especially within the context of cultural heritage and cultural resource management? For one reason, federal cultural resource laws give recognized tribes a higher status than non-recognized organizations. For instance, section 106 of the NHPA requires that federal agencies, prior to conducting any undertaking that uses federal funds, occurs on federal lands, or requires a federal license, must consider the effects of that undertaking on historic and archaeological resources eligible for inclusion in the National Register of Historic Places. The procedures for section 106 compliance are codified in title 36, part 800, of the US Code of Federal Regulations. One important requirement for compliance is consultation with the appropriate Indian tribes: "It is the responsibility of the agency official to make a reasonable and good faith effort to identify Indian tribes and Native Hawaiian organizations that shall be consulted in the section 106 process."[38] The Code of Federal Regulations then goes on to define who or what an "Indian tribe" is: "*Indian tribe* means an Indian tribe, band, nation, or other organized group or community, including a native village, regional corporation or village corporation, as those terms are defined in section 3 of the Alaska Native Claims Settlement Act (43USC1602), which is *recognized* [emphasis added] as eligible for the special programs and services provided by the United States to Indians because of their status as Indians."[39]

This does not mean, however, that federally unrecognized tribes are precluded from consulting on federal cultural resource projects. A variety of stakeholders can participate in or comment on heritage management programs conducted under the auspices of the federal government. These stakeholders, noted as "additional consulting parties" in the regulations, are those "certain individuals and organizations with a demonstrated interest in the undertaking" who "may participate as consulting parties due to the nature of their legal or economic relation to the undertaking or affected properties, or their concern with the undertaking's effects on historic properties."[40] The Chinook Indian Nation clearly falls under this definition and can, under the guidelines, express interest in the work conducted at Cathlapotle regardless of its unrecognized status.

Furthermore, federal recognition does not give a tribal organization the right to claim cultural affiliation to a region that was historically the homeland of an unrecognized tribe. As Anan Raymond notes, "When it comes to affiliating a site, so to speak, to a culture or a group of people, federal recognition does not trump a non-federally recognized tribe."[41] Nonetheless, under the regulations of both the National Historic Preservation Act and the standards of the Advisory Council on Historic Preservation (ACHP), the status of federal recognition does carry the *right* to participate in section 106 consultations.[42] Therefore, Raymond says, "What is required . . . by the law is that you must *at least* consult with federally recognized tribes. You must *at least* consider their interests."[43] As a result, the US Fish and Wildlife Service is now obligated to consult with the federally recognized Cowlitz Indian Tribe when a project is conducted within the boundaries of the refuge. The Fish and Wildlife Service chooses to treat the Chinook Indian Nation as a full consulting party. As Scott Aikin notes, "With the Chinook we continue on with this institutionalized relationship." He also notes, however, that the relationship with the Chinook Indian Nation does "not carry the same weight as a federally recognized body," and under the letter of the law the Fish and Wildlife Service could legally discontinue the partnership at any time.[44]

In addition to providing elevated legal status, federal acknowledgment also brings institutional authority and financial resources to recognized tribal organizations. Federally recognized tribes are eligible for programs and funding that can greatly improve their ability to participate in heritage management projects. Paying attention to cultural resources is an expensive proposition in terms of finances and personnel, and additional resources can potentially play a more important role in heritage management than a tribe's legal status. The additional financial support that came with federal recognition was likely influential in the Cowlitz Indian Tribe's claim to the site of Cathlapotle. As Raymond says,

about ownership of archaeological sites, Indigenous identity, and intellectual authority. My search for the history of these maps, created by colonial agents, reminded me that they were really a form of "cartographic illusion" that hid the complexity of Indigenous identity and place, typically to the benefit of colonial institutions.[1] I was also reminded that, regardless of the illusory nature of these maps, they and their other iterations ultimately became political reality, and Native American nations were forced to reconfigure centuries-old identities in order to cope with the new colonial landscape that these maps represented.

This chapter, then, is about maps. It is about maps and the identity and boundary fictions they create. It is about the legacies of anthropologists, historians, and ethnohistorians in that process. And it is about the way that maps continue to shape and guide governmental action in the present. While in some ways the story of this chapter begins with the first contact between Native Americans and Euro-Americans on the Columbia River, the most important connection between the past and present of maps in the context of this book begins with a somewhat overlooked nineteenth-century exploration expedition and the theoretical views of a twenty-one-year-old ethnologist who was a part of it.

THE US EXPLORING EXPEDITION OF 1838–1842

The US Exploring Expedition of 1838–42, sometimes called the Wilkes Expedition or shortened to "US Ex. Ex.," does not hold the same place in the annals of exploration as, for instance, the three maritime expeditions of James Cook. Nor does it hold nearly as prominent of a place in American memory as does Lewis and Clark's Corps of Discovery. Much of the somewhat forgotten status of the Wilkes Expedition is due to the commander of the expedition himself, Lt. Charles Wilkes. By most accounts Wilkes was a brilliant man, but he was also brash, impulsive, paranoid, imperious, and occasionally cruel. These traits, especially the last, led to the court-martial of Wilkes on a number of charges, including falsifying an entry in a ship log, scandalous conduct, mistreatment of subordinate officers, cruelty in killing Natives, and excessive punishment through whipping of crew members. Although Wilkes was acquitted on all but the last charge, the drama surrounding Wilkes's behavior served as a distraction from the expedition itself. Rather than being held up as a successful expedition worthy of national celebration, the US Ex. Ex. was viewed first and foremost through the lens of controversy. Despite the initial controversy attached to Wilkes, the expedition ultimately proved to be significant. Objects collected during the expedition were placed in the relatively young Smithsonian Institution and helped to enhance the burgeoning museum's prestige. The expedition also increased the overall standing of science in the United States as well as America's place in the international scientific community. Most importantly, for the purposes of this chapter, the expedition influenced the ways that Indigenous boundaries and identities in the Pacific Northwest were viewed and would continue to be viewed, as well as the role that anthropologists and bureaucrats would play in that process.[2]

Although the US Ex. Ex. did not set sail until 1838, its roots went back more than a decade earlier. Within some circles of the US government during the 1820s there was growing interest in the initiation of a large-scale exploring expedition on the high seas. One of the leading voices for exploration was John Quincy Adams, who was inaugurated as the sixth president in 1825 and who had served as secretary of state prior to that. Adams was an admirer of the great expeditions of European nations and strongly hoped that the United States would undertake a maritime expedition that would take its place alongside the likes of the voyages of Cook. While Adams continued to push for an expedition within the halls of government, there were somewhat unexpected allies operating elsewhere. One of these was John Cleves Symmes Jr., a somewhat eccentric philosopher and scientist who postulated that the earth was hollow and consisted of a series of inhabitable concentric solid spheres. According to Symmes's "hollow earth" theory, openings were located near both the north and south poles, and the other spheres could be visited by entering these openings. Thus, in his opinion, an expedition to locate these holes was imperative.[3]

Symmes gave public lectures on his hollow earth theory throughout the United States in an effort to convince both the general public and the scientific community of its veracity and the need for exploration. Although he was not a particularly effective speaker, Symmes did gain some converts to his theory. One of these was Jeremiah Reynolds, a midwestern journalist. Unlike Symmes, Reynolds was both outgoing and an engaging speaker. Reynolds took up Symmes's cause and set off on his own speaking tour. Through his determined efforts an expedition designed to locate Symmes's postulated polar openings nearly gained the approval of Congress in the mid-1820s. By the late 1820s, however, Reynolds had abandoned his belief in the hollow earth theory. He nonetheless remained an active and vociferous proponent of a federally funded maritime expedition and was very effective in gaining the support of scientists, whalers, businessmen, and politicians. In May 1836, to a large extent due to the years of continued efforts by Reynolds, Congress authorized the president to send out an expedition to explore the South Seas and the Pacific Ocean.[4] Just over two years later, in August 1838, the US Exploring Expedition, under the command of Wilkes, set sail from the Norfolk Navy Yard in Virginia. The expedition's six ships traveled first to the Madeira Islands, then to South America and around Tierra del Fuego and Cape Horn, then to numerous islands in the Pacific, after which it traveled to Antarctica, then went north to the Oregon Territory and south to San Francisco Bay. After leaving the American West Coast the expedition traveled to the Philippines and around the southern tip of Africa, finally arriving back to the East Coast of the United States in June 1842, completing the circumnavigation of the globe nearly four years after departing on the voyage.

While Symmes's view of a hollow earth may have provided an initial—although ultimately tangential—impetus for an exploring expedition, there were more pragmatic and demonstrable reasons for launching the expedition. Many of these centered on increasing business opportunities. The US Ex. Ex. was tasked with surveying and charting uncharted areas where American whalers and commercial traders were already sailing, and Wilkes's standing as a first-rate surveyor was one of the reasons he had been chosen to lead the expedition. Surveying these areas would lead to the production of more accurate maps, which would ultimately increase the safety and efficiency—and therefore profitability—of US maritime business ventures. The expedition was also designed to promote national expansion and militarism (although these were typically tied to business interests as well). Specifically, one of its goals was to address the unease created by the threat of a new French naval presence in the South Seas and to check any further French expansion in that region. The expedition was also intended to remind the British—who had a long-established naval presence—of America's growing naval interests as well as to increase US presence and discovery claims to the Pacific Northwest.[5] The expedition was also given a mandate to chart and map areas of California, specifically the area of the San Francisco Bay. This was done with the intent of US acquisition of California from Mexico, which at the time was newly independent, weak, and debt-ridden and therefore viewed as vulnerable. Finally, although the US Navy declared that the expedition was void of any military character, the vessels of the expedition carried fairly extensive military firepower. The firepower was intended as a warning to the Native inhabitants of the South Seas, evidence to them of American military might, and, if needed, a demonstration of what would happen to Natives if they attacked or mis-treated US mariners.[6]

In addition, it was intended that the expedition would have a strong scientific component, and, as historian Barry Alan Joyce notes, the "announcement of the voyage set off a wave of excitement within the scientific community."[7] Those excited by the possibilities of the expedition included some of the leading scientific minds of the day. For instance, Samuel G. Morton—who is often considered the father of American physical anthropology and is best known for his now discredited theories on the links between skull size, intelligence, and race—was extremely interested in the expedition. Morton hoped that the voyage would result in the extensive gathering of human remains, specifically the skulls of Indigenous people and especially American Indians, which he would then add to his cranial collections.[8] Members of the influential American Philosophical Society were also interested in the expedition and like Morton were especially fascinated with the identification and classification of Native Americans, questions surrounding comparisons between Native Americans and other races, and the hypothesized connections between Native Americans and the fabled Ten Lost Tribes of Israel.[9]

Initial plans for the expedition included the participation of up to twenty civilian scientists across a wide range of fields of study, and a number of scientists eagerly signed up for the opportunity and adventure. That number soon decreased, however, as a few scientists resigned before the expedition started, principally due to the appointment of Wilkes as commander and his reputation for being ambitious, arrogant, and petty. Wilkes also wished to streamline the expedition and limit the number of civilian participants. He therefore transferred any scientific studies that he felt were naval in any way—things like geography, astronomy, hydrography, and meteorology—away from civilian scientists and to naval officers. In the end, the number of scientists was reduced from nearly twenty to seven.[10] Those chosen for the expedition were mostly well-known scientists, and these included geologist James Dwight Dana, zoologist and naturalist Charles Pickering, conchologist Joseph Couthouy, horticulturalist William Brackenridge, naturalist Titian Peale, and botanist William Rich (who was a last-moment replacement for the well-known botanist Asa Gray, who resigned because of the appointment of Wilkes). Most importantly for the purposes of this chapter, the expedition included a twenty-one-year-old recent graduate of Harvard: the ethnologist and philologist Horatio Hale.[11]

HORATIO HALE AND HIS "ETHNOGRAPHICAL MAP"

Despite being younger than his other scientific shipmates, Hale was well respected among his peers. As Joyce notes, Hale's work with Algonquin Indians and his writings on Algonquin vocabulary, completed while he was only seventeen, had given him a reputation as an expert in both Native American languages and ethnology. Even at the young age of twenty-one he was considered extremely well qualified and was recommended for participation on the expedition by fellow members of the scientific community.[12] Hale did nothing during or after the expedition to diminish this reputation or the trust placed in him. In fact, Hale's book written on his findings from the Wilkes Expedition, published in 1846 (*Ethnography and Philology*, vol. 6), was probably the best received of all of the volumes produced after the expedition. For instance, while volumes one through five, written by Wilkes and collectively titled *Narrative of the United States Exploring Expedition*, were met with mixed reviews, and Charles Pickering's volume, *The Races of Man*, was widely criticized, *Ethnography and Philology* "was met with unqualified praise among the scientific and literary community."[13]

Hale was principally interested in language and worked under a framework that saw language—rather than race, as researchers like Samuel G. Morton were arguing at the time—as the most distinctive characteristic of humans. Hale believed that a thorough analysis of language, including the recording of Indigenous mythology and oral traditions, would provide the best means for drawing out the specific histories and cultures of groups and would serve as a much better system for comparative analysis than biology could. A people's history, as well as their connections or lack of connections to other people, is found in their language, and it is for this reason that Hale referred to the study of language as the true basis of ethnology.[14] For this study, the Oregon Territory was ideal in that it contained a wide range of Indigenous languages in a relatively confined space. As Hale noted, "In Oregon . . . the variety of idioms has been found to be much greater than was anticipated. Probably, as has been before remarked, no other part of the world offers an example of so many tribes, with distinct languages, crowded together within a space so limited."[15] Given the central place of the illuminative power of language in Hale's thinking, the Oregon Territory therefore provided an excellent place for study of human variability and an opportunity to draw out important ethnic histories.

The richness of the opportunity for study led Hale to ask for permission to leave the expedition in Oregon and remain there to continue his work. That request was granted, and as the US Ex. Ex. set sail on its final leg in November 1841 Hale stayed behind. For several more months he continued his research on the Indigenous languages of the Oregon Territory.[16] Hale's focus on language did not preclude him from commenting on the overall character of the people he was there to study, and, like Lewis and Clark had been before him, he was not generous in his opinions of the Native Americans of the region. His distaste for the Chinookans of the Columbia River is especially apparent:

> The people of this division are among the ugliest of their race. They are below the middle size, with squat, clumsy forms, very broad faces, low foreheads, lank black hair, wide mouths, and a coarse rough skin, of a tanned, or dingy copper complexion. This description applies more particularly to the tribes of the coast . . . the intellectual and moral characteristics of these natives are not more pleasing than the physical. They are of moderate intelligence, coarse and dirty in their habits, indolent, deceitful, and passionate. They are rather superstitious than religious, are greatly addicted to gambling, and grossly libidinous. All these disagreeable qualities are most conspicuous in the tribes near the mouth of the Columbia.[17]

Hale's negative view of the people of the Columbia River was fueled by the same type of ethnocentric and racist assumptions on what Native Americans should look like and how they should behave as had been held by Lewis and Clark. Business acumen was viewed as stubbornness and thievishness, complex cultural behaviors were simplified as superstitions, and the relatively strong roles of women were translated into lewdness.

Hale's misguided views about the Native Americans of the Pacific Northwest are not, however, of central interest for this chapter. The focus here is on Hale's development of an ethnographic map based on his work in the Oregon Territory, especially the influence this map has had on later anthropological work in the region as well as the role it has played in shaping conceptions of what constitutes tribal identity and boundaries and present-day discussions surrounding contested heritage. Two closely related versions of Hale's ethnographic map were produced and published in the volumes of the Wilkes Expedition. One version is included in Hale's volume, *Ethnography and Philology* (between pages 196–97) and is titled "Ethnographical Map of Oregon Showing the Limits of the Tribes and Their Affinities by Language." The other version is included in volume 4, written by Wilkes, and titled "Map of the Oregon Territory." Although this version of the map lists Charles Wilkes as the author, it includes the same

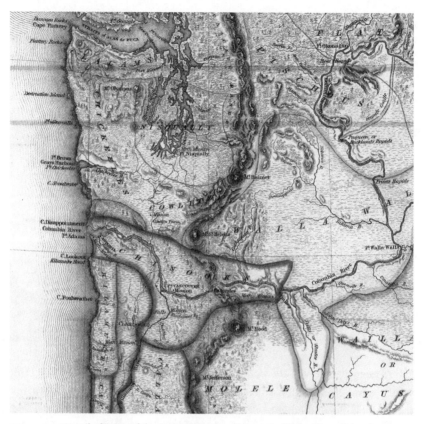

FIGURE 3. Detail of "Map of the Oregon Territory" from the Wilkes Expedition (1841). The map is based on the work of Horatio Hale and shows Indigenous language groups in bounded polygons (e.g., "Chinooks," "Cowlitz," etc.).

ethnographic information (with only slight modifications) that is on the one in Hale's volume, and it is based directly on his work (see figure 3).

These maps from the US Ex. Ex. are interesting for a number of reasons. First, they are the first maps of the region—and, as far as I can discern, some of the first maps in the world—to use language groupings as the primary unit of ethnographic identity for Indigenous cultures. This is, of course, a reflection and natural outgrowth of Hale's belief that the use of linguistic data is the best way to reconstruct ethnicity and ethnic histories and therefore the best indictor of shared identity. Second, Hale's map is the first of the region to visually articulate firm boundaries for language groups—language groups are defined in areal polygons with established boundaries. Rather than mapping specific points on the landscape—villages or even clusters of villages—Hale was interested in mapping and bounding the geographic extent of an entire language. Third, these maps are the first to use the label "Chinook" (or some variant of the word) to refer to an extended bounded geographic area. The map from Wilkes's volume 4 uses the term "Chinooks" to refer to an area extending both north and south along the Columbia River upriver to the Dalles, as well as along the downriver portion of the Willamette River (see figure 3). The legend in the map in Hale's *Ethnography and Philology* identifies that same bounded area as "Tshinuk" (to refer to the language family) while noting "Tshinuk" (Lower Chinook) and "Watlala" (Upper Chinook) on the map as divisions within the larger language family. The word "Chinook" initially referred to an individual village located near the mouth of the Columbia River. But through Hale's maps a word that had been specific to a particular village became instead visually associated with a larger geographic region and identified boundaries.

Anthropologists will find Hale's ethnographic maps instantly recognizable in their general form, if not in the specific regional details they present. These types of ethnographic maps, with bounded polygons representing language families (or some other indicator of assumed shared identity), became a staple of late-nineteenth-century anthropology, are intertwined with the growth of the field, and are still in use today. The revolutionary nature of Hale's ethnographic map at the time of its creation, however, should not be overlooked. For instance, we can compare Hale's maps with maps that preceded them. Lewis and Clark's original hand-drawn maps of the region from 1805 to 1806 identified individual Native American villages or very closely linked clusters of villages—for example "Quath-lah-poh-tle," "Mult-no-mah," and "Shoto nation"—rather than grouping them as one collected unit (see figure 4). Although the maps that were included with the first publication of Clark's journal in 1814 simplify the original hand-drawn maps by not denoting each individual village, they still identify Native populations based on village names and population clusters, rather than connection by language (see figure 5).[18] Later maps based in whole or in part on the travels of Lewis and Clark—such as the "Partie des Etats-Unis. No. 38" drawn in 1827 by Philippe M. G. Vandermaelen and the "Oregon Territory" created by David H. Burr and Illman & Pilbrow and published in 1835—follow the same pattern.[19] It is not until the appearance of Hale's maps as part of the record of the US Ex. Ex. that language becomes the primary visual designation of shared Native identity and that "Chinook" comes to designate a broad and bounded language cluster and not specifically a village and group at the mouth of the Columbia River.

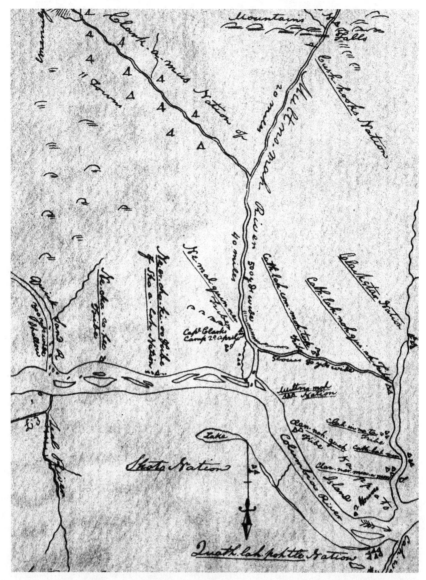

FIGURE 4. Hand-drawn map by William Clark (1806) showing the area where the Willa-mette ("Multnomah") River flows into the Columbia River. Indigenous villages or village clusters are noted (e.g., "Shoto Nation," "Quath.lah.pohtle Nation," etc.). North is to the bottom of the map. Courtesy of the Douglas County Museum, Roseburg, Oregon.

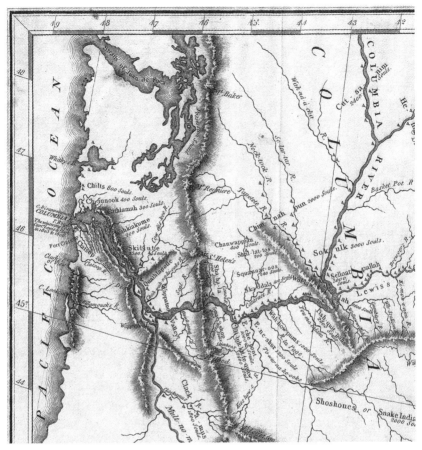

FIGURE 5. Detail of "A Map of Lewis and Clark's Track across the Western Portion of North America," from the 1814 publication of the history of the expedition by Paul Allen and Nicholas Biddle. Indigenous groups are designated by village clusters (i.e., "Chinnook," "Cathlamah," "Wahkiakume," "Clatsop," etc.).

Before delving into the repercussions of Hale's ethnographic maps, I want to briefly touch on Hale's life after the Wilkes Expedition and the publication of *Ethnography and Philology* in 1846. Despite the fact that Hale's work with the US Ex. Ex. was very well received, he quickly disappeared from the world of anthropology and did not publish anything related to the field for thirty-five years. Hale instead earned a degree in law, married, and then moved to Ontario, where he spent much of his time managing the properties of his wife. Hale, however, made his reappearance in the world of anthropology in the late 1860s when he began correspondence with Lewis Henry Morgan, perhaps the leading

American ethnologist of the time. While Hale and Morgan were friendly and respectful, they differed greatly in their views on culture and race. Hale strongly objected to Morgan's views on social evolution. Morgan argued that there were three stages in the progress of human culture—savagery, barbarism, and civilization—and that different groups of humans (and there was a strong racial component to this) moved through this hierarchy at different rates. Based on Hale's previous work, especially the work completed in the Oregon Territory, Hale rejected Morgan's claims, arguing instead that many of the cultural indicators Morgan used to demonstrate advanced cultural status—such as the superiority of patrilineal systems over matrilineal, and agricultural societies over hunting and gathering—did not work. Hale took a more relativistic approach and noted that high levels of complexity, such as the type of complexity he saw in language and kinship in the Oregon Territory, were present in any number of societies, including the ones that Morgan viewed as barbaric.[20]

Hale's correspondence with Morgan reintroduced him to the wider world of anthropology, and he soon became a member of the anthropology section of the British Association for the Advancement of Science. At the time that Hale joined the British Association it was actively supporting fieldwork designed to "scientifically" document American Indians before their presumed disappearance, representing the same form of "salvage anthropology" that was occurring throughout North America at the time. Hale was a central member of the committee formed to support these efforts at the British Association, and it was through this push for research that the now older Horatio Hale first came into contact with a young Franz Boas. The British Association hoped to fund someone to conduct fieldwork in the Pacific Northwest Coast, and given Hale's previous experience in the Oregon Territory it was initially expected that he would do the work himself. But Hale was nearing his seventies and feared he would no longer be physically able to make the trip. In January 1888 Hale instead contacted the energetic and ambitious Boas—not yet in his thirties—and asked him to do the fieldwork in the Pacific Northwest. At the time, Boas was in a somewhat precarious financial position and in a job that was not fulfilling. Additionally, Boas was looking for a research project that would finally and firmly place him on the anthropological map, so he quickly and enthusiastically agreed to Hale's offer.[21]

Hale became Boas's mentor and advisor for the fieldwork in the Northwest Coast, and the relationship between the two proved to be interesting and complex. Hale had a tendency to view Boas as a rash young man who was unwilling to follow his directions, and Boas often viewed Hale as a nuisance and busy-body who was getting in the way of his research. Anthropologist Jacob W. Gruber argues that this tension was due in part to the fact that Hale saw Boas as an extension of himself and therefore as a means to correct some of the research mistakes that Hale had made as a young man. Boas bristled at this. Still, as Gruber notes, Hale ultimately had a tremendous impact on Boas, and through this impact on Boas he also directly had an impact on the development of American anthropology itself.[22] While there is certainly much more that can be written on their complicated relationship, for the purposes of this chapter I will offer two brief examples of the correspondence between them. One of Hale's primary directives for Boas's work in the Northwest Coast region was, not surprisingly, a focus on languages as well as the development of a language-based ethnographic map similar to what Hale had created for the Wilkes Expedition. Hale had very specific instructions as to what he expected and offered his criticisms of Boas's initial work:

> I notice that you have given a great deal of space to the enumeration of small septs or subdivisions of two or three stocks, and to an account of the localities where these small septs reside. Such minute descriptions will, I think, be considered out of place in a general report, such as is now desired. Strictly speaking, these facts cannot be deemed scientific, in an ethnological sense,—any more than a list of all the towns and villages in Bavaria would be deemed appropriate to an account of the ethnology of Germany. Such particulars belong rather to geography or history than to anthropology. Of course whatever relates to gentes, in the proper sense, is of interest; but mere lists of villages or petty tribes, speaking similar dialects, are of no value for our purpose. . . . Do not make your ethnographic map unwieldy in size, or confuse it by inserting too many names.[23]

Hale's central interest in language, specifically language families rather than isolated dialects, is apparent in this letter. And he makes it clear that Boas's work should take a broad approach and not an interest in the particular details of individual villages or tribes. Much to the lingering frustration of Hale, however, Boas refused to follow Hale's suggestions to his satisfaction, as is evident from a letter Hale sent to Boas more than a year later: "I must earnestly enjoin you to follow implicitly the instructions you received from me. If you had done it last year—if you had kept the linguistic portion of your work strictly within the limits prescribed, and had made your ethnographic map to conform to my

Oregon map (as I requested)—you would have saved yourself and me a great deal of trouble, and would have produced a more satisfactory report. I cannot understand why you should persist in causing me an immense amount of useless trouble, as well as much annoyance."[24] These samples of correspondence not only hint at the complex and occasionally tense relationship between mentor and mentee, they also demonstrate why Hale's ethnographic maps from the Wilkes Expedition looked the way they did. The elements that were important to Hale were language and an indication of the geographic extent of that language. Any further details, such as the physical locations of villages or "tribes," were extraneous data that only served to needlessly obfuscate the centrality of language and its utility in illuminating shared identity.

THE REPERCUSSIONS OF HALE'S MAP

Hale's early work in the Pacific Northwest, combined with his direct mentorship of Franz Boas—with all of its complexities of personality and philosophical approach—ultimately plays a central role in the development of American anthropology. But my focus here is specifically on Hale's map and the direct repercussions of its creation. At its most fundamental level, Hale's map serves as the generative iteration for the ethnographic maps of the region that follow. These later maps typically either adopt Hale's language boundaries directly or present them with slight modifications only. For instance, the "Map Showing the Distribution of the Indian Tribes of Washington Territory" created in 1876 and sometimes referred to as the Gibbs map, because it was made to illustrate a paper written by the ethnologist George Gibbs, shows tribal boundaries based on language groupings (e.g., "Tsinuk") that closely approximate those of Hale (see figure 6).[25] Some other maps, such as James Mooney's "Distribution of Tribes of the Upper Columbia Region in Washington, Oregon and Idaho" from 1894, show a bit more detail and give boundaries for groups within larger families (e.g., Clatsop, Chinook, Wakiakum, and Kathlamet) but color-code the larger language family ("Chinookan") in boundaries that closely match Hale's map.[26] Finally, Hale's boundaries continue to be reflected in much more recent publications like the 1990 *Handbook of North American Indians*, vol. 7, *Northwest Coast*, published by the Smithsonian Institution.[27]

The repercussions of Hale's creation, however, go deeper than the production of a lineage of relatively similar looking maps. One of the central ramifications is that Hale's map—as well as the many other iterations that followed—helped to institute a set of anthropological assumptions about tribal

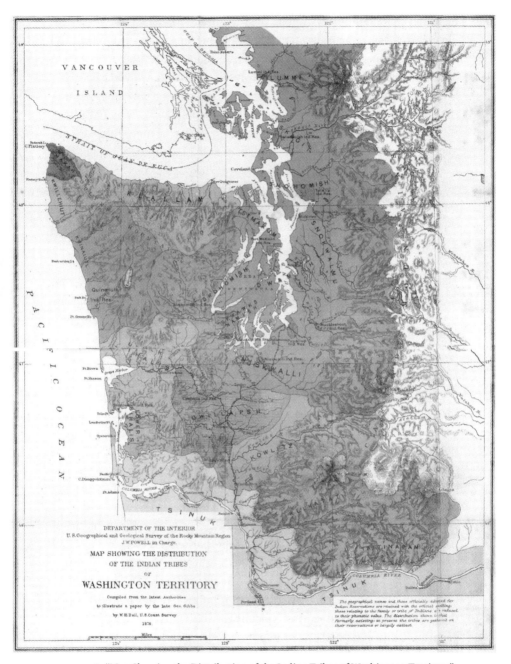

FIGURE 6. "Map Showing the Distribution of the Indian Tribes of Washington Territory" (1876), included in George Gibbs's "Tribes of Western Washington and Northwestern Oregon." The map is based directly on Horatio Hale's maps from the Wilkes Expedition. Courtesy of the Stephen S. Clark Library, University of Michigan Library.

define their various territories, and select the proper 'head chiefs' with whom to negotiate. This process, driven by political expediency rather than aboriginal reality, required the radical modification of Native institutions."[48] Hale's equation of language to identity to territory was a form of "radical modification" that made that process easier. Rather than dealing with the bureaucratic complexity of negotiating with individual autonomous villages and the multiple networks that in reality shaped Indigenous identity on the Columbia River, government agents fell back on that "process of creative misunderstanding" that made Indigenous identity both more simplified and abstract, while at the same time reconfiguring Indigenous places into larger, bounded, and more bureaucratically manageable units.

MAPS, ANTHROPOLOGISTS, AND CATHLAPOTLE

All of this brings us to where we started: the controversies over the cultural affiliation of the site of Cathlapotle. As outlined in chapter 2, archaeologists from both the US Fish and Wildlife Service and Portland State University believed that the Chinook Indian Nation provided the appropriate cultural continuity to serve as the primary consultants for the research work undertaken at Cathlapotle. While this was based partially on the active desire by the Chinook Indian Nation to participate, it was also based on generally accepted historical and ethnographic documents—including maps—that placed Chinookan-speaking peoples on both sides of the Columbia River from its mouth to the present-day location of The Dalles, Oregon. This includes areas now firmly located within the boundaries of the Ridgefield National Wildlife Refuge. Specifically, this is the version of the boundaries of Chinookan territory as established by Horatio Hale and subsequently reiterated and codified in a number of maps drawn by ethnologists, anthropologists and government agents.[49] Importantly, these maps also placed Cowlitz tribal boundaries a few miles north of the Columbia River and outside of the current boundaries of the refuge. The accuracy of the boundaries delineated on these maps, however, became an important element in discussions surrounding the cultural affiliation of the site of Cathlapotle, and the Cowlitz Indian Tribe challenged them. This was not, however, the first time that the accuracy of these boundaries had been debated, as the issue had been previously raised in a case presented before the Indian Claims Commission in 1969.

The Indian Claims Commission (ICC) was a "quasi-judicial branch of Congress created in 1946 to deal finally with the long-standing claims of Native

Americans against the Federal Government."[50] In order to deal with Native American land claims, a central mission of the ICC leaders was to establish acceptable geographic boundaries for tribal territories, especially by establishing the areas of "exclusive use and occupancy" for any Indigenous groups that had a claim before the ICC. Maps that were created by anthropologists and ethnographers, as well as details of the background fieldwork or research that had led to the creation of these maps, served as primary forms of evidence. In fact, the role of the anthropologically related scholar as "expert" witness (over even the direct testimony of Native Americans) grew tremendously within the context of the ICC. As anthropologist Nancy Lurie describes,

> it soon became obvious that evidence would consist of more than official documents or records and direct testimony of Indians or their neighbors. Such evidence required organization and interpretation by experts skilled in work of this type. Consequently, anthropological and historical analyses began to play an important part in claims litigation. Critical study of literature concerning given tribes was buttressed with ethnographic accounts. These offered more complete information and more accurate descriptions than the direct testimony of Indians taken according to the format of legal depositions. Archaeological investigations provided information where documentary and ethnographic information was incomplete. . . . The Court of Claims [which preceded the ICC] had used anthropological testimony on only three occasions and no precedents in testimony had been established in this regard, so that the role of expert witness was a new one for archaeologists, ethnologists, and ethnohistorians.[51]

But, as discussed above, determining Indigenous territories, especially in places like the Columbia River, was extremely complex if even possible. Therefore, it is no surprise that the "expert" witnesses often did not agree on tribal boundaries, and this is clearly demonstrated in the case that the Cowlitz Indian Tribe brought before the ICC in 1969.

At issue in this case—the documents of which are collected under the umbrella of Docket No. 218—was the determination of whether the Cowlitz Indian Tribe had aboriginal or "Indian" title to land located within the state of Washington, and, if so, whether those lands had been taken from them without just compensation. The decision of the ICC was that "the United States deprived the plaintiff Cowlitz Tribe of its original Indian title as of

March 3, 1855, without payment of any compensation therefore. Accordingly, plaintiff is entitled to a recovery under the provisions of Clause 4, section 2 of the Indian Claims Commission Act."[52] This decision, however, was not a complete victory for the Cowlitz Indian Tribe. There was a general consensus among government agents and expert witnesses that the areas encompassing the drainage of the Cowlitz River were clearly within the aboriginal territory of the Cowlitz Indian Tribe. In dispute, however, was the location of the southern boundary, specifically the drainage of the Lewis River that at its mouth encompasses the remains of the site of Cathlapotle. While the Cowlitz Tribe claimed this as an area of "exclusive use and occupancy," the ICC found that "the Lewis River area in the southern portion of the claimed tract was variously used and occupied by other Indian groups during the 1800s. Therefore, that area was not exclusively used and occupied by Cowlitz Indians."[53] As a result, the ICC excluded the Lewis River area from the lands to which the Cowlitz Tribe held title.[54]

In making its determination of boundaries for this case the ICC relied on the research and writings of numerous scholars. But most importantly they considered the testimony of two expert witnesses: Dr. Verne Ray for the Cowlitz Indian Tribe and Dr. Carroll Riley for the US government. Based on field research with the Cowlitz, Lower Chinook, and Klikitat Indians in 1931–37 and again in 1965–66, Ray concluded that the drainage of the Lewis River, which flows into the Columbia River just north of the site of Cathlapotle, had become Cowlitz territory by at least the 1830s. He describes how this happened and the relationship between shifting Chinookan and Cowlitz tribal boundaries:

> The Cowlitz border line follows the Columbia River from near Vancouver Lake to a point downstream a short distance beyond present Longview, Washington. This entire strip was held, prior to the 1830's, by Chinookan-speaking peoples, but the strip was a very narrow one. Beyond the dividing line the Cowlitz were firmly established and had been from time beyond memory. Specifically, the territory of the Chinookans can be indicated by locating the points on the several rivers where Chinookan villages ended and Cowlitz villages started. These are: Lewis River, five miles from the mouth. . . . In the 1830's the Chinookans lost this portion of the Columbia River, just as they did the segment immediately upriver. The Cowlitz moved in, to the exclusion of all other Indians, and maintained their possession

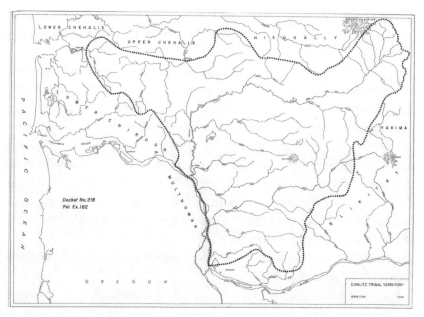

FIGURE 7. "Cowlitz Tribal Territory," showing the southwestern boundary of Cowlitz territory extending to the north shore of the Columbia River. The map is based on maps in Verne Ray's *Handbook of Cowlitz Indians* (1966) and was submitted as evidence in an Indian Claims Commission case for the Cowlitz Indian Tribe. National Archives, Records Group 279, ICC Docket 218.

from that time forward. Indeed, from the time they settled in this strip, there was no contest for possession until the disruption by the whites. The Cowlitz rapidly built up villages at and near the river mouths and by the 1840's these were among their largest settlements.[55]

Ray produced a map showing "Cowlitz Tribal Territory" extending to the Columbia River on the Washington side from roughly the present-day location of Longview, Washington, to Vancouver, Washington, placing the present-day Ridgefield National Wildlife Refuge well within these borders. This map was included as evidence for the ICC case (see figure 7). Ray also noted that an 1857 map drafted under the direction of Washington territorial governor and superintendent of Indian affairs Isaac I. Stevens notes that "the Lower Cowlitz ('Kowalitsk') are shown on the lower Cowlitz River and tributaries, the Kalama River and the lower Lewis ('Cathlapotle') River. . . . Chinookan peoples are not shown at any point on the north side of the Columbia River between present Cathlamet, Washington and the Cascades."[56]

The ICC and expert witnesses for the government did not, however, agree with Ray's assessment of tribal boundaries. The fundamental controversy surrounded the identity of a group referred to as the "Lewis River Indians" who lived near the confluence of the Lewis and Columbia Rivers. According to the ICC, Ray was incorrect in his determination that these were Cowlitz Indians:

> Plaintiff's expert, Dr. Ray, identifies the aborigines along Lewis River as "Lewis River Cowlitz." However, virtually all of the contemporary as well as the historical and anthropological reports have identified the aborigines on the Lewis River as belonging to other tribal groups—specifically the Chinook and the Klickitat. As Dr. Ray himself has stated the "Roving Klikitats" started moving into the general area in the first half of the nineteenth century. And the evidence indicates that the Klickitats were not just visitors or travelers passing through. They lived in the area and, as reported by Herbert Beaver, were farming the land in 1836–1838. . . . We cannot accept Dr. Ray's view. The overwhelming weight of the evidence indicates that the Lewis River area was used by various Indian groups throughout the first half of the nineteenth century. It could perhaps be described as a transitional area of shifting Indian use. But certainly it was not one of Cowlitz exclusive use and occupation.[57]

Riley, who served as primary witness for the United States, also disagreed with Ray's assignment of a Cowlitz tribal identity for the Lewis River groups, instead suggesting that they were

> a group of people speaking either Taitnapan or Klikitat dialects or both. . . . Dr. [Melville] Jacobs who did the ethnological work on the Taitnapan seems to call them Klikitat. They are variously referred to in the earlier documents usually as Klikitat or Taitnapan. At any rate they were Sahaptin speaking peoples. I do not know. I see no evidence whatsoever for considering these Cowlitz. I am in the strongest of disagreement with Dr. Ray—the most emphatic disagreement here. I do not believe these Lewis River people should ever be considered Cowlitz and I do not think on the basis of this evidence that we have here that they were so considered.[58]

Ray agreed that the Lewis River groups were Sahaptin-speaking populations, but he argued that they were Sahaptin-speaking Taitnapams who had intermarried and merged with Salish-speaking Lower Cowlitz populations. As a result, the modern Cowlitz Tribe includes both Salish and Sahaptin components. Furthermore, Ray argued that the misidentification of the Lewis River Cowlitz as "Roving Klikitats" was the result of the stereotypical views that white settlers held concerning Indian authenticity:

> The Indians west of the Cascade divide were considered by nearly all whites to be much inferior to the natives of the Interior and the Great Plains. The latter fitted the story-book concept of the Indian: mounted, colorfully dressed "warriors" of impressive stature and general appearance who always engaged in bold exploits. The "Roving Klikitat" pretty much fitted this stereotype; the Cowlitz not at all. The whites at the settlements and trading posts, seeing the "Roving Klikitat" arrive from the Lewis River quarter, even came to assume—perhaps quite naturally—that the Lewis River country was theirs. These whites never visited the more distant parts of the territory of the Lewis River Cowlitz, and the Cowlitz seldom or never came to the settlements. Indeed, as late as the 1850's there were some Lewis River Cowlitz who had never yet seen a white man. The "Roving Klikitats" being very well known, the Lewis River Cowlitz known almost not at all, it became quite customary for the Lewis River country to be called "Klikitat" country. There was another reason for the confusion just noted. All Sahaptin speakers were characteristically known by the coastal whites as Klikitat. This included the Yakima and Kittitas tribes, the Upper Cowlitz and the Lewis River Cowlitz. The early literature is replete with examples of this usage. Corrections and explanations are also rather numerous but this didn't change the practice. In fact, even ethnologist George Gibbs, who corrected the error in some of his writings, was guilty of perpetuating it at other times.[59]

Although the ICC and contemporary anthropologists disagreed with Ray's assessments, the issue of the identity of the Lewis River groups and Cowlitz tribal connections to the area did not disappear after this case. For instance, the issue resurfaced during the Cowlitz Indian Tribe's federal acknowledgment proceedings and also within the context of the tribe's proposal to have a 152-acre parcel of land located a few miles from Ridgefield, Washington placed in "fee-to-trust" status to serve as both the tribe's initial reservation and location for a proposed gaming center.[60] Most importantly for this chapter, however, Verne Ray's definitions of tribal identity and the map that he created to show the boundaries of that identity served as primary items of evidence for the Cowlitz Indian Tribe's claims of connection to the site of Cathlapotle. In a context where the ambiguous tribal identities and indeterminate and

shifting boundaries of the region became central issues in discussions surrounding the cultural affiliation of Cathlapotle—as well as the management
of heritage resources within the Ridgefield NWR and who should serve as
consulting partners on archaeological research conducted within the refuge—
the documents of anthropologist Ray played a crucial role.

CARTOGRAPHIC ILLUSIONS AND POLITICAL REALITIES

At its core, discussion of the appropriate cultural affiliation of Cathlapotle
came down to the differences between, on the one hand, a map and its later
iterations created by an anthropologist in the 1840s (Horatio Hale) and, on the
other, a map created by a different anthropologist (Verne Ray) in the 1960s.
The negotiations surrounding Cathlapotle were and are, of course, more complicated than this, and all of the parties involved recognized the complexity
of Indigenous identity, both precontact and post-contact, along the Columbia
River. Still, that does not diminish the principal role that maps played as
evidence in the controversy. Nor does it diminish the central argument here,
which is that Hale's map, Ray's map, and all of the intervening iterations
created by other anthropologists and government agents are forms of cartographic illusion. These cartographic illusions work to obscure the complexity
of Indigenous identity and senses of place (and do so typically to the benefit
of colonial institutions), create static and fixed images of Native boundaries,
attack Indigenous sovereignty by replacing Native views of territory with
anthropological ones, and continue to play a role in the present in arguments
over who should be considered an appropriate Native American "stakeholder"
in cultural heritage stewardship. Although illusory, these maps became political reality, and both the Chinook Indian Nation and the Cowlitz Indian Tribe
were forced to assert their connections of identity and connections of place
within the frameworks of these maps that they did not create.

The title for this chapter—"Where is your history?"—comes from a discussion that I had with former Chinook Indian Nation chair Gary Johnson. Johnson was describing to me the thousands of pages of documents that the
Chinook had gathered during the course of their efforts for federal acknowledgment, and he was pointing out that this compilation of history and lineage
was equal to or greater than that of any of the other Indigenous nations in the
region, federally recognized or not. In effect, he was asking for all of these
other groups to show where their documents were, where their history was
compiled. In this context, Johnson was most directly referring to records and

archives. But I also recognized that there was a spatial component to what he was saying; the *where* of his question referred not only to pieces of paper but to places on the landscape as well. Long-standing attachment to place is central to Indigenous communities and identities. It is intermeshed with assertions of sovereignty and rights of access to resources and landscapes, and it is what primarily distinguishes Indigenous populations from later colonial arrivals. But attachment to place becomes more complex in situations where colonial invasion has dramatically altered places, where people have been violently removed from the landscape through both death and physical dislocation, and where the determinations of who belong to places are no longer exclusively controlled by the communities themselves but rather by outsiders in a complex combination of anthropology, cartography, and government bureaucracy.

When discussing Horatio Hale, Jacob Gruber notes that Hale's work as demonstrated in the Pacific Northwest provided the conceptual foundations for a holistic study of humans and the "general anthropology" that would come after Hale and become the hallmark of anthropologists like Franz Boas and his students.[61] This type of holistic approach is evident in Hale's use of broad field surveys, his focus on the connections between language and identity, and his creation of general ethnographic maps that graphically illustrate those connections. The challenge, however, is that this holistic and generalized approach to anthropology is applied to the much more specific and lived realm of claims to places and sites, territorial boundaries, and tribal identity. Brian Thom argues that boundaries reflect embedded cultural experiences, and for Indigenous populations of the Pacific Northwest the cultural experience of boundaries is one of fluidity and flexibility. In the creation of ethnographic maps, however, "the fluid and flexible nature of indigenous thinking . . . is largely lost once mapped in the ethnographic tradition of fixed boundaries, which assumes a one-dimensional relationship between social organization and territory." In addition to the loss of fluidity and flexibility, Thom argues, the use of ethnographic maps in efforts to determine exclusive territory or Indigenous rights to places in the present often heightens tensions between Indigenous nations, transforming long-standing social and political relationships. Ultimately, the use of "single, polygonal representations of traditional territories—a practice that has long roots in the ethnographic mapping practiced by anthropologists since the late 19th century—has confounded negotiations and exacerbated relations among kin and neighbouring First Nations communities."[62]

As noted in chapter 2, the Chinook Indian Nation firmly asserts its long attachment to the site of Cathlapotle, and former chair Gary Johnson has described the connections that the Chinook have to Cathlapotle through both blood and marriage. All historical evidence points to the presence of Chinookan speakers on both shores of the Columbia River at least to The Dalles, as well as the presence of a complex set of networks based on kinship and trade. There is little question that the Chinook are culturally tied to the site. But I want to make it clear that my intent in this chapter has not been to weigh the merits of Chinookan claims to Cathlapotle against those of the Cowlitz Indian Tribe. Nor has it been to determine who is and who is not an appropriate Indigenous stakeholder for the site, or whether those claims to the site should be held exclusively or should be shared. Instead, my intent here has been to show how the insertion of anthropological ideas into conceptions of tribal identity, the creation of ethnographic maps that reflect that conception of identity, and the co-optation of those maps and conceptions for governmental purposes fundamentally altered the landscape and changed the terms of debate. The complexity of Indigenous identity became more hidden while formerly fluid and flexible borders became more rigid, and authority over who is sufficiently affiliated to places on the landscape shifted from the communities themselves to outside experts.

As demonstrated in the discussions over Cathlapotle, the legacies of colonial maps and colonial views of Indigeneity and space continue to be felt. Furthermore, they continue to create tensions, not just between Indigenous nations and non-Indigenous agents but also between the Indigenous communities that are now forced to assert identity within the framework of colonial assumptions. In the next chapter I move from the discussions of space and imposed Indigenous identity in the context of abstract colonial maps to the more concrete place of a site of public history: the Cathlapotle Plankhouse located on the grounds of the Ridgefield National Wildlife Refuge. The Cathlapotle Plankhouse has become a present-day site of reclamation for the Chinook Indian Nation, a place where they can more freely assert their identity (rather than have it imposed upon them) and live their heritage through ceremony and the performance of protocol. But despite the greater control over identity and heritage, the legacies of colonialism continue to be apparent at the plankhouse, as federal ownership of the land, occasionally competing visions of the goals and values of public memory, and lingering tensions with the Cowlitz Indian Tribe over the cultural affiliation of Cathlapotle result in an ambiguous place of heritage.

CHAPTER 4

"We honor the house"

Memory and Ambiguity at the Cathlapotle Plankhouse

ON MARCH 29, 2005, THE DOORS OF THE CATHLAPOTLE PLANKHOUSE were opened to the public for the first time. The plankhouse, a beautifully decorated 40-by-80-foot building constructed out of cedar, was erected within the boundaries of the Ridgefield National Wildlife Refuge in Washington State to serve as a site where visitors could learn about the natural and cultural history of the area. The date of the grand opening was not accidental. On this date 199 years earlier Lewis and Clark's Corps of Discovery landed their dugout canoes on the banks of the Chinookan town of Cathlapotle and visited with its inhabitants for approximately two hours.[1] The grand opening ceremony in 2005 was designed to not only celebrate and capitalize on this historic event, but also to publically celebrate the partnership between the Chinook Indian Nation, US Fish and Wildlife Service archaeologists and staff, the Friends of the Ridgefield National Wildlife Refuge, and a variety of other financial supporters who made the construction of the Cathlapotle Plankhouse a reality. Additionally, more than a hundred volunteers had offered thousands of hours of labor to the project, and the plankhouse would not have been built without their efforts. The important role that volunteers played in bringing this project to fruition was recognized during the grand opening.[2]

The Cathlapotle Plankhouse serves as a place of memory designed to provide a physical link to the Indigenous populations that once thrived in the area where the structure now sits. It is also a site of public education, and thousands of local schoolchildren have now visited it to learn about the cultural and natural heritage of the refuge and surrounding region, the practice of archaeology, and wildlife conservation. The plankhouse is a popular stopping point for the local population and other visitors to the refuge. Some come upon the plankhouse accidentally during their visits, but many travel to the refuge

FIGURE 8. Exterior of the Cathlapotle Plankhouse, Ridgefield National Wildlife Refuge, Ridgefield, Washington. The exterior includes a painted center support post and a traditional Chinookan oval-shaped doorway. Photograph by the author.

specifically to visit it. Well-attended public workshops and presentations on Chinookan culture and history are held regularly within its walls. And because of its connection to Lewis and Clark, the refuge in general and the plankhouse specifically have become a travel destination for tourists interested in the Corps of Discovery story and Cathlapotle's place in it. As a place of public history and education the Cathlapotle Plankhouse is an impressive achievement and has been recognized as such. The Cathlapotle Plankhouse Project Steering Committee was given the US Secretary of the Interior's Cooperative Conservation Award in 2006, and in 2015 First Lady Michelle Obama designated the Friends of the Ridgefield National Wildlife Refuge as "Preserve America Stewards" for its role in the development of the Cathlapotle Plankhouse.

The Cathlapotle Plankhouse is also, however, a place where competing visions of the past, the role and value of cultural resource stewardship, and the ownership and control of heritage come directly into focus. Furthermore, it is the place where these varied visions of heritage took on their most public face, especially within the context of Lewis and Clark Bicentennial celebrations. In addition to serving as a site for historical interpretation to the general public, the plankhouse has become a place of cultural reclamation for the Chinook Indian Nation, a cultural center where they hold nonpublic and public tribal events, share songs and dances, and practice the protocols that are so central to who they are. In this context the plankhouse is a place where heritage is *lived*. But the plankhouse sits on lands owned and controlled by the government of the United States, and the somewhat unresolved questions raised about the cultural affiliation of Cathlapotle remain present in the background. As a result, the legacies and continuing manifestations of colonialism are an ever-present reality that the Chinook Indian Nation confronts in its use of the plankhouse and in its efforts to control its own heritage. The Cathlapotle Plankhouse is, therefore, an ambiguous monument, a place where the legacies of both a rich tribal history and colonialism intersect and where efforts to reclaim culture in the present are occasionally hindered by a lack of tribal control. This chapter focuses on the Cathlapotle Plankhouse as a place of heritage, and my goal is to trace the development of the plankhouse as a site of memory and to explore the issues that led to battles over its use, identity, and value as a public monument.

MEMORY AND PLACE

My discussion about the construction and use of the Cathlapotle Plankhouse as a place of heritage is informed by a large body of scholarship on memory.[3] It is philosopher Edward Casey's work on the centrality of place and its connection to memory, however, that provides the central framework. Casey argues that there are four major forms of human memory: *individual memory*, in which the individual person is a unique rememberer; *collective memory*, where different people recall the same event, each in their own way; *social memory*, which entails memories held in common due to a group connection; and *public memory*, which is memory that occurs out in the open.[4] While each type of human memory plays a role in shaping the other three, social memory and public memory seem most useful in understanding the issues and controversies surrounding the Cathlapotle Plankhouse.

Casey argues that social memory

> is the memory held in common by those who are affiliated . . . by kinship ties, by geographical proximity in neighborhoods, cities, and other regions, or by engagement in a common project. In other words, it is memory shared

by those who are *already* related to each other, whether by way of family
or friendship or civic acquaintance or just an alliance between people for a
specific purpose. . . . Crucial here is that social memories are not necessarily
public: families can harbor memories that are known only to themselves;
such privacy is often itself prized as such, providing that intimacy and bond-
ing that are so important to the maintenance of family life.[5]

Casey notes that "sharing memories" does not mean that members of the group
have identical memories or even the same experience of memory. What it does
mean is that (1) these members have had the same history (even if this is via
the proxy of another family member), (2) there is a common place where that
history was enacted and experienced, and (3) there is an ability to bring the
"history-in-that-place" into words or other suitable means of communication
and expression.[6]

Social memory contributes to public memory, but there are fundamental
differences between the two:

To begin with, by saying "public" we mean to contrast such memory with
anything that takes place privately—that is to say, offstage, in the *idios
cosmos* of one's home or club, or indeed just by oneself (whether physically
sequestered or not). "Public" signifies out in the open, in the *koinos cosmos*
where discussion with others is possible—whether on the basis of chance
encounters or planned meetings—but also where one is exposed and vulnerable, where one's limitations and fallibilities are all too apparent. In
this open realm, wherever it may be—in town halls, public parks, or city
streets—public memory serves as an encircling horizon.[7]

Casey argues that memory—rather than being a purely temporal phenomenon—
is always embodied and therefore tied to place. In fact, memory cannot occur
without place: "public memory is not a nebulous pursuit that can occur anywhere; it always occurs in some particular place."[8] But often a multiplicity of
voices can be heard at these places of memory, a multiplicity that contains the
tensions that underlie competing visions of memory and differing views on
what constitutes heritage. As will be shown in the following pages, this is
certainly the case at the Cathlapotle Plankhouse with its use as a place for
public interpretation as well as a place of cultural reclamation for the Chinook
Indian Nation.

PLANKHOUSES IN THE PAST AND PRESENT

Before turning specifically to the Cathlapotle Plankhouse, it is necessary to provide some context on the general importance and social centrality of plankhouses in the Pacific Northwest both historically and in the present.[9] Large plankhouses, typically made of cedar, were a ubiquitous component of the Pacific Northwest landscape as early as three thousand to four thousand years prior to the encroachment of European and American settlers. These houses were typically multifamily dwellings—housing anywhere from a dozen to well over a hundred people—located along the coast and the shorelines of major rivers and tributaries. While plankhouses varied greatly in size and design, some were of staggering dimensions. One house in the Portland Basin reached a length of 470 feet, a house seen in 1808 on the Fraser River measured 60 feet by 640 feet, and the "Old Man House" built in Puget Sound in 1815 was roughly 520 feet by 60 feet. Two of the houses at the village of Cathlapotle measured in excess of 150 feet by 40 feet.[10] These houses were not only massive, they also would have required an incredible expenditure of labor to construct and maintain, as well as an extensive amount of lumber. It is estimated that the 45-by-115-foot plankhouse that stood at the Meier Site in present-day Oregon would have required more than forty thousand board feet of lumber to construct. In comparison, a modern three-bedroom house requires, on average, somewhere between ten thousand and twelve thousand board feet of lumber. In addition, the plankhouse at Meier stood for roughly four hundred years. During this long life, wall planks and house posts would have inevitably deteriorated and would have needed to be repaired or replaced. As much as a million board feet of lumber might have been required for this house over the course of its four-century life.[11]

The large multifamily plankhouses were more than just places for people to sleep and store their stuff. They were the center of life. As Wayne Suttles notes, a plankhouse was a "food-processing and storage plant, and it was a workshop, recreation center, temple, theater, and fortress."[12] Houses were also the political center of society and primary places for the transmission of culture and protocols from one generation to the next. In effect, the plankhouse itself reflected both the rules of the larger culture as it existed in the present, as well as the continuity of that culture into the future.

Because of their central and comprehensive role in precontact Northwest Coast cultures, plankhouses have been—and continue to be—a focal point for archaeological studies in the Pacific Northwest. Extensive archaeological

remembered the discussions that had occurred between Ames and Raymond about reconstructing a plankhouse, and she felt that it would be a great project for the Fish and Wildlife Service to undertake. Additionally, the upcoming Lewis and Clark Bicentennial would be in full swing during 2005–6. It was assumed that this bicentennial would draw numerous visitors to the Portland area and to the Ridgefield National Wildlife Refuge, and proponents of the reconstruction argued that a plankhouse on refuge grounds would serve as an excellent project for the bicentennial. More importantly, there was the potential for funding due to the large amount of monies attached to the bicentennial events. Raymond says, "Absent the Lewis and Clark Bicentennial we probably wouldn't have thought of it again or pursued the project. It probably wouldn't have been built. . . . We could see early on, four years before the event, that there was an opportunity to do something, and most likely money attached, to do something that wouldn't have been done otherwise. So that was the stimulus, for sure."[26]

The idea of building the plankhouse was supported by the Chinook Indian Nation, despite its ambivalence toward the Lewis and Clark Bicentennial. Like most tribal nations along the Lewis and Clark Trail, the Chinook Indian Nation was concerned about its representation in the Lewis and Clark story, the undue weight given to a temporally brief expedition rather than the hundreds of generations of occupation by Native peoples, and an accurate portrayal of the devastation that this expedition ultimately represents. They also noted the irony that although Chinookan peoples had helped Lewis and Clark's Corps of Discovery survive their winter at the coast during 1805–6, they remained federally unrecognized in the present. Additionally, the Chinook were upset that the Clatsop-Nehalem Confederated Tribes were included in the official and government-sanctioned Lewis and Clark Bicentennial events and had received a grant from the National Park Service for their participation in these events.[27] But despite these concerns, the Chinook Indian Nation recognized the opportunities that the bicentennial offered. Sam Robinson notes that the potential costs and benefits of the bicentennial for the Chinook were a topic of discussion among citizens of the Chinook Indian Nation:

> Well, we've got this Lewis and Clark thing coming up. What do we want to do? Do we want to participate? Do we not want to participate? . . . What did they ever do for Chinook people other than open up another path to get to our lands, you know? And I just told them, . . . we're not federally recognized, and it could give us a good avenue to get our story out about that.

And it did, it did that deeply. And it let us tell people what happened to us, and [it] gave a lot of venues to do that in . . . and it brought the plankhouse to us.[28]

The Chinook also realized, or at least hoped, that although the plankhouse would be attached to the bicentennial in its formative stages, it would outlast the event and serve as a constant reminder of the presence of Chinookan peoples along the Columbia River.[29] Interdisciplinary scholar James Clifford argues that for Indigenous populations, who have a history of being marginalized and made to disappear physically and ideologically by colonial institutions, the ability to say "we exist" publically is a powerful political act, and the Chinook Indian Nation felt that the Cathlapotle Plankhouse, despite the potential hazards of connection to the Lewis and Clark story, would provide a place where they could say "we exist" to both the general population at public Lewis and Clark events and to other Northwest Coast tribal nations at events like the Winter Gathering.[30]

The process moved forward from there as Anan Raymond and honorary chief Cliff Schneider of the Chinook Indian Nation attended Lewis and Clark Bicentennial planning events to pitch the idea. Meanwhile, Virginia Parks—an education and public outreach specialist working for the Region 1 Cultural Resources Team of the US Fish and Wildlife Service—searched for grants. An initial grant was acquired from the Hugh and Jane Ferguson Foundation, which supports nonprofit organizations dedicated to the preservation of nature and education about cultural heritage. Shortly thereafter the project also received monies from a Clark County, Washington, hotel tax fund, designed to support projects that would stimulate tourism in the area. With this initial funding, an idea that Raymond initially referred to as a fantasy took its first steps toward reality.[31]

TENSIONS IN BUILDING A PLACE OF MEMORY

Once it became apparent that funding opportunities might make construction of the plankhouse financially viable, the next step was to create a body that would oversee the project and initiate architectural design. The Cathlapotle Plankhouse Project Steering Committee—consisting of employees of the US Fish and Wildlife Service, representatives of the Chinook Indian Nation, local community members, and a representative from the Lewis and Clark Bicentennial Committee of Vancouver/Clark County—formed to guide the process.

Shortly thereafter, an architect named Art Peterson was hired for the project. Peterson had been involved in building other plankhouses in the region and had a reputation for working well with tribal organizations and designing "authentic" buildings. All parties involved agreed that he was a good match for the project.

The issue of authenticity was a central component of discussions surrounding the construction of the plankhouse from the beginning. *Authenticity* is one of those words often used in heritage and public interpretation circles, but there is little consensus on exactly what it means. The word is notoriously difficult to define, and its definition seems to change over time and varies widely between different groups.[32] Given that none of the historical Cathlapotle plankhouses remained and that the new plankhouse would be built away from the site of the village itself, the authenticity of the Cathlapotle Plankhouse would have to depend on something other than the use of original materials or location. Raymond and Ames envisioned an authentic plankhouse as one that was a historically accurate reconstruction. While the plankhouse would not be an exact replica of the plankhouses that stood at Cathlapotle, it would at least be very similar based on what was known from historical written accounts and drawings as well as the archaeological excavations at the site. In essence, an authentic plankhouse for Raymond and Ames would be one that provided visitors of the refuge with a relatively accurate picture of what plankhouses and Chinookan material culture would have looked like roughly two hundred years ago.[33]

The Chinook Indian Nation was also concerned with authenticity, although its interests in authenticity were less related to direct correlation with the archaeological record and more in constructing a house with "social integrity."[34] For the Chinook Indian Nation, social integrity would only be achieved if Chinooks guided the design and construction of the plankhouse and if all ideas about it were vetted by the Chinook Indian Nation's Culture Committee. In addition to tribal control, the plankhouse could only be authentic, Sam Robinson says, if it was "representative of the ancestors."[35] This did not mean that the plankhouse had to look exactly like plankhouses looked when the ancestors were living in them but rather that all of the appropriate protocols were conducted during its construction and that the house was thereafter maintained and brought to life by continued use by Chinookan people. It is the appropriate protocols and lived heritage attached to the house that are key to honoring the ancestors, not only the material form of the building. Archaeologist Neil Silberman notes that in recent years heritage discussions have "shifted the locus of significance and authenticity of an element (tangible or intangible) of cultural heritage to its meaningfulness as an expression of identity or connectedness by living or associated communities. Thus the shift has been to the social and cultural significance from the thing."[36] This shift was apparent in discussions regarding construction of the Cathlapotle Plankhouse. This is not to say that the Chinook were unconcerned with historical accuracy or the material form of the plankhouse. They certainly wanted to design a plankhouse that represented the historical record. But the key to authenticity and honoring ancestors at the plankhouse would be its use by present-day Chinooks. Just as it was the protocols and social actions attached to plankhouses (rather than their form) that first resulted in their destruction by colonial agents, it would be the protocols and social actions conducted by Chinooks that would give the Cathlapotle Plankhouse its authenticity today.

At an early stage in the design of the building, the Chinook Indian Nation's Culture Committee expressed concern about the feasibility of constructing an authentic plankhouse in a modern world. Greg Robinson, a Chinook Indian Nation citizen who served as project coordinator for the Cathlapotle Plankhouse project, noted that "modern codes create a tangled web of modifications to aboriginal structures, making it virtually impossible to build a pure plankhouse."[37] Of specific concern was the ramification of modern building codes on a large structure that housed open fires and featured small oval doors, both features that were important to protocols associated with the plankhouse. Tom Melanson, who was the manager of the Ridgefield National Wildlife Refuge at that time, suggested that compliance with construction codes would not be an issue due to the location of the project on federal lands, and eventually the Chinook Indian Nation Culture Committee was convinced. Melanson, however, was incorrect in his assessment of the applicability of modern building codes to the Cathlapotle Plankhouse, and, in the view of many members of the Chinook Indian Nation, what "ensued over the course of the next few years is a textbook example of a longstanding legacy of the government promising one thing, and delivering another."[38]

Three primary issues came to the forefront: the safety of open fires and resulting air quality issues, accessible doorways, and the use of volunteer labor to construct the building. The first compromise that the Chinook Indian Nation made to building integrity centered on the issue of accessible doorways. Traditional Chinookan plankhouse doorways, oval and relatively small, do not meet the standards of the Americans with Disabilities Act (ADA). Additionally, the doorways are located a few feet off of the ground and would therefore be impossible for wheelchair traffic. Greg Robinson noted that "in the past, we simply would have carried our disabled people into the houses, but such simplicity has no place in the world of code application."[39] The Chinook Culture Committee decided, however, that the inclusion of an ADA door would serve to keep the project moving forward, and therefore they agreed to change the design of the building to incorporate a wheelchair-accessible doorway and an interior ramp. Lighted exit signs were also installed over the doorways, with the exception of the traditional doorway, which was to have a "This Is Not an Exit" sign placed above it. The Chinook Indian Nation considered this sign above a traditional door as a great insult.[40] Fortunately US Fish and Wildlife Service officials decided that this sign would not be necessary.

A second issue was the involvement of volunteers in constructing the building. Volunteers were an integral component of the project, and more than one hundred volunteers, including many people from surrounding communities as well as Chinook Indian Nation citizens, participated in constructing the plankhouse. Together they logged over thirty-five hundred hours of labor. During organized "work parties," volunteers gathered to help produce wall planks, notch and shape upright beams, and paint the ridgepole. Volunteers fabricated nearly all of the wooden materials in the house.[41] When it came time for the actual erection of the structure, however, safety engineers with the US Fish and Wildlife Service determined that volunteer labor could not be used and that this portion of the project would need to be handled by professional contractors. Many members of the Chinook Indian Nation, however, saw this as another broken promise and a threat to the integrity of the building. In their view, these volunteers had given a gift to the tribe in the form of labor, and to banish them at this critical juncture of the project was a breach of protocol.

Perhaps the greatest challenge was the use of fires within the plankhouse. In traditional Chinookan fashion the building was constructed with large hearth boxes, set roughly a foot below floor level and running down the central axis of the house (see figure 9). The hearth boxes were the heart of the structure and their fires were used for cooking, warmth, and light. The hearth was also a community center, where people gathered to eat, socialize, and tell stories, especially during the long, dark, and rainy winters of the Pacific Northwest. Fires were initially allowed in the Cathlapotle Plankhouse and were lit and kept burning during the grand opening ceremonies. Safety engineers from the US Fish and Wildlife Service, however, soon prohibited the use of fires within the plankhouse. Their concerns were twofold: first, they worried about plankhouse visitors accidentally falling into the hearth pits and fires, and

FIGURE 9. Interior of the Cathlapotle Plankhouse, Ridgefield National Wildlife Refuge, Ridgefield, Washington. The house has two hearths located in the floor along the axis, carved and decorated support beams, and an "Ancestor" carving as a main support in the back wall. Courtesy of Tony A. Johnson.

second, they were worried about meeting Environmental Protection Act (EPA) air quality standards due to the levels of smoke in a "confined" structure. For both safety and legal reasons, the burning of fires within the plankhouse was prohibited until these concerns could be addressed to the satisfaction of safety engineers.

The prohibitions on open fires did not sit well with the Chinook Indian Nation. Chinooks felt that they had been given assurances by other US Fish and Wildlife Service employees that fires would not be a problem, in part because open fires had been used in structures like this before and had also been allowed on other federal properties. They were dismayed that now "the safety and engineering branch of the FWS began to emerge as players in the developing direction of the plankhouse."[42] In part, their concerns related to aesthetics and how the house feels when the hearth fires are blazing. I remember the first time I entered the house when the fires were burning, the way the light flickered on the walls and the surprising warmth the fires offered. I also remember being struck by the sound of rain sizzling on the fires, as the drops entered the house through the open smoke holes in the ceiling and evaporated as they neared the flames. It is only when the fires are burning—with their associated sights, sounds, and feel—that visitors to the plankhouse really get a sense of what living in these massive structures might have been like.

For the Chinook Indian Nation, however, it was not simply a question of aesthetics, light, and warmth, as important as they might be. The Chinook believe that plankhouses are living beings that require care and appreciation to live well, just as do any other living beings. And it is the fire that brings the house to life as a being and that continues to nourish it. In fact, before the plankhouse was even constructed a fire was constructed on-site to prepare the house for life. As Sam Robinson notes, "the life of the house, you know, is fire. And you have got to have that fire to really bring that house to life."[43] This view that the Cathlapotle Plankhouse has a life of its own is something that Robinson has stressed to the docents who work at the plankhouse and to the general public when he speaks there: "You know, there's a true soul in this house. You know, we've got fires here today and that helps the soul of the house. . . . I really appreciate the fact that the docents that work in this house over the years have really come to know that there's a soul in this house, and that when we refer to this as the plankhouse we're referring to this person here, this house, this entity. . . . The docents were able to share that with many schoolchildren over the years."[44]

Fires in the plankhouse, then, are not simply aesthetic pleasantries that provide heat, light, and a nice visitor experience but that are ultimately unnecessary for the use of the house. Instead, fires are central to the responsibilities that the Chinooks owe to the plankhouse, an indispensable protocol that brings life and nourishment to the house. The prohibition against fires, therefore, dramatically hindered what the Chinook Indian Nation saw as the primary value of the structure: a place where they could enact cultural revival through the performance of necessary and appropriate cultural practice.

Anan Raymond's concern about the prohibition on fires in the house focused on something else: he was upset that safety and engineering professionals emerged as players in plankhouse construction at a relatively late stage in the process. He stated that initially he did not expect that fires in the plankhouse would be a significant or insurmountable problem, primarily due to the historic and educational nature of the structure. He also admits, however, that this assumption was a bit naive:

> The conception and creation of the plankhouse was, at least initially, an organic thing, created by people who had no experience in building buildings on a national wildlife refuge. In hindsight we were naive. But at the same time we were concerned and upset that as the prospect of erecting and finishing this house was near we learned from the engineering/safety

office of the US Fish and Wildlife Service that burning a fire or fires inside this building was not a simple proposition. And in retrospect it's clear that we probably should have been able to anticipate this. . . . It's a commonsense thing when you think about it. The US Fish and Wildlife Service is a big federal agency and a big federal bureaucracy, and the idea of having a big structure with a large open fire inside it and a lot of people, a lot of members of the general public standing around kicking sticks into the fire, well, it's something that doesn't come easy. We didn't plan for that.[45]

Large metal fences were constructed around the hearth boxes to address the concerns about visitors falling into the fire. The fences, however, were a tremendous aesthetic distraction. Standing more than three feet high and constructed of solid metal, they dramatically altered the feel of the plankhouse. Furthermore, while the fences were designed so that they could be removed, they were fairly heavy, and the removal process was not easy. This made quick access to the fires—which is necessary for some cultural activities, such as tuning hide drums, not to mention feeding the fire with wood—extremely difficult. The fences were so distracting and cumbersome that it became standard practice at the plankhouse to entirely remove them and cover the hearths with planks rather than have the hearth boxes open with the fences present. Whenever the Chinook used the plankhouse, the first thing they would do was remove the fences if they were present.

To answer questions surrounding EPA air standards, US Fish and Wildlife Service personnel undertook a number of experiments to test air quality in the plankhouse. The house was built in traditional Chinookan style, with smoke holes in the roof above the hearths and a gap between the top of the wall planks and the roof eaves to encourage draw and circulation. The first experiment demonstrated that the air quality within the plankhouse met EPA standards even when the fires were burning. Engineering personnel were concerned, however, that the initial test was conducted under nonstandard conditions (there were only a few people in the building at the time) and that air circulation and quality could change if there were more individuals in the plankhouse. A second test was conducted, this time with more than eighty people in the building, and again air quality met EPA standards. Engineers then suggested that the weather could play a role in air circulation and that experiments needed to be conducted under differing weather conditions. Alternatively, they suggested that fans—which the Chinook Indian Nation stated would be unsightly and noisy—could be installed in the plankhouse smoke holes to ensure that smoke would be drawn from the fires. These fans proved to make no difference regarding air quality. Anan Raymond succinctly noted that they did not work: "They were a complete disaster."[46] The fans were ultimately removed from the plankhouse, and what the numerous air quality tests demonstrated overall was that the most efficient evacuation of smoke from the house came from simply leaving the structure alone.

Former Chinook Indian Nation chair Gary Johnson was not surprised that the knowledge of hundreds of generations of his ancestors had created structures that worked well, and he found it a bit strange that thousands of years of experience would be second-guessed. He also joked about all of the safety concerns, saying, "Our ancestors lived for a long time, and I don't think they suffered any from not having an exit sign, or worried about falling in the fire."[47] Fish and Wildlife Service safety engineers remained unsatisfied, however, and unwilling to accept this knowledge of generations, despite the results of the air quality experiments.[48] The concerns regarding the ADA and EPA were serious, however, and resulted in the resignation of Peterson, the project architect, as well as some members of the Cathlapotle Plankhouse Project Steering Committee. The Chinook Indian Nation also nearly pulled out of the project entirely. Anan Raymond states, "It was definitely painful at times. . . . We almost lost them, or lost each other."[49]

Tensions surrounding the use of fires inside the house came to a head during one of the public Lewis and Clark events at the refuge. On November 5, 1805, Lewis and Clark's Corps of Discovery first sighted the village of Cathlapotle as they headed downriver. Although they did not stop at the village, they were met on the water by seven canoes of village residents who had come out to speak and trade with them. Exactly two hundred years later, on November 5, 2005, citizens of the Chinook Indian Nation and members of one of the Lewis and Clark reenactment groups retracing the voyage restaged the meeting. It was a cold and rainy day, and miserable in the way that only a cold, rainy Washington November day can be. The reenactment of the "first meeting" was to be followed by ceremonies and a feast in the plankhouse. But since fires were not allowed in the plankhouse, by order of US Fish and Wildlife Service safety engineers, spectators and participants who had just spent more than an hour outside in the rain entered a cold, damp building. It was not a comfortable experience, and it was even potentially dangerous: there were fears that some participants might become hypothermic. This was a source of frustration and anger for the Chinook Indian Nation: "We did the reenactment with the Lewis and Clark people, and we came back, and our elders were freezing, and the drums were soft, and we were soaked, and there was no fire. . . . And on that day we put our foot down and said we will not have any tribal public events at that plankhouse until you resolve the fire issue."[50]

The "fire issue" is still not resolved. Although the Chinook Indian Nation builds fires in the plankhouse during its nonpublic tribal events (to the chagrin of some employees of the Fish and Wildlife Service), "no fires allowed" remains the official policy during public events.

Anan Raymond argues that one of the driving forces behind the types of difficulties encountered during the course of the plankhouse project is the organic nature of large bureaucracies like the US Fish and Wildlife Service. The project developed within the minds of a few individuals, and all of the early stages of planning occurred within a relatively comfortable and confined body of like-minded people. But as the process grew, the dynamics changed: "It was an organic process that began with lower-level staff people and members of the Chinook Tribe. As the plankhouse project grew . . . it worked its way up the chains of the agency . . . worked its way up the bureaucracy, and the people who really had the authority in the agency and can affect that, . . . they came back and said 'wait a minute here, not so fast.'"[51] The result was that the ground rules and visions for the plankhouse, initially established among a small group, changed along the way. The Chinook Indian Nation viewed this change as yet another example of continued colonialism, as the federal government promised one thing but delivered another.[52] Anan Raymond understands the tribe's concern: "The tribe felt like the rules had been changed midstream, . . . and I suppose that is exactly correct, that is what did happen."[53] Some might argue that disagreements over ADA compliance, the inclusion of volunteers in construction, and the use and safety of indoor fires are fairly insignificant issues, nothing more than bureaucratic annoyances. But this would be a misunderstanding of the situation and what was really at stake. These disagreements represent not only differing visions of how heritage is best practiced today, but they were also a direct challenge to the Chinook Indian Nation in its efforts to determine and guide culture. And the disagreements were significant enough that they almost led to the collapse of the project.

EXCLUSION AND INCLUSION

Fires, air quality, and ADA-approved doors were not the only controversies surrounding the Cathlapotle Plankhouse. As described in chapter 2, the Cowlitz Indian Tribe had contested the designation of the Cathlapotle archaeological site as the remnants of a Chinook village, arguing instead that the cultural identity of the village was not known with certainty and that its association with the modern-day Chinook Indian Nation was open to question. The Cowlitz Indian Tribe's claim to the site of Cathlapotle sparked a difficult and often emotional struggle over the sites of heritage located within the boundaries of the Ridgefield National Wildlife Refuge, and this included the development, interpretation, and control of the Cathlapotle Plankhouse.

In the wake of federal recognition in 2002, the Cowlitz Indian Tribe asserted that its voice be heard at the refuge, and this included participation in the planning, construction, and interpretation of the Cathlapotle Plankhouse. The primary Cowlitz concern was that the US Fish and Wildlife Service was presenting the plankhouse as an exclusively "Chinookan" structure and that the Chinook Indian Nation had been given full control over the use of the plankhouse. Additionally, the tribe noted that plans for the plankhouse did not include any acknowledgment or memory of a Cowlitz presence in the area.[54] The Cowlitz Indian Tribe threatened to block funding for the plankhouse unless they were recognized as full partners in the project.

The Washington State Department of Transportation (WSDOT) had awarded the US Fish and Wildlife Service a $220,000 grant to assist in building the plankhouse. The Cowlitz Indian Tribe protested this award, arguing that there were questions about cultural affiliation and that it was not being allowed to participate. In 2004 the tribe was able to convince an advisory committee of the WSDOT that the grant needed to be placed on hold until the issue could be fully resolved. This put the Cathlapotle Plankhouse project on hiatus, and Chinook citizen Greg Robinson, the project coordinator, was temporarily laid off.[55] Also at risk were matching funds through the Meyer Memorial Trust and M. J. Murdock Charitable Trust. Anan Raymond was not willing to accede to the Cowlitz Indian Tribe or diminish the Chinook Indian Nation's primacy in the plankhouse, and some US Fish and Wildlife Service employees felt that the actions of the Cowlitz Indian Tribe made them feel like they were being "strong-armed."[56] Mike Iyall, former director of natural and cultural resources for the Cowlitz Indian Tribe, however, viewed it differently, and he suggested that the Cowlitz Indian Tribe simply wanted to be recognized and included. He viewed the lack of inclusion of non-Chinook tribal organizations at the plankhouse as an abrogation of sovereignty:

> I think that for us it seemed to be a "them or us" choice. For instance, today the Chinook Nation is given control of the interior of the plankhouse. We

can't access it. We were told that the interior of the plankhouse belongs
to the Chinook tribe by Fish and Wildlife Service people. I mean, how does
that make you welcome? You know, it doesn't. . . . To me the presence of
the plankhouse, the way it's currently signed and marked by the Fish and
Wildlife Service . . . it's a temple to somebody else's god on the altar of my
church. That's the way I see the plankhouse. It's not an asset to us. We've
been excluded from it; we've been made to feel like outsiders around it.
I had worked to try and find inclusion for us and everybody else that would
have used the plankhouses in the area. I've had no success.[57]

For Iyall the position that the US Fish and Wildlife Service took regarding the
plankhouse demonstrated to him that "they would rather throw away a quar-
ter of a million dollars than let us be involved."[58]

Citizens of the Chinook Indian Nation were concerned about the Cowlitz
Tribe's claims regarding Cathlapotle and especially its desire to consult on the
construction of a Chinookan-style plankhouse. They also felt that federal
archaeologists seemed too eager to simply appease the Cowlitz Tribe and its
wishes, a position that was not lost on US Fish and Wildlife Service archaeologist Raymond:

> They were disillusioned that the agency was yielding to what to them
> appeared to be unreasonable demands or statements or positions by the
> Cowlitz Tribe. They were disillusioned 1) because it violated the consen-
> sus understanding of history and culture, and 2) because it sort of violated
> the long-standing relationship that we had with them. And I think they
> were objecting also, from a political perspective, in that Cathlapotle and
> the plankhouse represented a bit of a toehold that the Chinook tribe has in
> expressing their culture in the Vancouver [Washington] area. And to some-
> how lose this by the federal government yielding to a federally recognized
> Cowlitz Tribe would just be an indignity.[59]

Although the Chinook Indian Nation had been a consulting party since the
inception of the Cathlapotle Archaeological Project, it threatened to pull out
of the project entirely if the Cowlitz Tribe was included as a consulting party
on the plankhouse.

A series of meetings and negotiations between the US Fish and Wildlife
Service, the Chinook Indian Nation, and the Cowlitz Indian Tribe followed,
although the Chinook declined to participate directly in any meetings in

which the Cowlitz Indian Tribe was present. Negotiations between the Chinook Indian Nation and the Fish and Wildlife Service proceeded within the framework of a fourteen-year partnership, which proved invaluable, as trust and solid friendships had been built during this period. Despite their nonrecognized status, the Chinook expected the Fish and Wildlife Service to consult with them on a government-to-government basis, and generally they had been afforded that respect during this long-standing partnership. This is a central reason why the trust between the two parties was so strong. Negotiations with the Cowlitz Indian Tribe, however, proved more difficult as there were no previous relationships upon which to build. The meetings between the Fish and Wildlife Service and the Cowlitz Indian Tribe stalled for a time. The inclusion of David Nicandri, a neutral third party from the Washington State Historical Society, and Scott Aikin, tribal liaison for the Fish and Wildlife Service, introduced a sense of stability and calm to the negotiation process, and negotiations soon moved forward again.

The tangible result of the negotiation was a memorandum of understanding (MOU) between the Fish and Wildlife Service and the Cowlitz Indian Tribe. This document codified the relationship between the two parties and created a protocol for future cooperation. The MOU stated that the US Fish and Wildlife Service would "recognize that the Cowlitz are entitled to equal participation in the development, planning, and production of educational and interpretive materials relevant to the presence of the Cowlitz Indians in the area of the refuge" and stipulated that representatives of the Cowlitz Indian Tribe would be included on the cultural interpretation and education steering committee of the refuge.[60] The MOU also stated that the term *Chinook* would not be used to describe the residents of Cathlapotle and that the terms *Cathlapotle Nation* or *Cathlapotle Chinookans* would be used instead. This was an important point for Mike Iyall, who felt that the use of the term *Chinook* falsely created in the public mind a direct link between the people of Cathlapotle and the modern-day Chinook Indian Nation without addressing the historical complexities of identity within the region.[61] The MOU also made clear, however, that the inclusion of the Cowlitz Indian Tribe in the project did not exclude the involvement of other interested tribes and that the technical aspects of the plankhouse construction would continue to be guided by Kenneth Ames in consultation with the Chinook Indian Nation.[62]

Negotiations between the US Fish and Wildlife Service and the Chinook Indian Nation also resulted in an MOU, which was drafted and instituted before the MOU between the Fish and Wildlife Service and the Cowlitz Indian

Tribe had been finalized. The MOU with the Chinook Indian Nation noted that other interested tribes could be involved in the planning of interpretive and educational materials for the cultural resources of the refuge; the Chinook Indian Nation could not prevent other tribes from participating. Most importantly, however, the MOU clearly stated that control over the cultural use of the Cathlapotle Plankhouse resided with the Chinook and that the Chinook Indian Nation would be "the principal organization that exclusively embodies and perpetuates the traditional and modern culture of the Chinookans of the greater lower Columbia River, including the Cathlapotle Chinookans who historically lived on what is now the Refuge."[63]

Although the MOUs managed to move the process of building the plankhouse forward, no one was entirely satisfied. For instance, Mike Iyall argued that the US Fish and Wildlife Service continued to ignore the government-to-government relationship that is required with the Cowlitz Indian Tribe due to their recognized status, and that the Fish and Wildlife Service had failed to consistently involve them in consultations on educational and interpretive material as designated in the MOU. He also believed that there was a bias present in Fish and Wildlife Service publications regarding Cathlapotle, that archaeologists were not doing enough to inform the public of a Cowlitz history in the region, and that all that he and the Cowlitz Indian Tribe had asked for was inclusion in the plankhouse project, that it serve as a regional plankhouse for all the tribes, and that "the official name of the people that lived at the plankhouse be what Lewis and Clark called them, 'the Cathlapotle Nation.'"[64] His view was that Cowlitz inclusion in the educational material "never happened" and that many people associated with the plankhouse weren't aware of the terms of the MOU and therefore treated Cowlitz people like threatening outsiders when they came to the plankhouse, "so . . . eventually you don't go back."[65]

Gary Johnson of the Chinook Indian Nation also expressed concern that many people associated with the management of the plankhouse were unaware of the terms of the MOU, although his concern took a somewhat different direction than Iyall's: "As new people have come in [to participation in the plankhouse] they are not aware of the original agreements, where any changes within the plankhouse have to be approved by the [Chinook] tribe and the US Fish and Wildlife Service. We were aware and concerned that when you get new managers, new employees, new committee members, that they won't know how hard the tribe worked to have control over the story being told there."[66] Despite the reaffirmation of their voice as a consulting party,

have been in that house, you know. We're not going to dump the plankhouse for another site. It's just that the federal government can make it tough on you to exist as much as you want to there.[76]

On March 29, 2015, the Cathlapotle Plankhouse had its tenth anniversary. Over the course of those ten years the plankhouse has been a place of pride for the Chinook Indian Nation. It represents the legacies of a rich heritage and is a place where the Chinook can visibly affirm their continued presence on the Columbia River and in the region, both to other tribal nations and to the wider public. It is a place where they can continue to enact the protocols that are so fundamental to cultural survival and where they hold central events like the Winter Gathering. But it is also a place that serves as a reminder of a colonial history and its continuing effects. The physical displacement of the current plankhouse on federal lands, the lack of complete control over its purpose and use, and the continued connection between the house and the Lewis and Clark story of American expansion result in a site of memory that is somewhat ambiguous. In this sense, while the plankhouse might still serve as a place of heritage for the Chinook Indian Nation, it does not represent a place of decolonized heritage. In the next chapter I shift my discussion to the Chinook Indian Nation and the central importance of canoe resurgence in the late twentieth and early twenty-first centuries. Canoes have reappeared across the Indigenous landscape and waterways of the Pacific Northwest, and they have brought with them the renewal of an entire suite of cultural practices and the reassertion of the centrality of protocol. Canoe resurgence, therefore, has resulted in not just the revitalization of an aspect of culture but also in the culture itself. Most importantly, the return of the canoes reflects what the Chinook Indian Nation sees as the most fundamental components of heritage and what heritage looks like when it is disentangled from colonial control and colonial legacies. The return of the canoes, therefore, provides a vision of heritage that is more completely decolonized.

"There's no way to overstate how important Tribal Journeys is"

The Return of the Canoes and
the Decolonization of Heritage

ON SEPTEMBER 24, 2011, THE CHINOOK INDIAN NATION WELCOMED a new member into its tribal family—a thirty-seven-foot-long oceangoing canoe. On that day the Chinook held a ceremony for the canoe at Fort Columbia State Park, near Chinook, Washington. They circled the canoe five times—five is the central number in Chinookan culture—and ceremonially scrubbed and cleansed the canoe inside and out with fresh cedar boughs to make the canoe feel welcome and to remove any bad feelings that might be present. The canoe was also given a name: *Kthlmin. Kthlmin* was the name of a Chinookan chief who lived near the present-day Westport, Oregon.[1] It is also the Chinookan word for *moon*. Since canoe travel is guided by the tides, which good canoe navigators must respect and understand, the canoe name honors not only an ancestor but also the tide-controlling moon.

The canoe was a gift of reparation to the Chinook Indian Nation from the descendants of William Clark.[2] In March 1806, as members of the Corps of Discovery neared the end of their stay at Fort Clatsop, four members of the expedition—with the blessing of Lewis and Clark—stole a canoe from a nearby Clatsop village. The Corps members were preparing for their return voyage and needed an additional canoe for the trip. They could not, however, find any Clatsop willing to sell a canoe—canoes were considered the highest measure of value for them—so the Corps members decided to take one instead, and they did so while Clatsop chief Coboway was visiting Fort Clatsop.[3] Earlier that winter a few Clatsop had come across six elk that had been shot and left behind by members of the Corps of Discovery. Thinking that the elk had been abandoned and not wanting them to go to waste, the Clatsop took the six elk back to their village. Lewis and Clark rationalized the theft of the canoe as payment for what they considered stolen elk, and in doing so they conveniently forgot that Coboway, in an act of good faith, had already made restitution for the elk. Lewis and Clark also did not realize that when they approved the theft of the canoe they were not just approving the theft of a carved piece of cedar: they were approving the theft of a living thing and a member of a family.

Approximately two hundred years later, Chinook Indian Nation chairman Ray Gardner was speaking with Rick Holton. Both Gardner and Holton were actively involved in American Rivers, a nonprofit organization that works to protect and conserve US waterways. They were both also participants in the planning for Lewis and Clark Bicentennial events. Holton's wife, Carlota ("Lotsie") Clark, was a seventh-generation direct descendant of William Clark, and over conversations between the three of them the story of the stolen Chinookan canoe came up, as well as the central importance of canoes to Chinookan culture and the fact that canoes were considered to be living members of a family. Based on these conversations as well as positive interactions Lotsie had had with citizens of the Chinook Indian Nation in the context of Lewis and Clark Bicentennial events, she decided that something should be done to make reparation for her ancestor's role in the theft of the canoe. A new canoe would be built and returned to the Chinook Indian Nation. She organized an effort that resulted in the disbursement of nearly $30,000 from the Clark family trust, monies that were used to build *Kthlmin*. Descendants of William Clark, including Lotsie, were at the September 24 ceremony at Fort Columbia State Park. They were there to see the canoe returned, and they were there "to right a wrong."[4]

The focus of this chapter is the return of canoes to Pacific Northwest tribal nations in general and to the Chinook Indian Nation in specific. The reparative gifting of *Kthlmin* is just one small part of this story. As was the case with most aspects of Indigenous culture, the canoe culture of Pacific Northwest Indian nations was negatively impacted by colonialism and its associated polices of assimilation and genocide. Although canoes and the extensive and interwoven cultural practices associated with them never entirely disappeared in the face of colonial pressure—their centrality was maintained in the memories of many individuals and families—the presence of canoes on waterways and shorelines in the Pacific Northwest had nearly vanished in the decades following white invasion. In the last few decades, however, the canoes have returned, and they are most visibly present in events like Tribal Journeys, a weeks-long

FIGURE 11. *Kthlmin* on its maiden voyage on the Columbia River in June 2012, near the river's mouth. Saddle Mountain is in the background. *Kthlmin* was on its way to the Chinook Indian Nation's First Salmon Ceremony, held annually at Chinook Point. Courtesy of Sam Robinson, photograph by Mildred Robinson.

paddle and gathering of Indigenous nations that annually brings together thousands of Native American/First Nations citizens in the Pacific Northwest. The return of the canoes brought the return of all the cultural practices integrally connected with them: the skills of carving canoes and associated items, ceremonies surrounding canoe construction, dances and songs, understanding of waterways and tides, and the protocols of canoe travel and coming ashore. It has also brought a sense of cultural pride and well-being and serves as an effective means to combat the alcoholism and drug abuse that impacts many Indigenous communities. Overall, canoe resurgence has brought a demonstration of cultural resilience and a reaffirmation of tribal places, practices, and sovereignty. In this sense canoe resurgence is fundamentally an act of decolonization. As is suggested by the story of *Kthlmin*, canoe culture is fundamental to the Chinook Indian Nation and a central component of their heritage. The centrality of canoe revitalization to the Chinook effectively illustrates what they consider to be most important in terms of heritage, the significance of cultural resilience, and what heritage looks like when it is disentangled from colonial legacies and control.

THE CENTRALITY OF CANOE CULTURE

Anthropologists and historians have written pages and pages on some of the classic elements of Pacific Northwest Indigenous culture. It is not particularly difficult to find a long and extensive history of scholarly articles on the potlatch, the importance of salmon to Pacific Northwest cultures, the artistry and meaning of totem poles and carved masks, the archaeology of plankhouses, and the place of Northwest cultures within the realm of "complex hunter-gatherers." More rare are the writings on and discussions of the central importance of canoes to the people of the Northwest.[5] This dearth of writing on canoes has not gone unnoticed. As David Neel, the author of *The Great Canoes: Reviving a Northwest Coast Tradition*, states, "It's hard to explain why so little has been written about them, as they are probably the single most important aspect of Northwest Coast culture."[6] Neel notes that canoes were as important to Pacific Northwest culture as cars are to us today. They were the primary means of transporting people and conducting trade, and they fostered close connections between villages. But unlike what is typically the case with automobiles, canoes were items of great spiritual importance. They were beings that were treated with reverence and respect from the time the tree that would become the canoe was felled, to its long life as a finished vessel. Canoes also carried the knowledge of generations in them, as passed-down understandings of waterways, navigation, carving and craft, stories and songs, and necessary protocols were intimately tied to canoe culture. Additionally, traveling through waterways for hours at a time in a confined space—and in what were occasionally dangerous situations—necessitated the ability to work together and respect each other. Canoes taught people how to behave appropriately and as such served as a "metaphor for community."[7]

The canoes of the Pacific Northwest were dugout canoes typically made from a single log of western red cedar (*Thuja plicata*). Hilary Stewart argues that there is no other place in the world that dugout canoe making was developed to such a high level of sophistication and that no other people created "a dugout that could match the speed, capacity and seaworthiness—or the elegant grace—of the sleek canoes of the Northwest Coast Indian."[8] While the dugout canoe was the basic form all along the Pacific Northwest coast, canoe styles varied from place to place. Their forms were dictated in part by the local environment and the purpose they were designed to serve. Additionally, there was a remarkable level of aesthetic consistency within styles, although subtle stylistic touches by individual canoe carvers were visible to other canoe-carving experts. Stewart suggests that there were four basic styles of canoe along the coast. The northern style—used by people like the Haida and designed for crossing open stretches of rough water—had large vertical prows, high flaring sides, and rounded bottoms. These design elements added buoyancy, cut through high waves, and prevented excessive water from washing over the sides. Coast Salish canoes, which were used in waters typically more sheltered than that of the north, had rounded bottoms and a bow that was more gently sloped than that of the northern canoes. They were finely crafted, with the thickness of the wood at the gunwale often being less than the width of a finger. The West Coast canoe—also called the Chinook-style canoe—was used by groups like the Chinook, Quileute, and Makah. This canoe was designed for open water and sea travel and had a flat bottom, vertical stern, and beautifully flared sides. While the main portion of the canoe was crafted from a single piece of wood, elegantly carved stern and bow additions were added separately, fitted with watertight precision. The fourth style was the river or shovel-nose canoe, designed for traveling on the fresh waters of rivers and streams. This canoe was slender and more simply and quickly built than the other styles and had fewer sharp edges on the hull in order to make it less likely to be pushed off course by river currents. The sizes of canoes varied greatly. Some of the large northern-style canoes reached an excess of sixty feet in length and seven feet in height, while some of the smaller canoes were only a few feet in length and light enough to be portaged by an individual.[9]

The process of creating a canoe began with the careful selection of a suitable log by the canoe carver. The carver would look for a straight tree with minimum taper, of sufficient size for the planned canoe, and containing few knots and scars. Once the appropriate tree had been selected, the tree was felled, bark was removed, and the exterior lines of the canoe were roughed out and established. At this point the canoe was often left for a few months to allow the wood to mature. The next steps in the process included more detailed shaping of the canoe exterior as well as hollowing out the interior. Chisels and adzes were used to remove the interior wood—sometimes in segments or blocks—until the interior form took shape. Along some parts of the coast, controlled burning of the wood, often with hot rocks, assisted in the hollowing process. As the canoe came closer to the desired final shape, the carving process became more precise. The carver worked to assure elegant and symmetrical lines, while maintaining the appropriate thickness of canoe sides. Forms and equal-length pegs—drilled and placed into canoe walls as thickness-markers—were typically used to assure precise symmetry and equal wall thickness throughout.

When the carving of the canoe was completed to the canoe maker's satisfaction the canoe would be steamed and "spread" in order to give the craft greater width and increased stability. This ingenious process was accomplished by first filling the canoe with a few inches of water. Next, rocks were heated in nearby fires and then placed into the water in the canoe. This would cause the water to boil and steam, and the boiling water would be splashed along the interior of the hull. The steaming of the interior wood caused the canoe hull to soften, widen, and spread, and the canoe was typically covered with mats to intensify the effects of the process. At times this spreading was assisted by placing wooden rods or thwarts between the gunwales. As the canoe widened, both the bow and the stern would lift, creating ends that were slightly higher than the middle of the hull. Once the rocks cooled, additional heated rocks would be placed into the canoe to continue the steaming, and the process would be repeated until the canoe had widened to its full extent or to the satisfaction of the canoe maker. While this step of the process was risky—cracks often developed during steaming and spreading—it was a necessary and ingenious method for crafting spacious canoes with high carrying capacities. In addition it resulted in canoes that were incredibly stable and had gracefully curving lines. Final steps in canoe making included burning or scorching the hull exterior, which both hardened the wood and drew preservative oils from the interior. The charcoal from the burning also became the foundation for the black coloring so prevalent on Northwest Coast canoes. Final steps also included sanding and burnishing and the addition of oil (often seal, whale, or dogfish oil) for further preservation. Separate bow and stern pieces—which sometimes included intricate and beautiful carvings—were added to all but the smallest canoes, and most canoes were painted and otherwise decorated.[10] The canoe-making process required the skills of extremely talented experts, and the best canoe makers of today can only approximate the skill sets of canoe makers from the past.

The first Europeans to visit the Pacific Northwest were amazed by the craftsmanship and beauty of the canoes, as well as by the navigation skills of Indigenous paddlers. They noted the elegant and efficient lines of Northwest canoes and expressed their admiration for the abilities of canoe builders who could shape such symmetrical, well-proportioned, and fair vessels without the use of any familiar instruments of measure and with tools they considered simple and crude. It is important to note also that some of these early visitors to the coast were sailors, captains, and shipbuilders themselves, people who were well versed in navigation and maritime engineering. It has even been suggested that the Chinook-style canoe provided the basis for the American clipper ship.[11] Europeans were also startled by the sheer number of canoes that they saw on the coast. For instance, George Vancouver, while anchored off of Quadra Island, off of the east coast of what is now Vancouver Island, noted that eighteen canoes came out to visit his ship, while at least eighty canoes were still left on shore. Near a village off of the west coast of Vancouver Island, James Cook estimated that the roughly eighty canoes that came out to trade with his ship carried a total of at least five hundred people. The chief factor at Fort Langley along the Fraser River recorded instances of two hundred canoes passing by, and in 1791 Capt. Thomas Barnett, while sailing near the Queen Charlotte Islands, recorded an astounding six hundred Haida canoes surrounding his ship.[12] By all accounts it is clear that Pacific Northwest canoes were beautiful, seaworthy, and numerous.

Canoes were certainly ubiquitous along the lower Columbia River, and Tony Johnson notes "that in the past there were as many canoes as there were people in Chinook territory."[13] Additionally, the canoes of the lower Columbia were equal to the beauty and craftsmanship of those of the northern Pacific Coast. The artistry of these canoes was not lost on the members of Lewis and Clark's Corps of Discovery who marveled at the exquisite lines of Chinookan canoes and the skills of canoe-makers who crafted such symmetrical and seaworthy vessels by hand. On March 30, 1806, as the Corps passed what is present-day Sauvie Island near Portland, Oregon, Sgt. Patrick Gass, a member of the Corps, wrote in his journal that the "natives of this country ought to have the credit for making the finest canoes, perhaps in the world, both as to service and beauty; and are no less expert in working them when made."[14] Lewis and Clark wrote extensive details in their journals on the construction of Columbia River canoes, including drawings of the various types of canoes that they saw.[15] One of the styles of canoes they were particularly interested in was the "image canoe," a unique form of Columbia River canoe that had finely carved and detailed figures mounted on the bow or on both bow and stern. The carved figures often represented animals, such as bears or birds, but could also represent human figures. Tony Johnson and Adam McIsaac argue that the carvings on Columbia River image canoes are "of a scale unrivaled on the Northwest Coast."[16]

In addition to the aesthetics of Columbia River canoes, Lewis and Clark were captivated by their functionality and engineering as well as the skills of Chinookan paddlers. Lewis noted in his journal on February 1, 1806, "the natives inhabiting the lower portion of the Columbia River make their canoes remarkably neat light and well addapted for riding high waves. I have seen the natives near the coast riding waves in these canoes with safety and apparently without concern where I should have thought it impossible for any vessel of the same size to lived a minute."[17]

Lewis might have been remembering what the Corps had experienced in November 1805. Only a few miles from the mouth of the Columbia River and the Pacific Ocean, and just east of the present-day Washington-side base of the Astoria-Megler Bridge, the Corps was stranded by a heavy winter storm. The storm began on November 9, and the strength of the winds and the high waves forced the Corps to take refuge on the shore in a small, rugged, and barely sheltered inlet, which Clark, in his journal entry, later referred to as "this dismal nitich."[18] The storm raged for six days, and the Corps—wet, hungry, and confined to uneven ground by raging waters on one side and a steep rocky hillside on the other—feared for their safety. In the midst of this heavy storm, however, the trapped Corps was visited by five Kathlamet Chinookans traveling in a canoe. Lewis and Clark were astonished: not only had these Chinookans braved the waters that had kept the Corps trapped for days, they had traveled through those rugged waters from a village on the opposite side of the river at one of its widest spots. They sold thirteen salmon to the Corps—which greatly aided the Corps members in their desperate condition—and then got in their canoe and headed back out. Clark concluded his account of this amazing encounter: "The Indians left us and Crossed the river which is about 5 miles wide through the highest Sees I ever Saw a Small vestle ride, their Canoe is Small, maney times they were out of Sight before they were 2 miles off Certain it is they are the best canoe navigators I ever Saw."[19]

Pacific Northwest canoes were not solely beautiful and seaworthy. They were integral to the rich economy of Pacific Northwest Indigenous cultures. For people who made a substantial portion of their living on maritime and riverine resources, canoes provided both the necessary means to move people to those resources and to carry those resources back to people and across the wider landscape. Canoes were critical for the large-scale trade that occurred throughout the Pacific Northwest as they could easily carry massive quantities of goods. Some of the larger freight canoes could carry as much as six tons of cargo, an amount of tradable items that simply could not be matched traveling by land. Regularly, large parts of entire villages were moved via canoes, a process accomplished by lashing two or more canoes together, placing cedar wall planks (removed from the houses) between the canoes, and then setting all of the household goods on top of the planks. While not as conspicuous as the larger canoes, smaller canoes were just as important to the day-to-day economy of Pacific Northwest cultures. For instance, Chinookan women living at the village of Cathlapotle filled small canoes with large amounts of wapato, a staple of both consumption and trade. The canoes were then paddled back to the village via wetlands and streams or were light enough—even with their cargo—to be portaged a small distance back to a main stem of the river. Without canoes, large and small, the classic economy of the Pacific Northwest would not have been possible.[20]

Finally—and fundamentally—canoes were not just utilitarian tools of the economy. They were embedded in a cultural context that was deeply spiritual and community-oriented. Each canoe had its own spirit, its own life, and canoes have always been treated as family members. The sacredness surrounding canoes was inherent at the beginning of the process of making them. For instance, master canoe carvers did not acquire their skills through practice alone, guardian spirits helped to guide their hands. Furthermore, protocols and ceremonies directed the creation of a canoe at every step of the way. This included ceremonies to facilitate communication between the carver and the spirit of the tree even before the tree was felled, rituals that were followed by the carver during the canoe-making process, and the cleansing ceremonies attached to naming and launching the canoe. Will Sarvis notes the central importance of spirituality to these canoes: "The tree spirit never left the wood, but rather evolved from an entity inhabiting a growing tree to one inhabiting a fallen log, to one that lived inside the wood as the canoe builder began to render a vessel out of it, and finally to one inhabiting the finished canoe. In a sense, the canoe was always a sacred vessel, having spiritual qualities from the outset, and—facilitated by the effort, perception, and spiritual power of the canoe builder—transformed into a form of wood that embodied a specific canoe spirit."[21] Canoes, then, were not inanimate objects built simply to facilitate travel, trade, and the gathering of resources. They were living beings created by humans following appropriate protocols and guided by spirit helpers. Furthermore, they were cherished and respected members of the family and community.

The close connection between canoes, their owners, and spirituality is also evident in the use of canoes as places of interment. Along the lower Columbia, canoes were often used as the final resting place for the deceased. Shortly after death, the body was wrapped in skins, mats, or blankets and was placed inside a canoe. The canoes were then suspended from the boughs of trees or placed on support platforms created from posts, planks, and "spirit boards." Holes were drilled in the bottom of the canoe, which both "killed" the canoe and allowed for the drainage of rainwater. This also rendered the canoe unusable to anyone who might consider stealing it for personal use (a concern that principally happened after the arrival of white settlers). Often a second canoe would be placed upside down over the first to provide further protection from rainwater, and the two would be lashed together. Items of personal property—like paddles, bows and arrows, harpoons, and guns for men, and wooden bowls, blankets, cooking utensils, and kettles for women—were typically also included in the canoe and placed beside the body, or hung on the posts supporting the canoe.[22]

Given that canoes were a central component of Pacific Northwest cultures, it should come as no surprise that canoes, and all of the embedded cultural associations attached to them, were devastated by colonialism. Canoes were not subject to the same sort of direct attack as cedar plankhouses and the potlatch. There were no widespread government mandates that canoes be burned, nor were they outlawed as was the potlatch, but this is most likely because canoes were more useful to white settlers and occasionally used by them. Sarvis notes that canoes survived initial colonial invasion and that canoe building perhaps even thrived in the first decades after Euro-American contact. But by the late nineteenth century the presence of the sleek vessels on waterways and shorelines, as well as the skills needed to build them, began to decline. During the early decades of the twentieth century the speed of that decline dramatically increased to the point that cedar canoes, once the most ubiquitous symbol of the Indigenous Pacific Northwest, became a rarity.[23]

How did this happen? One standard explanation is that canoes simply gave way to more modernized forms of transportation: canoes, while beautiful and skillfully designed, could not compete with mechanized fishing boats. While this explanation is undoubtedly accurate at some level, it is simplistic and ignores the broader colonial context within which the demise of the canoe occurred. Literary scholar Misao Dean notes that the argument that the canoe was an inevitable victim of advancing technology

> leaves out the cultural and economic [colonial] forces that all but determined their loss. The economic role of the big canoes was lost: First Nations were encouraged to settle in one place and join the wage economy, working in canning factories or living on reserves where government agencies could conveniently deliver services. Individual reserves rarely included all of the

several different locations and townsites that the people would traditionally travel to at different times of the year, to harvest salmon, or clams, or berries, or oolichans, so First Nations people did not necessarily travel for economic reasons any more. . . . The social reasons for the big canoes were also lost: the potlatch was outlawed, so there was little need for ceremonial travel (and when potlatches were held, participants did not necessarily want to draw the attention of the local police).[24]

At the same time that Natives were being forced to assimilate to the terms of an imposed colonial economy and to give up many of their central ceremonies, their lands were being taken and were subject to wide-scale industrial harvesting of western red cedar, further separating communities from the material that was the soul of the canoe. Finally, the twin colonial forces of disease and alcohol led to the loss of many elders who were knowledgeable in the ways of the canoe, as well as the resulting disruption of the cultural mechanisms for passing down that knowledge.[25] The fading of canoe culture was not simply the result of an unavoidable transition in technology. It was the result of the active implementation of colonial forces that stripped away the economic and social reasons for canoes, took the material for the canoes themselves, and damaged the intellectual knowledge base that made canoes possible.

CANOE REVIVAL AND THE HISTORY OF TRIBAL JOURNEYS

Canoes and their central place in Pacific Northwest culture never entirely disappeared, despite the onslaught of colonial pressures. For instance, although some master carvers moved from traditional dugouts to mechanized crafts, they still carried with them generations of canoe-building knowledge. Tony Johnson notes that Chinook master carver and Bay Center, Washington, resident Joseph "Josie" George (1871–1945) transferred his expert knowledge of canoe building to the construction of modern fishing boats, and he says that it has become a source of pride to own one of George's expertly crafted vessels.[26] Additionally, Native communities scattered throughout the Pacific Northwest continued to travel by canoe to visit each other for ceremonies and gatherings (often referring to them as birthday parties or giving them other labels to make them more palatable to white officials), some small canoes continued to be carved and used, and modified canoes, which were longer and more narrow, were built for use in the relatively widespread intertribal canoe racing events that became popular during the mid-twentieth century.[27]

It was not until the end of the twentieth century, however, that canoe resurgence in the Pacific Northwest reached florescence and developed its most visible and extensive embodiment: Tribal Journeys. Tribal Journeys is a multiweek paddle and potlatch that has revitalized the ancient water highways of the Pacific Northwest. Indigenous communities from Alaska, British Columbia, Washington, and Oregon annually participate in the journey. In recent years participation has spread to California and even included Māoris from New Zealand, Native Hawaiians, and Ainu from Hokkaido. Each year one Native American village or community hosts the final destination of the journey, and the canoe families from the multitude of participating tribal communities make plans to arrive together on the host community's shore at a time predetermined by that community.[28] The landing at the host village, however, is really a midpoint in each Tribal Journeys as there are days of dances and gatherings afterward. The total time for Tribal Journeys can exceed three weeks. Before arriving at the host community each canoe and canoe family has already traveled many miles (and typically many days), often paddling directly from their own community or starting from another if they have accepted an invitation from that community to travel together. They have also already made multiple stops along the way, being hosted each night by the tribal community whose homelands they are passing through on their journey. Once all of the canoes have arrived at the final destination, the host community holds a weeklong gathering that includes feasting, dancing, and singing, with as many as ten thousand people (including both paddlers and nonpaddlers) and more than a hundred canoes.

The origins of Tribal Journeys are multiple, as the efforts of a number of individuals and the legacies of a number of tribal events eventually coalesced. Tom Heidlebaugh (now deceased), a central figure in Pacific Northwest canoe revitalization, traced the beginnings of Tribal Journeys back to a cultural revitalization project that he and some colleagues were working on near La Push, Washington, in the early 1970s. The project was at a remote village on the coast, and they used a refurbished canoe to travel to the site. The canoe ultimately became a central part of the project.[29] A few years later, in the mideighties, the well-known Haida artist Bill Reid (assisted by a number of other artists) carved *LooTas* (Wave Eater), a fifty-foot-long canoe. *LooTas* was based on the measurements of a Haida canoe in a museum collection, and its construction helped to spur a renaissance in canoe carving. *LooTas* became an important symbol and ambassador of Haida culture, even traveling up the Seine to Paris in 1989. Prior to that, *LooTas* was paddled as part of the 1986

World's Fair in Vancouver, British Columbia (Expo 86), which also included a canoe of the Heiltsuk Nation that had been paddled the roughly three hundred miles from its home in Bella Bella, British Columbia, to Vancouver.[30]

The event, however, that is most often credited for the creation of Tribal Journeys is the Paddle to Seattle that happened in 1989. The Paddle to Seattle was held as a part of the centennial celebrations of Washington State that occurred during the year.[31] In July 1989 canoes from the tribal communities of Hoh and La Push, Washington, left their Pacific Coast homes and paddled into the Salish Sea (Puget Sound), where they met up with canoes from the Heiltsuk, Lummi, Tulalip, and Suquamish nations. The flotilla of canoes traveled to Golden Gardens Park, located just outside of Seattle. Here they delivered a letter to the people of Washington State. Signed by representatives of twenty-one tribal communities from the state, it contained the words of the famous Duwamish and Suquamish leader Si'ahl (Seattle) and asked the residents and government of Washington to fulfill their obligations as responsible stewards of the earth. While numerous individuals were responsible for the organization of the Paddle to Seattle, Emmett Oliver, David Forlines, and Terri Tavener were central figures.[32]

At the Paddle to Seattle, Frank Brown—a member of the Heiltsuk Nation canoe—invited all of the canoe nations that were present that day to meet again in four years in Bella Bella (roughly ninety miles north of Vancouver Island), the home of the Heiltsuk Nation, for another gathering of canoes. After members of the other canoes discussed the proposal together, Brown's invitation was accepted. He was given the paddle of a senior Quileute elder and told that the canoes would arrive in Bella Bella in four years to retrieve the paddle. The proposed gathering came to be called the Qatuwas Festival—*Qatuwas* meaning "people gathered together in one place" in the Heiltsuk language. News of the Qatuwas Festival quickly spread, and Pacific Coast canoe nations began preparations for the gathering, and more tribal nations were building canoes and paddling again. In the summer of 1993 twenty-three canoes landed at Bella Bella and were welcomed on shore by Heiltsuk Nation chair Edwin Newman. In his welcoming speech he noted, "Native people are regaining their strength and culture, and this gathering is a sign that things are changing for our people."[33]

Close to two thousand people attended the Qatuwas Festival in 1993. Attendees quickly recognized the importance of the event and saw the potential for canoe resurgence and the gathering of Pacific Northwest tribes

Tokeland, Washington, the next evening). There is little question that Tribal Journeys has become a hub of the Chinook year.[38]

TRIBAL JOURNEYS AND COMMUNITY HEALING

An extremely important element of Tribal Journeys is the effect that the event has had on healing communities, especially in terms of its ability to combat drug and alcohol abuse. Unfortunately, the rates of drug and alcohol abuse are very high among American Indians and are a central area of concern for many tribal communities. While the causes of abuse are multifaceted, and certainly vary from community to community, they are ultimately directly related to colonialism. This includes a factor like the introduction of alcohol to communities who historically had little experience with it and therefore no social mechanisms for regulating its appropriate use. Socioeconomic aspects are also a likely contributor, as Native Americans experience higher rates of poverty and unemployment than the rest of the population. And the combined and continuing effects of attempted genocide take their toll, as tribal communities struggle with the legacies of boarding school abuse, loss of culture, constant exposure to racism, and the repercussions of multigenerational historical trauma.[39]

This legacy of colonialism is a problem both on reservations and in urban centers, and it affects people of all ages. Involvement in canoe culture, however, has had a dramatic and positive impact on the problem in recent years: "There's no way to overstate how important Tribal Journeys is in the sense of what it's doing for communities," Tony Johnson says. "If you come in and you look at it now you can't even see, necessarily, how important it is. Because you kind of have to go back thirty years or something to see just how bad the communities were, or just how bad off some places were, or just how rough things were."[40] The positive impact that Tribal Journeys and canoe resurgence has had is not just a fortunate, unexpected side effect. As Johnson notes, the leaders who were involved with the movement at the very beginning knew and expected that canoe culture would help to fix problems associated with drug and alcohol abuse, especially with the youth, and it was a primary reason for pushing for increased involvement with canoes:

> In my experience, sitting with these guys that I named earlier, Phil Red
> Eagle, Connie McCloud, Tom Heidlebaugh, Tom Jackson, Mary McQuillen,

Clint Hackney, and others, these folks were expressly about fixing our communities through the youth. And this is really what it's about, is fixing the communities. Getting rid of the garbage, encouraging the good stuff, discouraging the bad, and . . . it is the youth that have made the difference. I mean, . . . you have now a situation where the kids who might otherwise be complete, kind of, hoodlums in your community, wanting badly enough to be involved with the canoes, the singing and the dancing, whatever it is that got 'em. Because the bottom line is, it just gets you. For some of them it's just the physical aspect of it. They love being athletic and pushing themselves hard. For some it's that they love singing, and for some it's that they love dancing, and for some it's everything in between. But it has totally changed kids. . . . . So, a lot of the need for the canoe families, and the huge appeal, is the people that are trying to quit drink and drug and whatever. A canoe family that's 100 percent healthy could take you, if you were high off the street, the day that we left, we could take you in and plug you in the canoe, and sober you up, and get you into something positive and feeling good. And there are dozens, if not hundreds of people who have had that experience and never again thought about drink and drug and whatever. We've just absolutely got 'em.[41]

The primary reason why Tribal Journeys is so effective in combating drug and alcohol abuse is because it is an intervention method directly rooted in tribal and community values. Most previous attempts to address the problems of drug and alcohol abuse among Native Americans used intervention methods that had been successful among non-Native populations. But these methods tended not to work in tribal communities, typically because they assumed that the causes of abuse were the same in Native American populations as they were in the general population. They failed to look at the specific histories and cultures of each tribe, and they failed to consult with and directly include the communities affected.[42] Tribal Journeys, however, springs directly from tribal values and the specifics of canoe culture. Furthermore, the values that are emphasized to Tribal Journeys participants come directly from elders and other leaders of the community. In this approach culture is the only route for healing and the only thing that will be effective in the long term.[43]

The role of canoe resurgence in combating drug and alcohol abuse within the Chinook Indian Nation has certainly been evident, and, as I witnessed, this impact is not just among the youth. As described in the introduction, I had the honor of attending the Bay Center–Georgetown Paddle at Bay Center, Washington, on Saturday, August 23, 2008. Part of the work of that event was a naming ceremony for the Shoalwater Bay Tribe's first canoe in generations, and the celebration included a paddle across the Willapa Bay from Toke Point, Washington, to Bay Center. Six canoes carried dozens of tribal members, representing the Shoalwater Bay Tribe, the Chinook Indian Nation, and their relatives from the Confederated Tribes of Grand Ronde. When they arrived in Bay Center they were greeted with songs and drumming. The paddle was a revitalization of the water highway that had directly connected the Shoalwater and Chinook communities for millennia, and it was the first time in recent history that canoes traversed a path that had been traversed countless times in the past. A feast and ceremony was held after the paddle, and in what is a common practice in tribal ceremonies, attendees were asked if they would like to say some words or share what was on their minds. An older gentleman who had participated in the day's paddle got up to speak. He noted that he had also just recently participated in Tribal Journeys, and in a soft voice he described what it had meant to him, how it had created a sense of pride in his heritage and in his own abilities, and how it had altered his overall view on life. He also noted that after years and years of battling alcoholism, he had stopped drinking. It was a powerful moment—on a day of powerful moments—and one that I will never forget.

While there is no doubt that canoe resurgence and Tribal Journeys has had an overall positive effect on communities, it is not a solution that works for, or is appropriate for, everyone. As Tony Johnson notes, "It doesn't mean that there's not problems in any of our communities still. But the bottom line is [that] people want to participate in Tribal Journeys, and to do it they are willing to change their lives. Because you really have to do that."[44] The key here is that in order for it to be effective, people must change their lives. Through Tribal Journeys, Indigenous cultural values and practices are established as the way to change one's life, and it provides an observable road map for those who wish to make that change. This map is codified in "The Ten Rules of the Canoe," a set of protocols and rules of conduct that guide behavior while participating in Tribal Journeys. The rules cover behavior toward one another, behavior toward oneself, how to act in the canoe, and by extension how to act in life:

THE TEN RULES OF THE CANOE

Rule 1: Every stroke we take is one less we have to make. Keep going! Even against the most relentless wind, somehow a canoe moves forward. This mystery can only be explained by the fact that each pull forward is a real movement and not delusion.

Rule 2: There is to be no abuse of self or others. Respect and trust cannot exist in anger. It has to be thrown overboard, so the sea can cleanse it. It has to be washed off the hands and cast into the air, so the stars can take care of it. We always look back at the riptides we pulled through, amazed at how powerful we thought those dangers were.

Rule 3: Be flexible. The adaptable animal survives. If you get tired, ship your paddle and rest. If you get hungry, put in on a beach and eat a few oysters. If you can't figure one way to make it, do something new. When the wind confronts you, sometimes you are supposed to go the other way.

Rule 4: The gift of each enriches all. Every story is important. The bow, the stern, the skipper, cannot move without the power puller in the middle—everyone is part of the journey. The elder who sits in her cedar at the front, singing her paddle song, prays for us all, the weary paddler resting is still ballast. And there is always that time when the crew needs some joke, some remark, some silence to keep going. The least likely person provides.

Rule 5: We all pull and support each other. Nothing occurs in isolation. In a family of the canoe, we are ready for whatever comes. The family can argue, mock, ignore each other, at its worst, but that family will never let itself sink. The canoe that lets itself sink is certainly wiser never to leave the beach. When we know that we are not alone in our actions, we also know we are lifted up by everyone else.

Rule 6: A hungry person has no charity. Always nourish yourself. The bitter person, thinking that sacrifice means self-destruction, shares mostly anger. A paddler who doesn't eat at the feast doesn't have enough strength to paddle in the morning. Take that sandwich they throw at you at 2:00 a.m.! The gift of who you are only enters the world when you are strong enough to own it.

Rule 7: Our experiences are not enhanced through criticism. Who we are, how we are, what we do, why we continue, all flower in understanding. The canoe fellows who are grim go one way. Some men and women may sometimes go slow, but when they arrive they can still sing. And they have gone all over the sea, in the air with the seagulls, under the curve of the wave with the dolphin and down to the whispering shells, under the continental shelf. Withdrawing the blame acknowledges how wonderful a part if it all every one of us really is.

Rule 8: The journey is what we enjoy. Although the start is exciting and the conclusion gratefully achieved, it is that long, steady process we remember. Being part of the journey requires great preparation. Being done with a journey requires great awareness. Being on the journey, we are much more than ourselves. We are part of the movement of life, we have a destination, and for once, our will is pure, our goal is to go on.

Rule 9: A good teacher always allows the student to learn. We can berate each other, try to force each other to understand, or we can allow each paddler to gain awareness through the ongoing journey. Nothing sustains us like that sense of potential, that we can deal with things. Each paddler learns to deal with the person in front, the person behind, the water, the air, the energy, the blessing of the eagle.

Rule 10: When given a choice at all, be a worker bee—make honey![45]

The commitment to these ten rules is serious, and Tribal Journeys participants must promise to follow all of them during the journey. If they don't they are expected at a minimum to explain their actions and make restitution, or they may even be asked to leave. Additionally, Tribal Journeys is drug-free and alcohol-free. Anyone who cannot meet these expectations cannot continue to participate.

THE CANOE AS FAMILY AND COMMUNITY

The canoe is often described as a metaphor for the community, a group of people committed to working together and who depend upon each other to make progress.[46] Communities are by nature extensions and collections of families, and on Tribal Journeys people travel together as "canoe families." They paddle together, set up camp together, eat together, and perform protocol together. While some canoe families consist of people who aren't directly related by blood (instead brought together through shared interests and connections), many canoe families are directly tied together by blood relationships. For the Chinook Indian Nation the close connections of their canoe

FIGURE 14. Part of the Chinook Nation canoe family traveling in *Kthlmin* en route to Nisqually, Tribal Journeys, 2016. Photograph by Amiran White.

families, both at the immediate and extended family levels, are considered an asset. Tony Johnson says, "I think Chinook strength in the canoe journey is traveling as family. I mean, it's aunts, uncles, grandmas, grandpas, grandkids, moms, dads, whatever. And there is no thought about it. That is how we want it to be. Anything else, we wouldn't accept. It's just multigenerational family travel. We have canoe family elders, we have canoe family babies, and everything in between."[47] One of the benefits of having such a closely connected multigenerational canoe family is that it brings an already established level of familiarity and set of associations. Members of the canoe family can rely on a history of relationship and mutual concern to help navigate any problems that might come up, and there is a level of familiarity that in some ways is reminiscent of longhouse living.

Additionally, in a setting where people have long-standing relationships there is also a sense of control over the members of the canoe family, but it is a very specific type of control tied closely to expectations. Johnson says,

> To have a successful canoe family you have to have real control over the
> people involved. And I don't mean control over it like "we dictate what you
> do," but control over it in the sense of "we all have to know what people are

doing in their daily lives." We have to see them on a regular basis. We have to know what they are doing on a regular Friday night or a Saturday night or whatever. . . . Our canoe families are really successful because we have a genuine family relationship. We all know each other. We know what each other is doing, and the kids involved know the expectations and hold their friends to a certain line. . . . We have very high expectations of each other, and by the nature of a true tribal community—I mean, that's what it feels like to me—by the nature of the fact that we are living in a community, we are family, we are all together. You know, those expectations are actually followed through on and met.[48]

Close control over the canoe family and the requirement that canoe family members meet established expectations are necessary components of Tribal Journeys. Without them the successful completion of a canoe journey simply won't happen, primarily because the journey itself is extremely challenging. Tony Johnson says,

We all genuinely love each other in a Chinook canoe family. It is a group of people who are really, truly concerned with each other. And that's unique in the world, I think. But what we know is that if you don't feel that way, or if you are not actually together in that kind of committed way, the thing doesn't work. I mean, the nature of what we are doing is really hard. . . . The nature of Tribal Journeys makes it a spiritual journey, and you can't overstate that [because] you get up in the morning, based on the tide, and you travel. Sometimes it's just a number of hours. Sometimes it's a ridiculously long number of hours—twelve, thirteen, fourteen, fifteen, sixteen hours we might be in a canoe in a day, and off the water, setting up camp, living up to obligations, family needs, whatever. And then protocol. And the farther you go, the more people you pick up, and protocol becomes longer and later until really you are operating on very little sleep, physically pushing yourself really hard. This is all still not talking about the fact that it could be eighty-five degrees and the sun just blaring on you, or it could be fifty-five degrees, pissing rain and miserable.[49]

The physical and psychological challenges involved in Tribal Journeys are real, and travel on the water in a canoe can take a lot out of you. I have first-hand experience—albeit limited—of the difficulties, from my participation in the Chinook Paddle that annually occurs during the week before the Chinook Indian Nations' First Salmon Ceremony. During this paddle members of the Chinook Tribal Council, along with other Chinooks and invited friends, travel the Columbia River from Ridgefield, Washington, to Chinook, Washington, over the course of four days. Although in 2014 we were only on the water for a few hours each day, and on the relatively calm waters of the Columbia River (as opposed to being out on the ocean), the travel at times seemed endless. My arms, back, and shoulders ached, and occasionally I wasn't sure how I could manage even one more stroke. Although we were fortunate to have overall excellent weather on our trip, we still faced the near-constant winds of the Columbia, and at times it seemed like we were pulling and pulling, yet the shorelines to our left and right never appeared to move. Of course, the challenge is part of the point: it is the reason that the end of the voyage feels like such an accomplishment and instills a sense of pride. When you magnify the challenge to the level of days of eight or more hours on the water, as routinely happens during Tribal Journeys, and over the course of weeks rather than just a few days, the physical exhaustion, lack of sleep, and trials of living and working together in a confined space have the potential to pull a family apart. As Tony Johnson notes, "If you have all of that and a group of people that are not working for the best interest of each other, with each other, committed to the same ideas, it just comes apart at the seams."[50]

These situations can certainly lead to tensions and disagreements, and numerous canoe families have had to face moments of crisis.[51] But one of the strengths of Tribal Journeys for the Chinook is that canoe families rely on tribal teachings to address the tensions, and they do so by stressing truth-telling and providing gatherings where grievances can be directly addressed. As Johnson says,

> The traditional sensibility of our elders was not to lie, not to hide things. . . .
> If you believe these things, humans operate better together. It's what we
> are saying to each other. And by the way, there is a whole philosophy about
> how you live together in a canoe. There is a philosophy about how you live
> together in a longhouse. These things all play into it. But the bottom line is
> this: we tell each other we will circle up every single day and talk to each
> other as a group. If you have a beef, if there's a problem, you say it. You can
> say it to the person that you are having the problem with, and if you can't

resolve it that way, or if you don't want to, come to the skipper or somebody else, if you can do that. The other option is just in a circle, together. But if it's not important enough to do one of those things to bring it out, then you find a way to wash it away. You've got to dip it in the river, you've got to dip it in the creek, wash it in the ocean. Whatever it takes.[52]

It is important that canoe families work together and address any disagreements that might arise, not just for the reason of providing a harmonious experience but also because there can be very real and serious repercussions if tensions are present. Paddling in a small craft, in the midst of an ocean with large swells, is a dangerous venture, and lives have been lost on the journeys. Mary McQuillen has said that the canoe itself feels any tensions that might be present in canoe families and that those tensions must be addressed in order for the canoe to safely take care of the family:

> Each evening we would have a circle, so no one would bring any bad feelings into the canoe the next day. The canoe feels everything; the water feels everything, my grandfather used to say. The discipline and the prayer were very important. We took care of each other like a family. We made sure that for each one that traveled with us, our spiritual life was intact. We prayed for everyone even if we were upset; in this way we could travel in a good way. This way the canoe would take care of us, because it knows what we are feeling.[53]

The connection between entering a canoe with good feelings intact and having that canoe take care of you again reflects the metaphor of the canoe as a community. All of the lessons learned about truth-telling and prayer and addressing tensions while on the journey are meant to be applied to the lives of participants outside of the journey as well, and ultimately the community as a whole benefits.

The challenges of the journey—whether physical, social, or emotional—are, of course, what makes it such a good path for positive results. Participants encounter difficult physical challenges, including fatigue and exposure to the elements; they face their fears, whether that be the fear of water or of dancing, singing, and speaking in front of others; and they face the challenges of living and working together in close quarters. But during the process many learn that they can overcome these challenges, and they learn how to do so through culturally relevant and time-tested mechanisms. Successfully

facing these challenges, then, leads to a tremendous sense of pride in themselves and their culture. It is for these reasons that despite the challenges
and the hardships of the journey and the hours and hours of work, the result is
so positive. As Tony Johnson notes, "Ten percent of my time is awesome, just
a blast. Ninety percent of my time is probably miserable. And the ten percent
is so good that it outweighs the other."[54]

CULTURAL REVITALIZATION AND CULTURAL CONNECTION

The sense of accomplishment and pride that is achieved by overcoming challenges is one of the many positive attributes of Tribal Journeys and a primary
reason so many tribal citizens—especially the young—are drawn to it. The
ability to move forward in moments when you think you have reached your
breaking point is a tremendously uplifting experience. But there are other
impacts as well. Tony Johnson says, "It's amazing to watch and to see a crew
and what they are willing to do and take. You know, it's something else. When
you are seven or eight hours in and you still can't see where you are going,
it's very impressive what comes out of people that way. And then the other
part is, of course, [that] it inspires people to not just talk about the songs, the
dances, or whatever. There are new songs getting composed. There are old
dances being reinvigorated, you know what I mean? And it's just really fan-
tastic."[55] What Johnson is noting here is that canoes are not isolated material
objects. They are embedded within a cultural context and therefore necessarily connected to a suite of cultural practices that includes songs, dances,
and ultimately even one's view of the world. One of the many benefits of canoe
resurgence, then, is the associated resurgence of all those intertwined elements, and, as a result, the impact of the return of the canoes goes far beyond
the canoes themselves.

Canoe resurgence was certainly fueled, in part, by renewed interest in
the direct materiality of the canoes. Relearning the sophisticated process of
carving canoes, the engineering skills required to craft a seaworthy vessel,
and the intricate artistry attached to them motivated those in the vanguard
of canoe resurgence, individuals like Bill Reid, who meticulously studied
some of the few remaining canoes housed in museums before building one
himself.[56] Following the lead of Reid and other early resurgent canoe makers
in the Northwest—and directly driven by their desire to participate in Tribal
Journeys—numerous communities and individual canoe makers undertook
the laborious process of building new canoes. And the building of new canoes

inspired, necessarily, the carving of new paddles and the revitalization of artistic skills used for decorating canoe exteriors. It also required the relearning of the skills associated with traveling on the open water, skills like closely watching the water and the sky and gaining the ability to understand currents and tides.

The cultural importance of the canoe also expands into the revitalization of language, songs, and dances, which are all intimately tied to the performance of protocols on Tribal Journeys. As noted above, protocols occur when visiting nations come ashore and later in the evening in the host nation's longhouse. The protocols of coming ashore have encouraged greater interest in language, as it is becoming more and more common that the request to come ashore is given in the traditional language of the travelers. The evening protocols consist of the performance of songs and dances to the host community. But they are not just a demonstration of skills and talents: they are a gift to host community from their guests and a sign of recognition and thanks for the hosts' hospitality in providing food, shelter, and company. The performance of protocols in this context also helps to develop the skills of oration and speaking from the floor, an important and necessary skill for tribal leaders. Tribal leaders—and prospective leaders—get an opportunity to learn, practice, and hone their speaking abilities on the floor, in front of other Indigenous nations. In this sense the songs, dances, and oration connected to protocols reflect a larger tribal worldview. They are a reassertion of an expectation of reciprocity, a reflection of a system that provided the rules for relationships between Northwest Indigenous communities for centuries and long before the arrival of Euro-Americans, and a place for the emergence and development of tribal leaders. In effect, what canoe resurgence and Tribal Journeys accomplish is the revitalization of a *culture*, not just one aspect of it. Most importantly, this culture is now enacted, a lived heritage in which tribal citizens are "not just talking about it. It's real. And it really makes a difference."[57]

One of the ways that Tribal Journeys—and canoe travel in general—has made a difference is that it has strengthened the cultural connections that present-day citizens of the Chinook Indian Nation feel with their ancestors. The strong cultural connections seem to flow from physically moving over the water in a canoe. The act of retracing and reestablishing pathways that their ancestors traveled for millennia, seeing the shoreline and the world from the same vantage point as their ancestors did, serves as a powerful mechanism for reminding Chinooks of their long roots in place. When I speak with Chinook Indian Nation vice-chair Sam Robinson about his experiences on Tribal Journeys and his other travels by canoe, he always notes how important the canoes are to reaffirming those ancestral connections:

> With the Journeys there's been just so many different times that you know that your ancestors are there. You're traveling through that light fog out there and you just know that they are traveling with us [in Chinookan beliefs, fog is laid down by the ancestors as a means through which they travel]. . . . They're just glad to see us back again, out on the water. . . . One of the unique things for me is that we're traveling on the water and I'm hearing Chinook words. So you know that our ancestors were there through those trade routes . . . traveling up and down the coast. . . . So it's always a good day in the canoe. . . . For the Chinook Nation it helps us to get out there and to stay in touch with our culture.[58]

I have heard numerous accounts of paddlers hearing ancient words and ancient songs while in canoes on the water, from more than one person. The story that old songs that have not been heard for generations come alive again while canoe families are out on the water is one that is told consistently across the nations who have participated in the journeys. In this sense the canoe is a vessel for recovery, which provides a very tangible sense of cultural continuity.

My point here is that the canoe is only the beginning, a beginning that does not end with Tribal Journeys or with an isolated interest in the material form of canoes and paddles. Canoes are embedded within all the other aspects of Chinookan culture: songs, dances, languages, protocols, and a worldview that focuses on honesty and reciprocity. And the revitalization of canoes necessarily leads to revitalization of all of those other aspects as well. Furthermore, for the Chinook Indian Nation it is not the case that canoes simply get shelved after Tribal Journeys is complete each year, stored away in garages or sheds under tarps, forgotten and waiting to be uncovered and reintroduced a year later. Canoes have again become an integral part of Chinook life and are necessary components in ceremonies and events throughout the year. Canoes were an inseparable component of life to Chinookans in the past, and with their return canoes now have a central place in contemporary Chinookan culture, and their importance only continues to grow.

FIGURE 15. The Chinook Nation canoe family being welcomed ashore by the Nisqually Indian Tribe during final canoe landing protocols, Tribal Journeys, 2016. Photograph by Amiran White.

CANOE RESURGENCE AND DECOLONIZATION

The legacies of colonialism continue to affect Indigenous nations in the Pacific Northwest—including the Chinook Indian Nation—even after centuries of contact. This is the central theme of this book, and in the preceding chapters I have discussed how colonial mind-sets and institutions played a direct role in shaping and defining Indigenous identities through the processes of mapping, through determining who is sufficiently Indian to be federally recognized, and through deciding who are appropriate stakeholders when it comes to stewarding cultural resources and archaeological sites. The Chinook Indian Nation, in its efforts to control the practice and stories of its own heritage, faces these legacies of colonialism constantly. As Tony Johnson notes, however, a central aspect of canoe resurgence and Tribal Journeys is that they are fundamentally acts of decolonization: "I think there is a lot of [decolonization] in different aspects of Chinook life. I mean, I could feel like fishing, just fishing, just setting a net, is a kind of like rebellious or at least a take-back-my-rights act, right? Definitely, at that level, pulling in a canoe, village-to-village, reestablishing directly the connections that were either severed, damaged, or whatever over the years because of all this other garbage, the whole action

itself is kind of anticolonialism, right?"[59] The reestablishment of tribal connections that Johnson mentions is an extremely important component of
Tribal Journeys. Prior to colonial contact, waterways never served as boundaries between communities but instead were the primary means of connecting
peoples. By paddling through these ancient waterways from village to village
in canoes, the participants of Tribal Journeys are effectively redrawing the
colonial map of the entire region and reaffirming those connections that were
severed or altered by imposed and artificial colonial boundaries. Through a
series of canoe landings at tribal homelands—where visitors recognize the
host's legitimate right to that place through the performance of protocol—they
are reinscribing the landscape with an Indigenous map that asserts tribal pri-
macy and that predates colonial invasion. This is fundamentally an act of
decolonizing place.

Tribal Journeys and canoe resurgence also assert a decolonized enacted
heritage, in which time is ordered by the cycle of tides and the necessity of
performing protocols that may run late into the night rather than being
ordered by clocks. They present a world where actions are guided by Indigenous notions of reciprocity and truth-telling and where the paths to healing
from drug and alcohol abuse are rooted in Indigenous ceremonies and values.
One of the goals of colonization was to strip away all of those things that made
people Indian—a viewpoint embodied in the famous dictum "Kill the Indian,
and save the man." Whether it was through the institution of boarding schools
and efforts to remove Native children from their families, the attempted separation of tribal communities from their lands and languages, or direct efforts
at eradicating Native populations, colonialism worked to kill the Indian. Tony
Johnson argues, however, that Tribal Journeys and the return of canoes provide a path to decolonization, a way to remind people of their Indigeneity and
resilience: "Nowadays, one thing we say is 'Feed your Indian.' I mean, canoe
journeys, Tribal Journeys, being in the canoes, the Salmon Ceremony, things
we do—they feed your Indian. You have to find ways to do that."[60]

In this book I have also described some of the disputes that occasionally
arise between Indigenous nations, such as the tensions and disagreements
between the Chinook Indian Nation and the Cowlitz Indian Tribe over the
cultural affiliation and educational programs at Cathlapotle, and the Quinault
Indian Nation's opposition to Chinook recognition. But as I have pointed out,
we must place the colonial context of those disputes front and center. It is
incorrect to see these present-day disputes as simply cases of intertribal politics
instead of seeing them as a continuing manifestation of colonialism. But when

The resurgence of canoe culture that is reflected in Tribal Journeys is an extremely important form of enacted heritage that has worked to reestablish the ancient pathways that existed before colonial invasion. In the process it has removed anthropological and bureaucratic views of space and replaced them with Indigenous places. It asserts a form of heritage that is found in lived practice, one based in tribal cultural values of reciprocity and place, where Indigenous nations—rather than colonial agents—determine who is legitimately Indigenous. Ultimately, Tribal Journeys represents decolonized heritage. This trajectory toward the increasing decolonization of heritage as one moves through the chapters of the book is accompanied by the increasingly ubiquitous role played by protocol, those rules of behavior that ensure the maintenance of reciprocal responsibilities and offer a path forward. The centrality of protocol—the second primary theme of the book—is most evident in its connection to canoe resurgence, where it guides everything from the initial creation of the canoe, to travel on the water and recognition of the place of others on the landscape, to the maintenance and survival of family, community, and nation.

PROTOCOL, HERITAGE, AND PERFORMANCE

I will conclude with some final thoughts on the centrality of protocol and its connections to heritage, the relationship between humans and nonhumans, and the tangible and intangible. In my work with the Chinook Indian Nation, as well as my experiences with other Indigenous nations of the Pacific Northwest, I have been struck by the strong recognition by these groups that nonhuman objects (both animals and things) have an existence outside of humans. Nonhuman objects are not merely created by humans or placed here for human use; they exist independently of us. The canoe provides an example of this worldview. While the final shape of the canoe may be realized through human craftwork, the life of the canoe is not given to it by humans—its life was already there as a tree. Furthermore, the canoe is a being that has agency and can feel happiness, disappointment, and pain. But although the canoe and humans exist independently of each other, their lives are entangled by a sense of kinship and a series of reciprocal responsibilities. They rely on each other to make an appropriate path through the world. Rodney Harrison, who I noted in the introduction, refers to this entanglement of human and nonhuman actors as "connectivity ontologies" and describes this set of reciprocal responsibilities as "a series of diplomatic properties that emerge in the dialogue of heterogeneous human and non-human actors who are keeping pasts alive in the present, which function toward assembling futures."[4]

Harrison views this dialogue of human and nonhuman entanglement as the heart of an Indigenous approach to heritage. This reflects what I have seen as well, and I am in full agreement with him here. As I noted in the introduction, however, I choose to use the phrase *reciprocal heritage* to stress that the entanglement between humans and nonhumans is more than just connection and dialogue. It is centrally one of responsibilities. And during the course of my collaborations with the Chinook Indian Nation it became apparent that "the series of diplomatic properties," or *reciprocal responsibilities* in my phrasing, are codified in the rules and performance of protocols. Protocols are the requirement for appropriately fulfilling reciprocal relationships, and they are central to Chinookan views of heritage. As described in this book, they are present and fundamental in the Chinook Winter Gathering and First Salmon Ceremony, they serve to bring authenticity and life to the Cathlapotle Plankhouse, and they ensure the well-being of canoe families and recognition of Indigenous sovereignty on Tribal Journeys. Protocols, therefore, are more than simply a set of rules. They are the bridges that ensure reciprocity between humans and humans and between humans and nonhumans.

While protocols themselves can be considered as a form of intangible heritage, this does not mean that material objects are irrelevant to Chinookan views of heritage. In fact, quite the opposite is true. The physical canoe is important, the cedar plankhouse is important, the artifacts from the site of Cathlapotle are important, and the people of the community are important. But each is only as important as the relationships between them. And it is the requirement of reciprocity in these relationships that holds everything together, thus the intangible protocols, whose purpose is to ensure reciprocity between material agents, serve as the linchpin to heritage. For the Chinook Indian Nation, views of heritage focusing solely or principally on the preservation and categorization of material objects—a view that tends to underlie much of Western cultural heritage management—are simply not as meaningful since, in this view, material culture is disconnected from the intangible webs of reciprocity as defined in protocols. This approach to heritage, therefore, serves to destabilize any easy dichotomies between the tangible and intangible, the natural and cultural, and the human and nonhuman.[5] Furthermore, since heritage is attached to the *ongoing* relationships necessary for well-being, rather than static artifacts and objects from the past, heritage in this view is forward-looking. As Harrison writes, "Heritage emerges not as a process concerned with the past and present, but a future-oriented, emergent, contingent and creative endeavour. It is not a process of meaning-making that exists only in the human mind, but one in which multiple actors, both humans and non-humans, are equally implicated in complex processes that bind them across time and space."[6]

Finally, in this book I have used the word *performance* when speaking about protocols. I want to be clear, however, that when I use the term *performance* I do not use it in the sense of an action that is merely performed for others, in the way that an actor performs for an audience. Rather, I use the term in the sense of how one performs a duty, the action of fulfilling required responsibilities. This is an important distinction, especially within the context of twenty-first-century Indigenous claims to heritage. There can be a tendency to present these types of claims to heritage as something artificial, as invented political creations primarily constructed to convince others of their claims. As noted by James Clifford, in that view performance then becomes merely "a kind of self-marketing in systems of neoliberal tolerance. Performance is reduced to interpellation. Persons or groups are 'called' or 'hailed' to perform themselves as authentic cultural subjects."[7]

In my work with the Chinook Indian Nation, however, I never got the sense that the performance of protocols was an act created or designed to convince others of the rightfulness of Chinook claims. Instead it was required behavior done to ensure that the responsibilities of relationships between actors, both human and nonhuman, were fulfilled. And it was required behavior that was done in both events open to the public (with the public watching) and in Chinook private ceremonies (in the presence of community members only). The Chinook certainly want to remind others that they continue to exist. That is a central message that is often repeated at public and private events. The rules of protocol, however, were not created for that purpose. For the Chinook, humans did not create protocols for the purposes of political theater, but rather they exist independently, and humans are responsible for recognizing and following them. For this reason, the performance of protocols in gatherings like Tribal Journeys and at the Cathlapotle Plankhouse are not self-marketing performances of Indigeneity for the benefit of the non-Indigenous, nor are they a form of historical reenactment. They are simply a required responsibility and the most fundamental aspect of heritage. And it is this form of enacted and lived heritage—centered on the responsibility of the performance of protocols—that produces cultural resilience and that connects the Chinook Indian Nation's past to its present, and to its continued survival in the future.

NOTES

INTRODUCTION

1 A more complete presentation of my critiques of the Vancouver Land Bridge dedication ceremony, as well as other aspects of the Confluence Project, are found in Jon Daehnke, "Reflections on the *Confluence Project*: Assimilation, Sustainability, and the Perils of a Shared Heritage," *American Indian Quarterly* 36, no. 4 (2012): 503–24.

2 I use *Chinook* specifically in reference to the modern-day Chinook Indian Nation. The Chinook are the descendants of the Indigenous nations that were living along the westernmost portion of the Columbia River, from roughly Oak Point, Washington, to the river's mouth (and north and south along the Pacific coast). *Chinookan* refers to a larger grouping that includes any of the villages and people that spoke Chinookan-language dialects. These people lived along the Columbia River from its mouth to approximately the location of The Dalles, Oregon (as well as up the Willamette River to the Willamette Falls).

3 In this book I follow the example of other recent discussions of tribal resilience, continuity, and revitalization in the Pacific Northwest and elsewhere. See especially Charlotte Coté, *Spirits of Our Whaling Ancestors: Revitalizing Makah and Nuu-chah-nulth Traditions* (Seattle: University of Washington Press, 2010); Christine Dupres, *Being Cowlitz: How One Tribe Renewed and Sustained Its Identity* (Seattle: University of Washington Press, 2014); Les Field, *Abalone Tales: Collaborative Explorations of Sovereignty and Identity in Native California* (Durham: Duke University Press, 2008); Michelle M. Jacob, *Yakama Rising: Indigenous Cultural Revitalization, Activism, and Healing* (Tucson: University of Arizona Press, 2013); Charles Wilkinson, *The People Are Dancing Again: The History of the Siletz Tribe of Western Oregon* (Seattle: University of Washington Press, 2010).

4 Linda Tuhiwai Smith, *Decolonizing Methodologies: Research and Indigenous Peoples*, 2nd ed. (London: Zed Books, 2012), 1.

5 One of the classic discussions of the tensions between Indigenous communities and anthropologists is presented in Vine Deloria Jr., *Custer Died for Your Sins: An Indian Manifesto* (Norman: University of Oklahoma Press, 1988), 78–100. For examples of more recent discussions, see Les W. Field, "Complicities and Collaborations: Anthropologists and the 'Unacknowledged Tribes' of California," *Current Anthropology* 40, no. 2 (1999): 193–209; Les W. Field, "Unacknowledged Tribes, Dangerous Knowledge: The Muwekma Ohlone and How Indian Identities are 'Known,'" *Wicazo Sa Review* 18, no. 2 (2003): 79–94; Ian J. McNiven and Lynette Russell, *Appropriated Pasts: Indigenous Peoples and the Colonial Culture of Archaeology* (New York: AltaMira Press, 2005); Susan Roy, *These Mysterious People: Shaping History and Archaeology in a Northwest Coast Community* (Montreal: McGill-Queen's University Press, 2010). For a musical discussion of the topic, I direct the reader to Floyd Red Crow Westerman, "Here Come the Anthros," http://floyd redcrowwesterman.com/music.php.

6 Field, "Complicities and Collaborations," 195.

7 For other discussions of the complex entanglements between colonialism, tribal identity and authenticity, and western assumptions—especially in the greater Pacific

Northwest—see Andrew H. Fisher, *Shadow Tribe: The Making of Columbia River Indian Identity* (Seattle: University of Washington Press, 2010); Alexandra Harmon, *Indians in the Making: Ethnic Relations and Indian Identities around Puget Sound* (Berkeley: University of California Press, 2000); Paige Raibmon, *Authentic Indians: Episodes of Encounter from the Late-Nineteenth-Century Northwest Coast* (Durham: Duke University Press, 2005). For a classic study of issues surrounding tribal identity, see James Clifford, *The Predicament of Culture: Twentieth-Century Ethnography, Literature, and Art* (Cambridge: Harvard University Press, 1988), 277–346.

8   Smith, *Decolonizing Methodologies*, 11.

9   Gary Johnson, interview by author, September 5, 2006, Chinook, Washington.

10   A thorough discussion of heritage and its history is found in Rodney Harrison, *Heritage: Critical Approaches* (London: Routledge, 2013). Another excellent source for the topic is Laurajane Smith, *Uses of Heritage* (London: Routledge, 2006).

11   Harrison, *Heritage*, 14.

12   Ibid., 6.

13   Ibid., *Heritage*, 14–20; Smith, *Uses of Heritage*, 29–34.

14   In recent years there have been attempts to address the overemphasis on tangible heritage and to more widely recognize the value of intangible heritage. For instance, in 2003 UNESCO produced the Convention for the Safeguarding of the Intangible Cultural Heritage. These efforts, however, have not been without critique. See Harrison, *Heritage*, 114–39. See also Laurajane Smith and Natsuko Akagawa, eds., *Intangible Heritage* (London: Routledge, 2009).

15   Harrison, *Heritage*, 22. For more discussion on this, especially the role that archaeology has played in minimizing Indigenous histories, see Bruce Trigger, "Alternative Archaeologies: Nationalist, Colonialist, Imperialist," *Man* 19, no. 3 (1984): 355–70.

16   See Harrison, *Heritage*; Rodney Harrison, "Beyond 'Natural' and 'Cultural' Heritage: Toward an Ontological Politics of Heritage in the Age of Anthropocene," *Heritage and Society* 8, no. 1 (2015): 24–42; Rodney Harrison and Deborah Rose, "Intangible Heritage," in *Understanding Heritage and Memory*, ed. Tim Benton (Manchester: Manchester University Press, 2010), 238–75; Deborah Bird Rose, "On History, Trees, and Ethical Proximity," *Postcolonial Studies* 11, no. 2 (2008): 157–67; Deborah Bird Rose, *Wild Dog Dreaming: Love and Extinction* (Charlottesville: University of Virginia Press, 2011).

17   Harrison and Rose, "Intangible Heritage," 264–65.

18   Claire Poirier, "Drawing Lines in the Museum: Plains Cree Ontology as Political Practice," *Anthropologica* 53, no. 2 (2011): 294.

19   My thinking on the topic at the formative stages was heavily influenced by the work of Edward Casey. Specifically, see Edward Casey, *Getting Back into Place: Toward a Renewed Understanding of the Place-World* (Bloomington: Indiana University Press, 1993); Edward Casey, "How to Get from Space to Place in a Fairly Short Stretch of Time: Phenomenological Prolegomena," in *Senses of Place*, ed. Steven Feld and Keith H. Basso (Santa Fe: School of American Research Press, 1996), 13–52; Edward Casey, *The Fate of Place: A Philosophical History* (Berkeley: University of California Press, 1998); Edward Casey, *Remembering: A Phenomenological Study*, 2nd ed. (Bloomington: Indiana University Press, 2000); Edward Casey, "Public Memory in Place and Time," in *Framing Public Memory*, ed. Kendall R. Phillips (Tuscaloosa: University of Alabama Press, 2004).

20   In my talks with Chinook Indian Nation chair Tony Johnson, he has stated that he thinks the more standard American approach to landscape is to homogenize it; all lands within political boundaries are in some sense the same, and all are open to becoming possible

homes. Consequently, this leads to an overall lack of roots for many Americans. He also notes that for many Indigenous people that type of homogenized view of landscape and place is almost incomprehensible.

21 Jon Daehnke, "Public Outreach and the 'Hows' of Archaeology: Archaeology as a Model for Education" (master's thesis, Portland State University, 2002).

22 Jon Daehnke, *Cathlapotle . . . Catching Time's secrets* (Sherwood, OR: US Fish and Wildlife Service Cultural Resources, Region 1, 2005).

23 See Lynn Meskell, "Archaeological Ethnography: Conversations around Kruger National Park," *Archaeologies* 1, no. 1 (2005): 81–100; Lynn Meskell, "Falling Walls and Mending Fences: Archaeological Ethnography in the Limpopo," *Journal of Southern African Studies* 33, no. 2 (2007): 383–400; Lynn Meskell, "The Nature of Culture in Kruger National Park," in *Cosmopolitan Archaeologies*, ed. Lynn Meskell (Durham: Duke University Press, 2009), 89–112; Lynn Meskell, "Archaeological Ethnography: Materiality, Heritage, and Hybrid Methodologies," in *Archaeology and Anthropology: Past, Present and Future*, ed. by David Shankland (London: Berg, 2012), 133–44.

24 Examples of archaeological ethnographies done by non-archaeologists include Nadia Abu el-Haj, *Facts on the Ground: Archaeological Practice and Territorial Self-Fashioning in Israeli Society* (Chicago: University of Chicago Press, 2001); O. Hugo Benavides, *Making Ecuadorian Histories: Four Centuries of Defining Power* (Austin: University of Texas Press, 2004); Lisa Breglia, *Monumental Ambivalence: The Politics of Heritage* (Austin: University of Texas Press, 2006). In addition to the work by Meskell, examples of archaeological ethnographies done by trained archaeologists include Denis Byrne, *Surface Collection: Archaeological Travels in Southeast Asia* (Lanham: AltaMira Press, 2007); Alfredo Gonzales-Ruibal, "The Dream of Reason: An Archaeology of the Failures of Modernity in Ethiopia," *Journal of Social Archaeology* 6 (2006): 175–201; Kathryn Lafrenz Samuels, "Trajectories of Development: International Heritage Management of Archaeology in the Middle East and North Africa," *Archaeologies* 5 (2009): 68–91.

25 Meskell, "Archaeological Ethnography," (2005): 84.

26 Lynn Meskell, *The Nature of Heritage: The New South Africa* (Oxford: Wiley-Blackwell, 2012), 4.

27 See Charlotte Andrews, "Heritage Ethnography as a Specialised Craft: Grasping Maritime Heritage in Bermuda," in *Heritage Studies: Methods and Approaches*, ed. Marie Louise Stig Sorensen and John Carman (London: Routledge, 2009), 140–63; Charlotte Andrews, "Community Uses of Maritime Heritage in Bermuda: A Heritage Ethnography with Museum Implications" (PhD diss., University of Cambridge, 2010).

28 See Les W. Field, "Beyond 'Applied' Anthropology," in *A Companion to the Anthropology of North American Indians*, ed. Thomas Biolsi (Malden, M: Blackwell, 2004), 472–89; Les W. Field, *Abalone Tales: Collaborative Explorations of Sovereignty and Identity in Native California* (Durham: Duke University Press, 2008); Les W. Field, "'Side by Side or Facing One Another': Writing and Collaborative Ethnography in Comparative Perspective," *Collaborative Anthropologies* 1 (2008): 32–50.

29 Field, *Abalone Tales*, 6.

30 James Clifford broached discussion of the possibility and potential importance of shifting authority from anthropologists to communities by creating "polyphonic ethnographies" a few decades ago. See Clifford, *The Predicament of Culture: Twentieth-Century Ethnography, Literature, and Art* (Cambridge: Harvard University Press, 1988). Since that time, participation in and discussion of collaborative methods has increased dramatically. For instance, see discussions in Sonya Atalay, *Community-Based Archaeology:*

Research with, by, and for Indigenous and Local Communities (Berkeley: University of California Press, 2012); Luke Eric Lassiter, *The Chicago Guide to Collaborative Ethnography* (Chicago: University of Chicago Press, 2005)

31 Field, *Abalone Tales*, 6.

32 Katrine Barber, "Shared Authority in the Context of Tribal Sovereignty: Building Capacity for Partnerships with Indigenous Nations," *Public Historian* 35, no. 4 (2013): 26.

33 Ibid., 29.

34 SB 5433 is an amendment to Washington's HB 1495, which was passed in 2005. While HB 1495 "encouraged" Washington school districts to teach Pacific Northwest tribal histories, it did not make it mandatory.

35 In his April 21, 2004, testimony before the Committee on Indian Affairs of the US Senate on S. 297, Kevin Gover, the former assistant secretary for Indian affairs, stated that the Chinooks were deserving of recognition and that the limitations of the federal recognition process wrongfully led to their recognition being rescinded. S. 297 was written to provide reform and new resources to the Federal Acknowledgment Process. *Hearing by the Committee on Indian Affairs, United States Senate, One Hundred Eighth Congress, Second Session, on S. 297, to Provide Reforms and Resources to the Bureau of Indian Affairs to Improve the Federal Acknowledgment Process* (Washington: Government Printing Office, 2014), https://www.gpo.gov/fdsys/pkg/CHRG-108shrg93280/html/CHRG-108shrg93280.htm.

CHAPTER I

1 For more about Chinookan peoples and culture, see Robert T. Boyd, Kenneth M. Ames, and Tony A. Johnson, eds., *Chinookan Peoples of the Lower Columbia* (Seattle: University of Washington Press, 2013). To date this is the most complete volume on Chinookan history, and it provides an exhaustive set of references. Another excellent source is Robert T. Boyd, *Cathlapotle and Its Inhabitants, 1792–1860*, Cultural Resource Series 15 (Portland, OR: US Fish and Wildlife Service, 2011). Robert H. Ruby and John Brown, *The Chinook Indians: Traders of the Lower Columbia River* (Norman: University of Oklahoma Press, 1978) is a bit dated but still useful. Andrew Fisher, *Shadow Tribe: The Making of Columbia River Identity* (Seattle: University of Washington Press, 2010) focuses on history and Indigenous identity farther upriver on the Columbia, and Gray H. Whaley, *Oregon and the Collapse of Illahee: U.S. Empire and the Transformation of an Indigenous World, 1792–1859* (Chapel Hill: University of North Carolina Press, 2010) provides a good regional history of the effects of colonial contact.

2 See Kenneth M. Ames and Herbert D. G. Maschner, *Peoples of the Northwest Coast: Their Archaeology and Prehistory* (London: Thames and Hudson, 1999); Kenneth M. Ames, "The Northwest Coast," *Evolutionary Anthropology* 12 (2003): 19–33; Leland Donald, "The Northwest Coast as a Study Area: Natural, Prehistoric, and Ethnographic Issues," in *Emerging from the Mist: Studies in Northwest Coast Culture History*, eds. R. G. Matson, Gary Coupland, and Quentin Mackie (Vancouver: University of British Columbia Press, 2003), 289–327.

3 Ames, "Northwest Coast" (2003), 20. For an in-depth look at the Oregon and Washington coasts, see Paul D. Komar, *The Pacific Northwest Coast: Living with the Shores of Oregon and Washington* (Durham: Duke University Press, 1998).

4 R. G. Matson and Gary Coupland, *The Prehistory of the Northwest Coast* (San Diego: Academic Press, 1995), 21.

5   Ames and Maschner, *Peoples of the Northwest Coast*, 45–46.

6   R. F. Schalk, "The Structure of an Anadromous Fish Resource," in *For Theory Building in Anthropology*, ed. Lewis Binford (Orlando: Academic Press, 1977), 209. See also Ames, "Northwest Coast" (2003), 20; B. P. Finney et al., "Fisheries Productivity in the Northeastern Pacific Ocean over the Past 2,200 Years," *Nature* 416 (2002): 729–33; Wayne Suttles, "Coping with Abundance: Subsistence on the Northwest Coast," in *Man the Hunter*, eds. Richard B. Lee and Irven DeVore (Chicago: Aldine Press, 1968), 56–68.

7   Alfred Kroeber, "Cultural and Natural Areas of Native North America," *University of California Publications in American Archaeology and Ethnology* 38 (1939); F. Clark Wissler, *The American Indian: An Introduction to the Anthropology of the New World* (New York: McMurtrie, 1917). See also Ames and Maschner, *Peoples of the Northwest Coast*, 113.

8   Gregory Monks, "Prey as Bait: The Deep Bay Example," *Canadian Journal of Archaeology* 11 (1987): 119–42.

9   Hilary Stewart, *Indian Fishing: Early Methods on the Northwest Coast* (Vancouver, BC: Douglas & McIntyre, 1977); Alan D. McMillan, *Since the Time of the Transformers: The Ancient Heritage of the Nuu-chah-nulth, Ditidaht, and Makah* (Vancouver: University of British Columbia Press, 1999); Madonna Moss, "Shellfish, Gender, and Status on the Northwest Coast: Reconciling Archaeological, Ethnographic, and Ethnohistorical Records of the Tlingit," *American Anthropologist* 95 (1993): 631–52.

10   For example, see Philip Drucker, "Culture Element Distributions 26: Northwest Coast," *University of California Anthropological Records* 9 (1950): 157–294; Alfred Kroeber, "American Culture and the Northwest Coast," *American Anthropologist* 25 (1923): 1–20; Kroeber, "Cultural and Natural Areas of Native North America"; F. Clark Wissler, "Material Cultures of the North American Indians," *American Anthropologist* 16 (1914): 447–505; Wissler, *American Indian*.

11   Donald, "Northwest Coast as a Study Area," 297–98.

12   Ames, "Northwest Coast" (2003), 19.

13   David R. Huelsbeck, "The Surplus Economy of the Central Northwest Coast," *Research in Economic Anthropology* supplement 3 (1988): 149–77.

14   Jerry R. Galm, "Prehistoric Trade and Exchange in the Interior Plateau of Northwestern North America," in *Prehistoric Exchange Systems in North America*, eds. T. G. Baugh and J. E. Ericson (New York: Plenum Press, 1994) 275–306.

15   G. F. MacDonald, "The Epic of Nekt: The Archaeology of Metaphor," in *The Tsimshian: Images of the Past, Views of the Present*, ed. M. Seguin (Vancouver: University of British Columbia Press, 1984), 65–81. See also Stewart, *Indian Fishing*; Scott Byram and David G. Lewis, "Ourigan: Wealth of the Northwest Coast," *Oregon Historical Quarterly* 102 (2001): 127–57.

16   Charles Wolcott Brooks, *Japanese Wrecks Stranded and Picked up Adrift in the North Pacific Ocean, Ethnologically Considered as Furnishing Evidence of a Constant Infusion of Japanese Blood among the Coast Tribes of Northwestern Indians* (San Francisco: Academy of Sciences, 1876); George I. Quimby, "Japanese Wrecks, Iron Tools, and Prehistoric Indians of the Northwest Coast," *Arctic Anthropology* 22 (1985): 7–15.

17   Steven Acheson, "The Thin Edge: Evidence for Precontact Use and Working of Metal on the Northwest Coast," in *Emerging from the Mist: Studies in Northwest Coast Culture History*, eds. R. G. Matson, Gary Coupland, and Quentin Mackie (Vancouver: University of British Columbia Press, 2003), 213–29.

18   Kenneth M. Ames, "Slaves, Chiefs and Labour on the Northern Northwest Coast," *World Archaeology* 33 (2001): 1–17; Kenneth M. Ames, "Slavery, Household Production, and

Demography on the Southern Northwest Coast: Cables, Tacking, and Ropewalking," in *Invisible Citizens: Captives and Their Consequences*, ed. Catherine M. Cameron (Salt Lake City: University of Utah Press, 2008) 138–58; Leland Donald, "The Slave Trade on the Northwest Coast of North America," *Research in Economic Anthropology* 6 (1984): 121–58; Leland Donald, *Aboriginal Slavery on the Northwest Coast of North America* (Berkeley: University of California Press, 1997); Yvonne P. Hajda, "Slavery in the Greater Lower Columbia Region," *Ethnohistory* 52 (2005): 563–88; Donald Mitchell, "Predatory Warfare, Social Status, and the North Pacific Slave Trade," *Ethnology* 23 (1984): 39–48.

19   For discussion of the development and timing of Chinuk Wawa, see George Lang, *Making Wawa: The Genesis of Chinook Jargon* (Vancouver: University of British Columbia Press, 2008); Sarah G. Thomason, "Chinook Jargon in Areal and Historical Context," *Language* 59 (1983): 820–70; Henry Zenk and Tony A. Johnson, "A Northwest Language of Contact, Diplomacy, and Identity: Chinuk Wawa/Chinook Jargon," *Oregon Historical Quarterly* 111 (2010): 444–61; Henry B. Zenk and Tony A. Johnson, "Chinook Wawa and Its Roots in Chinookan," in Boyd, Ames, and Johnson, *Chinookan Peoples of the Lower Columbia*, 272–87.

20   Regna Darnell, "The Pivotal Role of the Northwest Coast in the History of Americanist Anthropology," *BC Studies* 125/126 (2000): 33–52.

21   The results of this fieldwork are Franz Boas, *Chinook Texts*, Bureau of American Ethnology Bulletin 20 (Washington DC: Bureau of American Ethnology, 1894); Franz Boas, *Kathlamet Texts*, Bureau of American Ethnology Bulletin 26 (Washington DC: Bureau of American Ethnology, 1901).

22   See Darnell, "Pivotal Role of the Northwest Coast." For additional discussions of the early connections between the Pacific Northwest and the development of anthropology, see Ames and Maschner, *Peoples of the Northwest Coast*, 19–22; Michael Harkin, "Past Presence: Conceptions of History in Northwest Coast Studies," *Arctic Anthropology* 33 (1996): 1–15; Paige Raibmon, *Authentic Indians: Episodes of Encounter from the Late-Nineteenth-Century Northwest Coast* (Durham: Duke University Press, 2005), 5–14; Regna Darnell, *And Along Came Boas: Continuity and Revolution in Americanist Anthropology* (Philadelphia: Benjamins, 1998); Regna Darnell, *Invisible Genealogies: A History of Americanist Anthropology* (Lincoln: University of Nebraska Press, 2001).

23   See Raibmon, *Authentic Indians*, 5–14. For discussion of collecting, see Douglas Cole, *Captured Heritage: The Scramble for Northwest Coast Artifacts* (Seattle: University of Washington Press, 1985); Jon Daehnke and Amy Lonetree, "Repatriation in the United States: The Current State of the Native American Graves Protection and Repatriation Act," *American Indian Culture and Research Journal* 35 (2011): 88–91; Ann M. Tweedie, *Drawing Back Culture: The Makah Struggle for Repatriation* (Seattle: University of Washington Press, 2002).

24   Quoted in James Riding In, "Our Dead Are Never Forgotten: American Indian Struggles for Burial Rights and Protections," in *"They Made Us Many Promises": The American Indian Experience, 1524 to the Present*, ed. Philip Weeks (Wheeling, IL: Harlan Davidson, 2002), 306.

25   Ibid.

26   The term *complex hunter-gatherer* first appears in T. D. Price, "Complexity in 'Non-complex' Societies," in *Archaeological Approaches to the Study of Complexity*, ed. S. E. van der Leuw (Amsterdam: Universiteit van Amsterdam, 1981), 55–99. For a thorough yet concise discussion of "complex hunter-gatherers" and their place in anthropological

research, see Kenneth M. Ames, "Complex Hunter-Gatherers," in *Encyclopedia of Global Archaeology*, ed. Claire Smith (New York: Springer, 2014), 1613–21.

27   See Kenneth M. Ames, "The Northwest Coast: Complex Hunter-Gatherers, Ecology, and Social Evolution," *Annual Review of Anthropology* 23 (1994): 209–29; Kent G. Lightfoot, "Long-Term Developments in Complex Hunter-Gatherer Societies: Recent Perspectives from the Coast of North America," *Journal of Archaeological Research* 1 (1993): 167–200.

28   Lightfoot, "Long-Term Developments," 168.

29   See C. M. Aikens and S. N. Rhee, eds., *Pacific Northeast Asia in Prehistory: Hunter-Fisher-Gatherers, Farmers, and Sociopolitical Elites* (Pullman: Washington State University Press, 1992); Jeanne Arnold, ed., *Emergent Complexity: The Evolution of Intermediate Societies* (Ann Arbor: International Monographs in Prehistory, 1996); S. Koyama and D. H. Thomas, eds., *Affluent Foragers: Pacific Coasts East and West*, Senri Ethnological Studies (Osaka, Japan: National Museum of Ethnology, 1981); T. D. Price and J. A. Brown, eds., *Prehistoric Hunter-Gatherers: The Emergence of Cultural Complexity* (San Diego: Academic Press, 1985); T. D. Price and G. M. Feinman, eds., *Foundations of Social Inequality* (New York: Plenum Press, 1995).

30   Raibmon, *Authentic Indians*, 5.

31   For example, see Susan Roy, *These Mysterious People: Shaping History and Archaeology in a Northwest Coast Community* (Montreal: McGill-Queen's University Press, 2010) for discussion of the role that anthropology and archaeology played in disassociating the Musqueam people from their own history.

32   Elizabeth A. Sobel, Kenneth M. Ames, and Robert J. Losey, "Environment and Archaeology of the Lower Columbia," in Boyd, Ames, and Johnson, *Chinookan Peoples of the Lower Columbia*, 23; Katrine Barber, *Death of Celilo Falls* (Seattle: University of Washington Press, 2005), 19.

33   Sobel, Ames, and Losey, "Environment and Archaeology of the Lower Columbia," 23.

34   Ibid., 25.

35   Richard M. Pettigrew, *A Prehistoric Culture Sequence in the Portland Basin of the Lower Columbia Valley*, University of Oregon Anthropological Papers 22 (Eugene: University of Oregon, Dept. of Anthropology, 1981), 5.

36   See Barber, *Death of Celilo Falls*, for an excellent discussion of the history and impacts of dam construction on the lower Columbia River.

37   David H. French and Kathrine S. French, "Wasco, Wishram, and Cascades," in *Handbook of North American Indians*, vol. 12, *Plateau*, ed. Deward Walker Jr. (Washington, DC: Smithsonian Institution, 1998), 368.

38   Robert T. Boyd, "Lower Chinookan Disease and Demography," in Boyd, Ames, and Johnson, *Chinookan Peoples of the Lower Columbia*, 245; Yvonne Hajda, "Social and Political Organization," in Boyd, Ames, and Johnson, *Chinookan Peoples of the Lower Columbia*, 146.

39   Michael Silverstein, "Chinookans of the Lower Columbia," in *Handbook of North American Indians*, vol. 7, *Northwest Coast*, ed. Wayne Suttles (Washington, DC: Smithsonian Institution, 1990), 533–46; French and French, "Wasco, Wishram, and Cascades," 360–77.

40   See Yvonne Hajda, "Regional Social Organization in the Greater Lower Columbia, 1792–1830" (PhD diss., University of Washington, 1984); Hajda, "Social and Political Organization."

41 Hajda, "Regional Social Organization," 14.

42 See note 19.

43 William Wuerch, "History of the Middle Chinooks to the Reservation Era" (master's thesis, University of Oregon, 1979), 3–4.

44 For discussion of head flattening and other forms of Chinookan ceremonialism, see Robert T. Boyd, "Lower Columbia Chinookan Ceremonialism," in Boyd, Ames, and Johnson, *Chinookan Peoples of the Lower Columbia*, 181–98. For discussion of the Chinookan art style, see Tony A. Johnson and Adam McIsaac, "Lower Columbia River Art," in Boyd, Ames, and Johnson, *Chinookan Peoples of the Lower Columbia*, 199–225.

45 One of the largest centers for Indigenous trade in North America was located near present-day The Dalles, Oregon. For discussion of the timing, extent, and nature of trade and exchange, see Yvonne Hajda and Elizabeth A. Sobel, "Lower Columbia Trade and Exchange Systems," in Boyd, Ames, and Johnson, *Chinookan Peoples of the Lower Columbia*, 106–24. The central role of trade in Chinookan life is also discussed in Ruby and Brown, *The Chinook Indians*, and Philip Drucker, *Cultures of the North Pacific Coast* (San Francisco: Chandler Publishing, 1965), 168–75.

46 Verne Ray, "The Historical Position of the Lower Chinook in the Native Culture of the Northwest," *Pacific Northwest Quarterly* 28 (1937): 371.

47 Yvonne Hajda notes that kinship on the lower Columbia River was predominantly "bilateral": descent was traced bilaterally, through both parents. Bilateral kinship, she writes, "creates a series of overlapping kindreds: each person's set of parents, siblings, cousins, and so on differs to some extent from everyone else's. Unilineal societies, while recognizing relationships through the other parent, trace 'legal' kin through mother or father only and so tend to develop mutually exclusive lineages and clans. The networks of kin created in bilateral societies thus tend to be more extensive than those found in unilineal societies." Hajda, "Social and Political Organization," 153.

48 See Hajda, "Regional Social Organization"; Hajda, "Social and Political Organization."

49 Hajda, "Social and Political Organization," 147–48.

50 See Robert T. Boyd, preface to Boyd, Ames, and Johnson, *Chinookan Peoples of the Lower Columbia*, xv–xvii. For an extended discussion of the connections between colonialism and the creation and transformation of indigenous identity, especially as it relates to the Columbia River, see Fisher, *Shadow Tribe*.

51 William L. Lang, "The Chinookan Encounter with Euro-Americans in the Lower Columbia River Valley," in Boyd, Ames, and Johnson, *Chinookan Peoples of the Lower Columbia*, 250–71, provides an extensive survey of contact on the Lower Columbia River.

52 Ibid., 250. For further discussion of early contact and shipwrecks, see Brooks, *Japanese Wrecks*; Jon Erlandson, Robert Losey, and Neil Peterson, "Early Maritime Contact on the Northern Oregon Coast: Some Notes on the 17th Century Nehalem Beeswax Ship," in *Changing Landscapes: Telling Our Stories*, ed. Jason Younker, Mark Tveskov, and David G. Lewis (North Bend, OR: Coquille Indian Tribe, 2001), 45–53; Quimby, "Japanese Wrecks."

53 Ruby and Brown, *Chinook Indians*, 31–32.

54 Lang, "Chinookan Encounter with Euro-Americans," 250–52.

55 When Broughton entered the estuary of the Columbia he encountered the *Jenny*, a British merchant ship captained by James Baker. Euro-American trade with Chinookans at the river's mouth proceeded rapidly after first contact with Gray. Ibid., 253.

56 Broughton, quoted in George Vancouver, *A Voyage of Discovery to the North Pacific Ocean and Round the World, 1791–1795* (London: Hakluyt Society, 1984), 755–56.

57 Lang, "Chinookan Encounter with Euro-Americans," 253.

58 Ibid.

59 Boyd, *Cathlapotle and Its Inhabitants*, 16. The Corps of Discovery traveled the lower Columbia from October 30, 1805, to April 12, 1806. Their accounts of this time period can be found in Gary E. Moulton, ed., *The Definitive Journals of Lewis and Clark*, vols. 5–7 (Lincoln: University of Nebraska Press, 1988–91).

60 Moulton, *Definitive Journals of Lewis and Clark*, vol. 6, 23.

61 Ibid., vol. 7, 26–28.

62 Ibid., vol. 6, 49.

63 Ibid., 50. See also Lang, "Chinookan Encounter with Euro-Americans," 256.

64 William L. Lang, "Lewis and Clark on the Columbia River: The Power of Landscape in the Exploration Experience," *Pacific Northwest Quarterly* 87 (1996): 141–48.

65 See James P. Ronda, *Lewis and Clark among the Indians* (Lincoln: University of Nebraska Press, 1984), 163–213. See also Lang, "Chinookan Encounter with Euro-Americans," 254–62.

66 Ibid. According to Ronda, Concomly, a Chinookan headman and the person who would emerge as the most important Chinookan in the years after Lewis and Clark, never visited Lewis and Clark at Fort Clatsop (Ronda, *Lewis and Clark*, 195).

67 Lang, "Chinookan Encounter with Euro-Americans," 262–64. For further discussion of Ilchee's marriage to McDougall, as well as the effects of colonial invasion on gender, race, and sexuality on the river, see Gray Whaley, "'Complete Liberty'? Gender, Sexuality, Race, and Social Change on the Lower Columbia River, 1805–1838," *Ethnohistory* 54 (2007): 669–95.

68 Lang, "Chinookan Encounter with Euro-Americans," 264–66.

69 Boyd, *Cathlapotle and Its Inhabitants*, 60.

70 Whaley, *Oregon and the Collapse of Illahee*, 74–83.

71 Ibid., 83–91.

72 See Nathan Reynolds, *"More Dangerous Dead than Living": The Killing of Chief Umtuch* (Longview, WA: Cowlitz Indian Tribe, 2007).

73 Robert Boyd has done the most extensive and thorough work on contact-related diseases affecting Native Americans in the Pacific Northwest. See Robert T. Boyd, "The Introduction of Infectious Diseases among the Indians of the Pacific Northwest, 1774–1874," (PhD diss., University of Washington, 1985); Robert T. Boyd, "Demographic History, 1774–1874," in *Handbook of North American Indians*, vol. 7, *Northwest Coast*, ed. Wayne Suttles (Washington, DC: Smithsonian Institution, 1990), 135–48; Robert T. Boyd, *The Coming of the Spirit of Pestilence: Introduced Infectious Diseases and Population Decline among Northwest Coast Indians, 1774–1874* (Seattle: University of Washington Press, 1999); Robert T. Boyd, "Lower Chinookan Disease and Demography," in Boyd, Ames, and Johnson, *Chinookan Peoples of the Lower Columbia*, 229–49. This section relies heavily on Boyd's extensive work.

74 Boyd, "Demographic History," 137–42; Boyd, *Spirit of Pestilence*, 21–60, 160–201; Boyd, "Lower Chinookan Disease," 235–38. There is still controversy over the exact timing and vehicle of arrival of smallpox both in the Pacific Northwest in general and along the Columbia River specifically. For instance, some argue that smallpox was introduced to the Columbia River by Spanish ships in the mid-1770s, while others suggest that it arrived instead from the plains in the early 1780s. A recently discovered oral history suggests that it may have first been introduced by a European ship carrying sick passengers in the early 1780s. See Boyd, "Lower Chinookan Disease," 236.

75   Ibid., 84.

76   Wuerch, "History of the Middle Chinooks," 94–95.

77   Burt Barker, ed., *Letters of Dr. John McLoughlin, Written at Fort Vancouver, 1829–1832* (Portland, OR: Binfords and Mort, 1948), 175. See also Boyd, *Spirit of Pestilence*, 91.

78   Boyd, *Spirit of Pestilence*, 84. See also William Bowen, "The Oregon Frontiersman: A Demographic View," in *The Western Shore: Oregon Country Essays Honoring the American Revolution*, ed. Thomas Vaughan (Portland: Oregon Historical Society Press, 1975), 181–98.

79   Wuerch, "History of the Middle Chinooks," 119.

80   Hajda, "Regional Social Organization," 35–46.

81   Andrew Fisher and Melinda Marie Jetté, "'Now You See Them, Now You Don't': Chinook Tribal Affairs and the Struggle for Federal Recognition," in Boyd, Ames, and Johnson, *Chinookan Peoples of the Lower Columbia*, 288–306. For an excellent discussion of the type of limited title rights Congress considered Native Americans to have to their homelands, see Robert L. Miller, *Native America, Discovered and Conquered: Thomas Jefferson, Lewis and Clark, and Manifest Destiny* (Lincoln, NE: Bison Books, 2008). Miller demonstrates the connection between US views of aboriginal title and long-standing beliefs in the Doctrine of Discovery.

82   David G. Lewis, "Clackamas and Cascades Treaties," in Boyd, Ames, and Johnson, *Chinookan Peoples of the Lower Columbia*, 320.

83   See David G. Lewis, Eirik Thorsgard, and Chuck Williams, "Honoring our Tilixam," in Boyd, Ames, and Johnson, *Chinookan Peoples of the Lower Columbia*, 307–8; Lewis, "Clackamas and Cascades Treaties," 320–22; Wuerch, "History of the Middle Chinooks," 119–39.

84   See Fisher and Jetté, "Now You See Them," 290–91. See also C. F. Coan, "The First Stage of the Federal Indian Policy in the Pacific Northwest, 1849–1852," *Quarterly of the Oregon Historical Society* 22 (1921): 58–61.

85   Fisher and Jetté, "Now You See Them," 291.

86   Ibid., 291–92.

87   Katherine Elliott, interview by author, Issaquah, Washington, July 30, 2013. See also "The Chehalis River Treaty 1855," Chinook Nation, www.chinooknation.org/justice /week1/day4.html.

88   Fisher and Jetté, "Now You See Them," 292. See also C. F. Coan, "The Adoption of Reservation Policy in the Pacific Northwest, 1853–1855," *Quarterly of the Oregon Historical Society* 23 (1922): 17–18.

89   Fisher and Jetté, "Now You See Them," 293.

90   Ibid., 292–93.

91   Boyd, preface, xvi. See also Chuck Williams, in Boyd, Ames, and Johnson, "The Cascade Indians," in *Chinookan Peoples of the Lower Columbia*, 314.

92   Tony A. Johnson, "The Chinook People Today," in Boyd, Ames, and Johnson, *Chinookan Peoples of the Lower Columbia*, 6.

93   See the Chinook Indian Nation website, www.chinooknation.org.

94   Tony Johnson, "Chinook People Today," 7, 16; "Kill the Indian, and Save the Man: Capt. Richard H. Pratt on the Education of Native Americans," *History Matters*, http://history matters.gmu.edu/d/4929.

95   Quoted in ibid., 4.

96   Ibid., 19.

97   Elliott interview.

(London: Penguin Books, 2003). The connection between the expedition and the development of the field of anthropology is nicely covered in Barry Alan Joyce, *The Shaping of American Ethnography: The Wilkes Expedition, 1838–1842* (Lincoln: University of Nebraska Press, 2001).

3   Joyce, *Shaping of American Ethnography*, 12–13; Philbrick, *Sea of Glory*, 18–20.

4   Joyce, *Shaping of American Ethnography*, 13; Philbrick, *Sea of Glory*, 30.

5   At this time the Pacific Northwest was a center of imperial designs, and the colonial ownership and boundaries of the region were not yet determined. Both England and the United States made claims to the area drained by the Columbia River, as well as some of the other large rivers in the region, and both jointly occupied the area. The issue was not settled until the Oregon Treaty of 1846, which established the 49th Parallel as the boundary between American and British territories (except the portion of Vancouver Island south of the 49th, which remained under British control). For an interesting discussion of the role of cartography in the boundary contention, see Daniel Clayton, "The Creation of Imperial Space in the Pacific Northwest," *Journal of Historical Geography* 26, no. 3 (2000): 337–46. See also Daniel Clayton, *Islands of Truth: The Imperial Fashioning of Vancouver Island* (Vancouver: University of British Columbia Press, 2000), 205–23.

6   Joyce, *Shaping of American Ethnography*, 13-14.

7   Ibid., 14–15.

8   Morton and other collectors were especially interested in the artificially flattened skulls of many of the Native American cultures of the Pacific Northwest, including Chinookans along the Columbia River. Human remains were collected expressly against the wishes and beliefs of Native Americans, and therefore collectors typically worked covertly or at night to avoid being caught. One of the times collectors were caught was during the Wilkes Expedition, when expedition members who were collecting remains from a Chinookan burial site on the Columbia River (referred to as Mount Coffin) let one of their campfires spread. The fire ended up destroying an estimated thee thousand burial canoes. This offense and destruction was devastating to the Chinookan communities, who were already reeling from deaths due to disease. See Wendi A. Lindquist, "Stealing from the Dead: Scientists, Settlers, and Indian Burial Sites in Early-Nineteenth-Century Oregon," *Oregon Historical Quarterly* 115, no. 3 (2014): 336. The widespread theft of Native American remains is one of the most shameful legacies of anthropology, and it is one that continues to haunt the discipline to this day.

9   Joyce, *Shaping of American Ethnography*, 16.

10   Ibid., 23.

11   Wilkes wanted to drop Hale from the expedition, as he believed that a philologist was unnecessary and that crew members could just as easily collect vocabularies and observe customs and behaviors. The scientific community led by the politically influential John Pickering—uncle of Charles Pickering and a former president of the Academy of Natural Science—appealed the decision of Wilkes and stressed the importance of having a trained specialist in languages on the expedition. Wilkes relented, and Hale was included as a member of the expedition (Joyce, *Shaping of American Ethnography*, 23–25).

12   Joyce, *Shaping of American Ethnography*, 25.

13   Ibid., 155.

14   Discussion of Hale's views on language and ethnology, as well as the role that these views played on Franz Boas and the development of American anthropology, is found

in Jacob W. Gruber, "Horatio Hale and the Development of American Anthropology," *Proceedings of the American Philosophical Society* 111, no. 1 (1967): 5–37.

15   Horatio Hale, *Ethnography and Philology*, vol. 6 (Philadelphia: C. Sherman, 1846), 223.

16   Gruber, "Horatio Hale," 9; Joyce, *Shaping of American Ethnography*, 138.

17   Hale, *Ethnography and Philology*, vol. 6, 198. As Hale aged, his view on the Native Americans of the Pacific Northwest softened. In his seventies he wrote to Boas, "I do not know if you have seen my account of the Oregon tribes written more than forty years ago. . . . My impression is that I rated the character of those Indians too low. I was then a young man of 24, fresh from College, and ethnological science was far behind the present stage" (letter from Horatio Hale to Franz Boas, March 1, 1888, Franz Boas papers, American Philosophical Society, Philadelphia).

18   Paul Allen, Nicholas Biddle, William Clark, and Meriwether Lewis, *History of the Expedition under the Command of Captains Lewis and Clark: To the Sources of the Missouri, Thence across the Rocky Mountains and down the River Columbia to the Pacific Ocean* (Philadelphia: Bradford and Inskeep, 1814). Digital version of the map ("Map of Lewis and Clark's Track"): David Rumsey Map Collection, www.davidrumsey.com/luna/serv let/detail/RUMSEY~8~1~978~50039:A-Map-of-Lewis-and-Clark-s-Track,-A#.

19   Philippe Marie Guillaume Vandermaelen, "Partie des Etats-Unis. No. 38" (1827), Digital Emerson, http://digitalemerson.wsulibs.wsu.edu/items/show/2037; David H. Burr; Illman & Pilbrow, "Oregon Territory" (1835), David Rumsey Map Collection, www .davidrumsey.com/luna/servlet/detail/RUMSEY~8~1~3313~400130.

20   Hale's post–US Ex. Ex. life is discussed in Joyce, *Shaping of American Ethnography*, 157–61, and Gruber, "Horatio Hale," 11–37.

21   Gruber, "Horatio Hale," 23–25.

22   Ibid., 5–37.

23   Horatio Hale to Franz Boas, May 21, 1888. The original letters are part of the "Franz Boas Papers" collection at the American Philosophical Society in Philadelphia. The Franz Boas Papers have recently been digitized by the APS. Microfilm copies of the letters are also available at the Cecil H. Green Library at Stanford University, which is where I accessed them.

24   Horatio Hale to Franz Boas, July 13, 1889.

25   The map appears in George Gibbs, "Tribes of Western Washington and Northwestern Oregon," *Contributions to North American Ethnology* 1 (1877): 157–361. Gibbs mentions Hale in the second sentence of the first paragraph.

26   James Mooney, "Distribution of Tribes of the Upper Columbia Region in Washington, Oregon and Idaho: Including All Those of the Smohalla and Shaker Religions (1894)," Washington, DC: GPO, 1896, Washington State University Libraries, Digital Exhibits, http://digitalexhibits.libraries.wsu.edu/items/show/1600.

27   Wayne Suttles, ed., *Handbook of North American Indians*, vol. 7, *Northwest Coast* (Washington DC: Smithsonian Institution, 1990), ix.

28   Les W. Field, *Abalone Tales: Collaborative Explorations of Sovereignty and Identity in Native California* (Durham: Duke University Press, 2008), 34, 36.

29   Andrew Fisher, *Shadow Tribe: The Making of Columbia River Indian Identity* (Seattle: University of Washington Press, 2010), 25.

30   Yvonne Hajda, "Regional Social Organization in the Greater Lower Columbia, 1792–1830" (PhD diss., University of Washington, 1984), 9.

31   Fisher, *Shadow Tribe*, 24.

32 Hajda, "Regional Social Organization," 9. Hale was not, however, the first person to use the village name "Chinook" to refer to an extended group. Hajda notes that in 1795 Charles Bishop used "Chinook" to refer to a number of villages along the river, as did Lewis and Clark and Alexander Henry in 1814. See Yvonne Hajda, "Social and Political Organization," in Boyd, Ames, and Johnson, *Chinookan Peoples of the Lower Columbia*, 147.

33 Leslie Spier, *Tribal Distribution in Washington*, General Series in Anthropology 3 (Menasha, WI: George Banta, 1936), 6.

34 Joel Berreman, "Tribal Distribution in Oregon," *Memoirs of the American Anthropological Association* 47 (1937): 11, 15.

35 Hajda, "Regional Social Organization," 11–12.

36 For instance, Gibbs states that in western Washington alone there were fourteen languages that came from five distinct language families. Gibbs, "Tribes of Western Washington," 163.

37 Hajda, "Regional Social Organization," 14.

38 Fisher, *Shadow Tribe*, 29.

39 Ibid., 15.

40 For instance, see Ian J. Barrow, *Making History, Drawing Territory: British Mapping in India, c. 1756–1905* (Oxford: Oxford University Press, 2003); D. Graham Burnett, *Masters of All They Surveyed: Exploration, Geography, and a British El Dorado* (Chicago: University of Chicago Press, 2000); Matthew H. Edney, *Mapping an Empire: The Geographical Construction of British India, 1765–1843* (Chicago: University of Chicago Press, 1997); Cole Harris, *Making Native Space: Colonialism, Resistance, and Reserves in British Columbia* (Vancouver: University of British Columbia Press, 2002); Cole Harris, "How Did Colonialism Dispossess? Comments from an Edge of Empire," *Annals of the Association of American Geographers* 94, no. 1 (2004): 165–82; Thongchai Winichakul, *Siam Mapped: A History of the Geo-Body of a Nation* (Honolulu: University of Hawaii Press, 1994).

41 Clayton, "The Creation of Imperial Space," 338.

42 Ibid., 345. Emphasis in original.

43 Martin Brückner, *The Geographic Revolution in Early America: Maps, Literacy, and National Identity* (Chapel Hill: University of North Carolina Press, 2006), 204–6.

44 Ibid., 237.

45 James V. Walker, "Henry S. Tanner and Cartographic Expression of American Expansionism in the 1820s," *Oregon Historical Quarterly* 111, no. 4 (2010): 437.

46 Brückner, *Geographic Revolution*, 238.

47 Ibid., 256–57.

48 Andrew Fisher, "Tangled Nets: Treaty Rights and Tribal Identities at Celilo Falls," *Oregon Historical Quarterly* 105, no. 2 (2004): 182.

49 In addition to the maps I have already noted, Hale's version of boundaries is also shown in Alfred Kroeber, "Cultural and Natural Areas of Native North America," *University of California Publications in American Archaeology and Ethnology* 38 (1939), and John R. Swanton, *The Indian Tribes of North America*, Smithsonian Institution Bureau of American Ethnology Bulletin 145 (Washington DC: Smithsonian Institution, 1952).

50 Harvey D. Rosenthal, "Indian Claims and the American Conscience: A Brief History of the Indian Claims Commission," in *Irredeemable America: The Indians' Estate and Land Claims*, ed. Imre Sutton (Albuquerque: University of New Mexico Press, 1985), 35. For further history of the ICC, see Nancy O. Lurie, "The Indian Claims Commission Act," *Annals of the American Academy of Political and Social Science* 311 (1957): 56–70;

Nancy O. Lurie, "The Indian Claims Commission Act," *Annals of the American Academy of Political and Social Science* 436 (1978): 97–110; Harvey D. Rosenthal, *Their Day in Court: A History of the Indian Claims Commission* (New York: Garland, 1990).

51 Lurie, "The Indian Claims Commission Act" (1957), 59–60. For further discussion of the connection between the ICC and the rise of the anthropologist as expert witness, see Lawrence Rosen, "The Anthropologist as Expert Witness," *American Anthropologist* 79, no. 3 (1977): 555–78; Helen Hornbeck Tanner, "In the Arena: An Expert Witness View of the Indian Claims Commission," in *Beyond Red Power: American Indian Politics and Activism since 1900*, eds. Daniel M. Cobb and Loretta Fowler (Santa Fe: School for Advanced Research, 2007), 178–200. Michael Harkin argues that the field of ethnohistory owes its development to the ICC. Michael Harkin, "Ethnohistory's Ethnohistory: Creating a Discipline from the Ground Up," *Social Science History* 34, no. 2 (2010): 113–28.

52 Herbert C. Taylor, *Coast Salish and Western Washington Indians III* (New York: Garland, 1974), 370.

53 Ibid., 390.

54 Ibid., 366.

55 Verne Ray, *Handbook of Cowlitz Indians* (Seattle: Northwest Copy, 1966), A1–A2.

56 Ibid., B47.

57 Taylor, *Coast Salish and Western Washington Indians III*, 365–66.

58 Quoted in ibid., 385.

59 Ray, *Handbook of Cowlitz Indians*, A10.

60 See Bureau of Indian Affairs, "Historical Technical Report, Cowlitz Indian Tribe," Bureau of Indian Affairs, n.d., 25, 54–67, http://bia.gov/cs/groups/public/documents /text/idc-001694.pdf; Penny J. Coleman, "Re: Cowlitz Tribe Restored Land Opinion," memorandum to Philip N. Hogen, chairman, from Penny J. Coleman, acting general counsel, National Indian Gaming Commission, November 22, 2005, www.nigc.gov /images/uploads/indianlands/09_cowlitztribe.pdf.

61 Gruber, "Horatio Hale," 32.

62 Brian Thom, "The Paradox of Boundaries in Coast Salish Territories," *Cultural Geographies* 16 (2009): 181, 183.

CHAPTER 4

1   See Gary E. Moulton, ed., *The Journals of the Lewis and Clark Expedition*, vol. 7 (Lincoln: University of Nebraska Press), 26–30, for Lewis and Clark's account of their visit to Cathlapotle.

2   A "Volunteer Appreciation Gala and Preview" open only to volunteers, Chinook Nation tribal members, and US Fish and Wildlife Service staff was held a few days prior, on March 26. The public grand opening event, however, also recognized the important role of volunteers in the project.

3   See Craig E. Barton, ed., *Sites of Memory: Perspectives on Architecture and Race* (New York: Princeton Architectural Press, 2001); John Bodnar, *Remaking America: Public Memory, Commemoration, and Patriotism in the Twentieth Century* (Princeton: Princeton University Press, 1992); Paul Connerton, *How Societies Remember* (Cambridge: Cambridge University Press, 1989); Maurice Halbwachs, *On Collective Memory*, trans. Lewis A. Coser (Chicago: University of Chicago Press, 1992); Michael Kammen, *Mystic Chords of Memory* (New York: Alfred A. Knopf, 1991); Edward T. Linenthal, *The Unfinished*

Bombing: Oklahoma City in American Memory (Oxford: Oxford University Press, 2001); Kendall R. Phillips, ed., *Framing Public Memory* (Tuscaloosa: University of Alabama Press, 2004); Patricia Rubertone, ed., *Archaeologies of Placemaking: Monuments, Memories, and Engagement in Native North America* (Walnut Creek, CA: Left Coast Press, 2008).

4   Edward Casey, "Public Memory in Place and Time," in *Framing Public Memory*, ed. Kendall R. Phillips (Tuscaloosa: University of Alabama Press, 2004).

5   Ibid., 21–22.

6   Ibid., 22.

7   Ibid., 25.

8   Ibid., 32. For more on Casey's discussion of the connections between memory and place see Edward Casey, *Getting Back into Place: Toward a Renewed Understanding of the Place-World* (Bloomington: Indiana University Press, 1993); Edward Casey, "How to Get from Space to Place in a Fairly Short Stretch of Time: Phenomenological Prolegomena," in *Senses of Place*, ed. Steven Feld and Keith Basso (Santa Fe: School of American Research Press, 1996), 13–52; Edward Casey, *The Fate of Place: A Philosophical History* (Berkeley: University of California Press, 1998); Edward Casey, *Remembering: A Phenomenological Study*, 2nd ed. (Bloomington: Indiana University Press, 2000).

9   While many Northwest Coast archaeologists tend to use the term *plankhouse*, many Native American groups prefer the term *longhouse*. See D. Ann Trieu Gahr, Elizabeth A. Sobel, and Kenneth Ames, introduction to Sobel, Trieu Gahr, and Ames, *Household Archaeology on the Northwest Coast*, 5. I primarily use the term *plankhouse* in this book for two reasons: the official name of the building on the Ridgefield National Wildlife Refuge is the Cathlapotle Plankhouse, and citizens of the Chinook Nation typically refer to it as a plankhouse. I will occasionally use the term *longhouse* when referring to specific structures that use that term (and, of course, in direct quotations).

10 See Yvonne Hajda, "Notes on Indian Houses of the Wappato Valley," *Northwest Anthropological Research Notes* 28 (1994): 184; Wayne Suttles, "The Shed-Roof House," in Wright, *A Time of Gathering*, 212; Kenneth M. Ames, Cameron M. Smith, William L. Cornett, Elizabeth A. Sobel, Stephen C. Hamilton, John Wolf, and Doria Raetz, *Archaeological Investigations at 45CL1 Cathlapotle (1991–1996), Ridgefield National Wildlife Refuge, Clark County, Washington: A Preliminary Report*, Cultural Resource Series 13 (Sherwood, OR: US Fish and Wildlife Service, 1999).

11 Kenneth Ames, Doria F. Raetz, Stephen C. Hamilton, and Christine McAfee, "Household Archaeology of a Southern Northwest Coast Plank House," *Journal of Field Archaeology* 19 (1992): 275–90. For additional discussion of the labor and material requirements of plankhouses, see Kenneth Ames, "Life in the Big House: Household Labor and Dwelling Size on the Northwest Coast," in *People Who Lived in Big Houses: Archaeological Perspectives on Large Domestic Structures*, ed. G. Coupland and E. G. Banning (Madison, WI: Prehistory Press, 1996), 131–50; D. Ann Trieu Gahr, "From Architects to Ancestors: The Life Cycle of Plank Houses," in Trieu Gahr, Sobel, and Ames, *Household Archaeology on the Northwest Coast*, 57–79.

12 Suttles, "The Shed-Roof House," 214. See also Kenneth M. Ames and Herbert D. G. Maschner, *Peoples of the Northwest Coast: Their Archaeology and Prehistory* (London: Thames and Hudson, 1999), especially chapter 6.

13 Trieu Gahr, Sobel, and Ames, introduction to *Household Archaeology on the Northwest Coast*, 53. A number of edited volumes on household archaeology have been produced in the last few decades. For examples, see Coupland and Banning, *People Who Lived in*

Big Houses; Rosemary A. Joyce and Susan D. Gillespie, eds., *Beyond Kinship: Social and Material Reproduction in House Societies* (Philadelphia: University of Pennsylvania Press, 2000); Sobel, Trieu Gahr, and Ames, *Household Archaeology on the Northwest Coast*.

14 For descriptions of plankhouses, see J. C. Beaglehole, ed., *The Journals of Captain James Cook on His Voyages of Discovery* (Cambridge: Cambridge University Press/Hakluyt Society, 1955); Paul Kane, *Wanderings of an Artist among the Indians of North America* (Edmonton: Hurtig Publishers, 1968); Gary E. Moulton, ed., *The Journals of the Lewis and Clark Expedition*, vols. 5–7 (Lincoln: University of Nebraska Press, 1988–91); James G. Swan, *The Northwest Coast, or, Three Years Residence in Washington Territory* (Seattle: University of Washington Press, 1972).

15 Yvonne Marshall, "Transformations of Nuu-chah-nulth Houses," in *Beyond Kinship: Social and Material Reproduction in House Societies*, eds. Rosemary A. Joyce and Susan D. Gillespie (Philadelphia: University of Pennsylvania Press, 2000), 88.

16 See Noel Purser, "Bringing Back the Canoe: A Suquamish Story," in *Tribal Canoe Journeys*, 8–9 (Suquamish Tribe, 2009); Derek Sheppard, "New Longhouse Opens for Suquamish Tribe," *Seattle Times,* March 11, 2009; Leonard Forsman, "History of Western Washington Native Peoples," in Wright, *A Time of Gathering*, 208.

17 Marshall, "Transformations of Nuu-chah-nulth Houses," 88.

18 Ibid., 101–2.

19 Yvonne Marshall (ibid.,102) notes that in the early twentieth century, Nuu-chah-nulth longhouses were transformed from being residential units to being places for ceremony such as the potlatch. A longhouse continued to serve as a place for symbolic capital, and while people no longer resided within the structure it remained part of the political and social core of the society. Marshall also notes, however, that this was a short-lived phenomenon, as colonial policies of assimilation and attacks on tribal identity continued.

20 Jonathan Clapperton, "Building Longhouses and Constructing Identities: A Brief History of the Coqualeetza Longhouse and Shxwta:selhawtxw," *University of the Fraser Valley Research Review* 2, no. 2 (2009), 95–118; Mary Ellen Flanagan and Nicholas C. Zaferatos, "Appropriate Technologies in the Traditional Native American Smokehouse: Public Health Considerations in Tribal Community Development," *American Indian Culture and Research Journal* 24, no. 4 (2000): 69–93; Sheppard, "New Longhouse Opens for Suquamish Tribe."

21 Patricia Pierce Erikson, "Welcome to This House: A Century of Makah People Honoring Identity and Negotiating Cultural Tourism," *Ethnohistory* 50, no. 3 (2003), 524, 526, emphasis in original. Clapperton, "Building Longhouses and Constructing Identities," also provides an interesting discussion of the living nature of modern plankhouses and the value (and occasional tension) of longhouses for the education of both Native and non-Native audiences.

22 Sam Robinson, interview by author, August 18, 2009.

23 Sam Robinson, interview by author, August 27, 2008.

24 Anan Raymond, interview by author, March 6, 2007.

25 Ibid.

26 Ibid.

27 Associated Press, "Oregon Tribe Withdraws from Lewis and Clark Bicentennial," *Seattle Times*, November 29, 2004.

28 Sam Robinson interview, August 27, 2008.

29 Ibid. Anan Raymond also hoped that the plankhouse would outlive the focus on Lewis and Clark: "One of the selling points of this plankhouse . . . was that we weren't creating

just a thing or event that would somehow die after the bicentennial. We were creating a place that would live on long after the bicentennial and deliver a conservation, cultural and natural history message. Lewis and Clark was just the stimulus." Raymond interview, March 6, 2007.

30   James Clifford, "Looking Several Ways: Anthropology and Native Heritage in Alaska," *Current Anthropology* 45 (2004): 9.

31   Raymond interview, March 6, 2007.

32   See David Lowenthal, "Authenticities Past and Present," *CRM: The Journal of Heritage Stewardship* 6 (2009), 6–17.

33   Raymond interview, March 6, 2007. For further discussion of the use of "reconstructions" for historical interpretation, see John H. Jameson Jr., ed., *The Reconstructed Past: Reconstructions in the Public Interpretation or Archaeology and History* (Walnut Creek, CA: AltaMira Press, 2004). The connection between reconstructions and authenticity is also noted in paragraph 86 of *Operational Guidelines for the World Heritage Convention* (Paris: UNESCO, 2015). This paragraph states that, in terms of authenticity and nomination to the World Heritage List, "the reconstruction of archaeological remains or historic buildings or districts is justifiable only in exceptional circumstances. Reconstruction is acceptable only on the basis of complete and detailed documentation and to no extent on conjecture."

34   Gary Johnson, interview by author, September 5, 2006.

35   Sam Robinson interview, August 27, 2008.

36   Neil Silberman, "Process Not Product: The ICOMOS Ename Charter (2008) and the Practice of Heritage Stewardship," *CRM: The Journal of Heritage Stewardship* 6, no. 2 (2009): 12.

37   Greg Robinson, "The Cathlapotle Plankhouse Project: A Bittersweet Victory," *Chinook Tillicums: The Voice of the Chinook Tribe*, Fall 2004, 1.

38   Ibid.

39   Ibid.

40   Ibid., 3.

41   Raymond interview, March 6, 2007.

42   Greg Robinson, "The Cathlapotle Plankhouse Project," 3.

43   Sam Robinson interview, August 27, 2008.

44   Sam Robinson, "Welcome Statement," tenth anniversary celebration of the Cathlapotle Plankhouse, Ridgefield, Washington, March 29, 2015.

45   Raymond interview, March 6, 2007.

46   Ibid.

47   Gary Johnson interview.

48   The Swinomish people also had concerns about air quality issues at their longhouse. The Swinomish longhouse is located on tribal lands, and members of the tribe brought the concerns. In that case tests did indicate high levels of smoke and particulates. They ultimately solved the problem by constructing belowground air inflow pipes to the fire pits. See Flanagan and Zaferatos, "Appropriate Technologies in the Traditional Native American Smokehouse."

49   Raymond interview, March 6, 2007.

50   Sam Robinson interview, August 27, 2008.

51   Raymond interview, March 6, 2007.

52   Greg Robinson, "The Cathlapotle Plankhouse Project," 1.

53 Raymond interview, March 6, 2007.

54 Mike Iyall, interview by author, July 25, 2006.

55 See Dean Baker, "Cowlitz Want Role in Plank House," *Vancouver Columbian*, February 18, 2004; Foster Church, "Plank House Work to Resume: Grants Will Allow Construction to Begin Again on the Cathlapotle House after Protests by the Cowlitz Tribe Stopped Work," *Oregonian*, March 3, 2004.

56 Scott Aikin, interview by author, July 14, 2006.

57 Iyall interview.

58 Ibid.

59 Anan Raymond, interview by author, January 9, 2006.

60 US Fish and Wildlife Service, "Memorandum of Understanding between the U.S. Fish and Wildlife Service and the Cowlitz Indian Tribe," n.d., copy filed at the US Fish and Wildlife Service Cultural Resources Team Office, Sherwood, Oregon.

61 Delineating tribal identity in the Pacific Northwest can be particularly complex, both precontact and post-contact. Prior to contact the largest political unit of organization was typically the village. Additionally, villages were often multilingual, with high levels of intermarriage between villages. As a result, individuals had a number of interconnections within and across villages and a multiplicity of identities. See Yvonne Hajda, "Regional Social Organization in the Greater Lower Columbia, 1792–1830" (PhD diss., University of Washington, 1984). Colonial actors, including government agents and ethnographers, struggled with this complexity of identity and attempted to impose their own simplified views of tribal boundaries (most often based on language) to suit their own administrative purposes. For an excellent discussion of the issue slightly upriver from Cathlapotle, see Andrew H. Fisher, *Shadow Tribe: The Making of Columbia River Indian Identity* (Seattle: University of Washington Press, 2010). In part, the Cowlitz Tribe argued that US Fish and Wildlife, by presenting Cathlapotle as a "Chinook" village, was not recognizing the complexity of tribal identity along the Columbia River.

62 US Fish and Wildlife Service, "Memorandum of Understanding between the U.S. Fish and Wildlife Service and the Cowlitz Indian Tribe."

63 US Fish and Wildlife Service, "Memorandum of Understanding between the U.S. Fish and Wildlife Service and the Chinook Indian Tribe," n.d., copy filed at the US Fish and Wildlife Service Cultural Resources Team Office, Sherwood, Oregon.

64 Iyall interview.

65 Ibid.

66 Johnson interview, 2006.

67 Johnson interview; Robinson interview, 2008.

68 Johnson interview.

69 Sam Robinson, BirdFest presentation at the Cathlapotle Plankhouse, Ridgefield, Washington, October 9, 2011.

70 Anan Raymond, interview by author, March 6, 2007.

71 Sam Robinson, interview by author, July 25, 2010.

72 US Fish and Wildlife Service, "Memorandum of Understanding between the U.S. Fish and Wildlife Service and the Chinook Indian Tribe."

73 Aikin interview.

74 Greg Robinson, "The Cathlapotle Plankhouse Project," 3.

75 Sam Robinson, interviews by author, August 27, 2008; August 18, 2009; July 25, 2010.

76 Sam Robinson interview, August 27, 2008.

CHAPTER 5

1   In Chinookan culture it would normally not be acceptable to use a family name in this
     way. But since the chief Kthlmin had no heirs it was appropriate to pass his name on to
     this canoe.

2   In one of our conversations, Chinook chair Tony Johnson noted to me that while the
     Chinook are extremely appreciative of the Clarks gift of the canoe, they believe that
     the debt was really owed by—and should have been paid by—the US government,
     not the Clark family.

3   The story of the canoe theft is told in James P. Ronda, *Lewis and Clark among the Indians*
     (Lincoln: University of Nebraska Press, 1984), 210–12.

4   Edward Stratton, "Clarks Make Good on Stolen Canoe: Family Makes Gift of Reparation
     to Chinook Nation," *Daily Astorian*, September 26, 2001. The story of the return of the
     canoe was covered by newspapers nationally and internationally.

5   There are, of course, sources on Northwest Coast canoes. For example, see Bill Durham,
     Indian Canoes of the Northwest Coast (Seattle: Copper Canoe Press, 1960); George Dur-
     ham, "Canoes from Cedar Logs: A Study of Early Types and Designs," *Pacific Northwest
     Quarterly* 46, no. 2 (1955): 33–39; Bill Holm, "Historical Salish Canoes," in Wright, *A
     Time of Gathering*, 238–47; Bill Holm, "Canoes of the Northwest Coast," in *Anthropology
     of the North Pacific Rim*, eds. William W. Fitzhugh and Valerie Chaussonnet (Washington
     DC: Smithsonian Institution Press, 1994), 259–64; Ronald L. Olson, *Adze, Canoe, and
     House Types of the Northwest Coast*, University of Washington Publications in Anthropol-
     ogy 2, no. 1 (Seattle: University of Washington Press, 1927); Thomas T. Waterman and
     Geraldine Coffin, *Types of Canoes on Puget Sound* (New York: Museum of the American
     Indian Heye Foundation, 1920). Will Sarvis, however, argues that these types of writings
     focus on physical form and construction rather than providing the reader with a broader
     understanding of the cultural and spiritual importance of canoes. Will Sarvis, "Deeply
     Embedded: Canoes as an Enduring Manifestation of Spiritualism and Communalism
     among the Coast Salish," *Journal of the West* 42, no. 4 (2003): 74.

6   David Neel, *The Great Canoes: Reviving a Northwest Coast Tradition* (Vancouver, BC:
     Douglas & McIntyre, 1995), 1.

7   Ibid., 1–2.

8   Hilary Stewart, *Cedar: Tree of Life to the Northwest Coast Indians* (Vancouver, BC: Doug-
     las & McIntyre, 1995), 48.

9   Ibid., 50–52. While Stewart suggests that there are four primary types, Bill Holm argues
     that there are at least a dozen. Holm, "Canoes of the Northwest Coast," 259.

10   Stewart, *Cedar*, 52–57, offers a thorough and illustrated account of the canoe-making
     process. The JayHawk Institute, a nonprofit foundation dedicated to sharing the his-
     tory, art and culture of Pacific Northwest Indigenous groups, has available online a
     series of helpful videos documenting the recent carving of a canoe. See "JayHawk
     Institute-NW Coast Indian Canoe Legacy Project," Vimeo, http://vimeo.com/album
     /2481973. See also "Short Films and Videos," JayHawk Institute, www.jayhawkinstitute
     .org/index.html.

11   Silas B. Smith, son of pioneer Solomon H. Smith and Celiast (a Clatsop woman who was
     the daughter of Clatsop leader Coboway), stated, "It is a historical fact that the model
     of the clipper ships, the finest model of all ships, was taken from the early Chinook
     canoe." Oregon Historical Society, *Proceedings of the Oregon Historical Society* (Salem:
     W. H. Leeds, 1900), 94.

12 Stewart, *Cedar*, 48. Thomas Barnett's claim may very well have been an exaggeration, but even so it still points to the ubiquitous nature of canoes in the Pacific Northwest. See also Kenneth M. Ames, "Going by Boat: The Forager-Collector Continuum at Sea," in *Beyond Foraging and Collecting: Evolutionary Change in Hunter-Gatherer Settlement Systems*, eds. Ben Fitzhugh and Junko Habu (New York: Kluwer Academic/Plenum Publishers, 2002), 31–32.

13 Tony Johnson, "The Chinook People Today," in Boyd, Ames, and Johnson, *Chinookan Peoples of the Lower Columbia*, 14.

14 Gary E. Moulton, ed., *The Definitive Journals of Lewis & Clark*, vol. 10, *The Journal of Patrick Gass* (Lincoln: University of Nebraska Press, 1996), 203–4.

15 Gary E. Moulton, ed., *The Definitive Journals of Lewis and Clark*, vol. 6 (Lincoln: University of Nebraska Press, 1996), 262–72.

16 Tony A. Johnson and Adam McIsaac, with Kenneth M. Ames and Robert T. Boyd, "Lower Columbia River Art," in Boyd, Ames, and Johnson, *Chinookan Peoples of the Lower Columbia*, 221.

17 Moulton, *The Definitive Journals of Lewis and Clark*, vol. 6, 262.

18 Ibid., 49.

19 Ibid., 40.

20 For an excellent discussion of the importance of canoes as a means of transportation and production, see Ames, "Going by Boat," 19–52.

21 Sarvis, "Deeply Embedded," 75. See also Johnson, "The Chinook People Today," 14. In a conversation about canoes with Tony Johnson, he told me that Chinooks believe that a cedar trees aspires to be a canoe. As he put it, a cedar tree smiles on the idea of becoming a canoe.

22 Robert T. Boyd, "Lower Columbia Chinookan Ceremonialism," in Boyd, Ames, and Johnson, *Chinookan Peoples of the Lower Columbia*, 194–95.

23 Sarvis, "Deeply Embedded," 77. See also Durham, *Indian Canoes of the Northwest Coast*, 78.

24 Misao Dean, *Inheriting a Canoe Paddle: The Canoe in Discourses of English-Canadian Nationalism* (Toronto: University of Toronto Press, 2013), 164–65.

25 Ibid. See also Sarvis, "Deeply Embedded," 74, 77.

26 Johnson, "The Chinook People Today," 14.

27 See Dean, *Inheriting a Canoe Paddle*, 165; Sarvis, "Deeply Embedded," 78. For more on racing canoes, see Emmett Oliver, "Reminiscences of a Canoe Puller," in Wright, *A Time of Gathering*, 248–53.

28 A community interested in hosting a future Tribal Journeys must announce its intention to host on the floor of Tribal Journeys. The prospective host community then typically sends representatives to other communities to make an official invitation and to let them know the date of the canoe landing. This is effectively a renewal of the potlatch that was prevalent and central throughout the Pacific Northwest.

29 *Tribal Journeys Handbook and Study Guide* ([Tacoma, WA]: Cedar Media, 2011), 3.

30 Neel, *Great Canoes*, 2–3; Dean, *Inheriting a Canoe Paddle*, 166–67.

31 Emmett Oliver, one of the foundational figures of the Paddle to Seattle, knew that celebrations of the Washington State centennial would include replicas of the tall-masted sailing ships that were symbolic of colonialism and empire. He wanted to be sure that Native Americans and their canoes also had a presence at the centennial. See Richard Walker, "Pullers Brave Rough Waters to Honor Warriors in Paddle to Quinault," *Indian Country Today*, August 5, 2013, http://indiancountrytodaymedianetwork.com/.

32 Neel, *Great Canoes*, 2–3.

33 Ibid., 3. See also David Neel, "Bella Bella: The Rebirth of the Northwest Coast Canoe," *Native Peoples Magazine* 7, no. 2 (1994): 10–18.

34 Sam Robinson, BirdFest presentation, October 9, 2011.

35 Tony Johnson, interview by author, January 22, 2014, Ilwaco, Washington. Emmett Oliver passed away on March 7, 2016, at the age of 102. His role in canoe revitalization and his positive impact on tribal nations is incalculable. For a brief history, see Richard Walker, "Emmett Oliver, Founder of Paddle to Seattle, Walks on at 102," *Indian Country Today Media Network*, http://indiancountrytodaymedianetwork.com.

36 Tony Johnson interview.

37 Ibid.

38 It is important to note that while Tribal Journeys has fueled a broader interest in canoe culture among Chinooks, canoe resurgence in the community had begun earlier. Canoes were being built before the beginning of the Journeys, and canoes also played a central role in events like the First Salmon Ceremony. Still, Tribal Journeys helped to fuel that resurgence and broaden its participation among Chinooks.

39 See Fred Beauvais, "American Indians and Alcohol," *Alcohol Health and Research World* 22, no. 4 (1998): 253–59; Dakotah C. Lane and John Simmons, "American Indian Youth Substance Abuse: Community Driven Interventions," *Mount Sinai Journal of Medicine* 78 (2011): 362–72. For discussion of historical trauma, see Maria Yellow Horse Brave Heart and Lemyra M. DeBruyn, "The American Indian Holocaust: Healing Historical Unresolved Grief," *American Indian and Alaska Native Mental Health Research* 8, no. 2 (1998): 56–78.

40 Tony Johnson interview.

41 Ibid.

42 See Lane and Simmons, "American Indian Youth Substance Abuse," 362–72.

43 The importance of collaboration between Native American communities and health care researchers and providers, especially within the context of canoe culture and efforts to combat drug and alcohol abuse, is discussed in several publications. For instance, see Elizabeth H. Hawkins and C. June La Marr, "Pulling for Native Communities: Alan Marlatt and the Journeys of the Circle," *Addiction Research and Theory* 20, no. 3 (2012): 236–42; Heather S. V. Lonczak, Lisa Rey Thomas, Dennis Donovan, Lisette Austin, Robin L. W. Sigo, Nigel Lawrence, and the Suquamish Tribe, "Navigating the Tide Together: Early Collaboration between Tribal and Academic Partners in a CBPR Study," *Pimatisiwin: A Journal of Aboriginal and Indigenous Community Health* 11, no. 3 (2013): 395–409; June La Marr and G. Alan Marlatt, *Canoe Journey Life's Journey: A Life Skills Manual for Native Adolescents* (Center City, MN: Hazelden Publishing and Educational Services, 2007); Lisa R. Thomas, Dennis Donovan, Robin L. W. Sigo, Lisette Austin, G. Alan Marlatt, and the Suquamish Tribe, "The Community Pulling Together: A Tribal Community-University Partnership Project to Reduce Substance Abuse and Promote Good Health in a Reservation Tribal Community," *Journal of Ethnicity in Substance Abuse* 8, no. 3 (2009): 283–300; Lisa R. Thomas, Dennis M. Donovan, and Robin L. W. Sigo, "Identifying Community Needs and Resources in a Native Community: A Research Partnership in the Pacific Northwest," *International Journal of Mental Health and Addiction* 8, no. 2 (2010): 362–73. See also Healing of the Canoe, www.healingofthecanoe.org, a collaboration between the Suquamish Tribe, Port Gamble S'Klallam Tribe, and the University of Washington's Alcohol and Drug Abuse Institute.

44 Tony Johnson interview.

45 *Tribal Journeys Handbook and Study Guide*, 4–5.

46 Neel, *Great Canoes*, 2.

47 Tony Johnson interview.

48 Ibid.

49 Ibid.

50 Ibid.

51 See *Pulling Together*, directed by James M. Fortier with the Muckleshoot Indian Tribe (Turtle Island Productions, 2004), DVD. This documentary includes some discussion of the challenges and tensions that canoe families face on the journey.

52 Tony Johnson interview.

53 Quoted in Neel, *Great Canoes*, 15.

54 Tony Johnson interview.

55 Ibid.

56 Neel, *Great Canoes*, 23.

57 Tony Johnson interview.

58 Sam Robinson, interview by author, July 25, 2010.

59 Tony Johnson interview.

60 Ibid.

61 Sam Robinson, interview by author, August 27, 2008.

62 Robinson interview, July 25, 2010.

CONCLUSION

1 Chinook Indian Nation, letter to the President Barack Obama, n.d., www.chinooktribe .org/justice/chinook_executive_justice_recognition_project%20.html.

2 An index of all of the letters is located at www.chinooktribe.org/justice/cejrp_index .html.

3 My use of the term *episodes* comes from Paige Raibmon, who uses "episodes of encounter" as a way to frame her discussion of the negotiation of Native American "authenticity" along the Pacific Northwest coast. See Paige Raibmon, *Authentic Indians: Episodes of Encounter from the Late-Nineteenth Century Northwest Coast* (Durham: Duke University Press, 2005).

4 Rodney Harrison, "Beyond 'Natural' and 'Cultural' Heritage: Toward an Ontological Politics of Heritage in the Age of the Anthropocene," *Heritage and Society* 8, no. 1 (2015): 27, 28.

5 For further discussion on these false dichotomies, see Rodney Harrison, *Heritage: Critical Approaches* (London: Routledge, 2013), 204–26; Harrison, "Beyond 'Natural' and 'Cultural' Heritage," 24–42; Rodney Harrison and Deborah Rose, "Intangible Heritage," in *Understanding Heritage and Memory*, ed. Tim Benton (Manchester: Manchester University Press, 2010), 238–75.

6 Harrison, *Heritage*, 222.

7 James Clifford, *Returns: Becoming Indigenous in the Twenty-First Century* (Cambridge: Harvard University Press, 2013), 46–47.

BIBLIOGRAPHY

Abu el-Haj, Nadia. *Facts on the Ground: Archaeological Practice and Territorial Self-Fashioning in Israeli Society*. Chicago: University of Chicago Press, 2001.

Acheson, Steven. "The Thin Edge: Evidence for Precontact Use and Working of Metal on the Northwest Coast." In *Emerging from the Mist: Studies in Northwest Coast Culture History*, edited by R. G. Matson, Gary Coupland, and Quentin Mackie, 213–29. Vancouver: University of British Columbia Press, 2003.

Advisory Council on Historic Preservation. *Consultation with Indian Tribes in the Section 106 Review Process: A Handbook*. Washington, DC: Advisory Council on Historic Preservation, 2012.

Aikens, C. M., and S. N. Rhee, eds. *Pacific Northeast Asia in Prehistory: Hunter-Fisher-Gatherers, Farmers, and Sociopolitical Elites*. Pullman: Washington State University Press, 1992.

Aikin, Scott. Interview by author. Portland, Oregon, July 14, 2006.

Alexanderson, Al. "Cowlitz Indians in Clark County." Unpublished manuscript in possession of author, n.d.

Allen, Paul, Nicholas Biddle, William Clark, and Meriwether Lewis. *History of the Expedition under the Command of Captains Lewis and Clark: To the Sources of the Missouri, Thence across the Rocky Mountains and down the River Columbia to the Pacific Ocean*. Philadelphia: Bradford and Inskeep, 1814.

Ames, Kenneth M. "Complex Hunter-Gatherers." In *Encyclopedia of Global Archaeology*, edited by Claire Smith, 1613–21. New York: Springer, 2014.

———. "Going by Boat: The Forager-Collector Continuum at Sea." In *Beyond Foraging and Collecting: Evolutionary Change in Hunter-Gatherer Settlement Systems*, edited by Ben Fitzhugh and Junko Habu, 17–50. New York: Kluwer Academic/Plenum Publishers, 2002.

———. Interview by author. Portland, Oregon, June 28, 2006.

———. "Life in the Big House: Household Labor and Dwelling Size on the Northwest Coast." In *People Who Lived in Big Houses: Archaeological Perspectives on Large Domestic Structures*, edited by G. Coupland and E. G. Banning, 131–50. Madison, WI: Prehistory Press, 1996.

———. "The Northwest Coast." *Evolutionary Anthropology* 12 (2003): 19–33.

———. "The Northwest Coast: Complex Hunter-Gatherers, Ecology, and Social Evolution." *Annual Review of Anthropology* 23 (1994): 209–29.

———. "Slavery, Household Production, and Demography on the Southern Northwest Coast: Cables, Tacking, and Ropewalking." In *Invisible Citizens: Captives and Their Consequences*, edited by Catherine M. Cameron, 138–58. Salt Lake City: University of Utah Press, 2008.

———. "Slaves, Chiefs and Labour on the Northern Northwest Coast." *World Archaeology* 33 (2001): 1–17.

Ames, Kenneth M., and Herbert D. G. Maschner. *Peoples of the Northwest Coast: Their Archaeology and Prehistory*. London: Thames and Hudson, 1999.

Ames, Kenneth M., Doria F. Raetz, Stephen C. Hamilton, and Christine McAfee. "Household Archaeology of a Southern Northwest Coast Plank House." *Journal of Field Archaeology* 19 (1992): 275–90.

Ames, Kenneth M., and Cameron Smith. "The Nature and Spatial Distribution of Activities

———. "Past Presence: Conceptions of History in Northwest Coast Studies." *Arctic Anthropology* 33 (1996): 1–15.

Harley, J. B. "Historical Geography and the Cartographic Illusion." *Journal of Historical Geography* 15, no. 1 (1989): 80–91.

Harmon, Alexandra. *Indians in the Making: Ethnic Relations and Indian Identities around Puget Sound.* Berkeley: University of California Press, 2000.

Harris, Cole. "How Did Colonialism Dispossess? Comments from an Edge of Empire." *Annals of the Association of American Geographers* 94, no. 1 (2004): 165–82.

———. *Making Native Space: Colonialism, Resistance, and Reserves in British Columbia.* Vancouver: University of British Columbia Press, 2002.

Harrison, Rodney. "Beyond 'Natural' and 'Cultural' Heritage: Toward an Ontological Politics of Heritage in the Age of Anthropocene." *Heritage and Society* 8, no. 1 (2015): 24–42.

———. *Heritage: Critical Approaches.* London: Routledge, 2013.

Harrison, Rodney, and Deborah Rose. "Intangible Heritage." In *Understanding Heritage and Memory,* edited by Tim Benton, 238–75. Manchester: Manchester University Press, 2010.

Hawkins, Elizabeth H., and C. June La Marr. "Pulling for Native communities: Alan Marlatt and the Journeys of the Circle." *Addiction Research and Theory* 20, no. 3 (2012): 236–42.

Holm, Bill. "Canoes of the Northwest Coast." In *Anthropology of the North Pacific Rim,* edited by William W. Fitzhugh and Valerie Chaussonnet, 259–64. Washington DC: Smithsonian Institution Press, 1994.

———. "Historical Salish Canoes." In *A Time of Gathering: Native Heritage in Washington State,* edited by Robin K. Wright, 238–47. Seattle: University of Washington Press, 1991.

Hudziak, Robert, and Clarence Smith. "Archaeological Site Form (45CL1)." 1948. On file at the Washington State Department of Archaeology and Historic Preservation, Olympia, Washington.

———. "Archaeological Site Form (45CL4)." 1948. On file at the Washington State Department of Archaeology and Historic Preservation, Olympia, Washington.

Huelsbeck, David R. "The Surplus Economy of the Central Northwest Coast." *Research in Economic Anthropology,* supplement 3 (1988): 149–77.

Interior Board of Indian Appeals. "In re Federal Acknowledgment of the Chinook Indian Tribe/Chinook Nation." 36 IBIA 245, August 1, 2001.

Iyall, Mike. Interview by author. Olympia, Washington, July 25, 2006.

Jacob, Michelle M. *Yakama Rising: Indigenous Cultural Revitalization, Activism, and Healing.* Tucson: University of Arizona Press, 2013.

Jameson, John H., Jr. *The Reconstructed Past: Reconstructions in the Public Interpretation of Archaeology and History.* Walnut Creek, CA: AltaMira Press, 2004.

Johnson, Gary. Interview by author. Chinook, Washington, September 5, 2006.

Johnson, Jean. "Eyes on the Prize: Cowlitz and Warm Springs Move toward Portland Gaming Market." *Indian Country Today,* September 27, 2004.

Johnson, Tony A. "The Chinook People Today." In Boyd, Ames, and Johnson, *Chinookan Peoples of the Lower Columbia,* 4–20.

———. Interview by author. Ilwaco, Washington, January 22, 2014.

Johnson, Tony A., and Adam McIsaac (with Kenneth M. Ames and Robert T. Boyd). "Lower Columbia River Art." In Boyd, Ames, and Johnson, *Chinookan Peoples of the Lower Columbia,* 199–225.

Joyce, Barry Alan. *The Shaping of American Ethnography: The Wilkes Expedition, 1838–1842.* Lincoln: University of Nebraska Press, 2001.

Joyce, Rosemary. "Solid Histories for Fragile Nations: Archaeology as Cultural Patrimony." In Meskell and Pels, *Embedding Ethics*, 253–73.

Joyce, Rosemary A., and Susan D. Gillespie, eds. *Beyond Kinship: Social and Material Reproduction in House Societies*. Philadelphia: University of Pennsylvania Press, 2000.

Kammen, Michael. *Mystic Chords of Memory*. New York: Alfred A. Knopf, 1991.

Kane, Paul. *Wanderings of an Artist among the Indians of North America*. Edmonton: Hurtig, 1968.

Klopotek, Brian. *Recognition Odysseys: Indigeneity, Race, and Federal Tribal Recognition Policy in Three Louisiana Indian Communities*. Durham: Duke University Press, 2011.

Komar, Paul D. *The Pacific Northwest Coast: Living with the Shores of Oregon and Washington*. Durham: Duke University Press, 1998.

Koyama, S., and D. H. Thomas, eds. *Affluent Foragers: Pacific Coasts East and West*. Senri Ethnological Studies. Osaka, Japan: National Museum of Ethnology, 1981.

Kroeber, Alfred. "American Culture and the Northwest Coast." *American Anthropologist* 25 (1923): 1–20.

———. "Cultural and Natural Areas of Native North America." *University of California Publications in American Archaeology and Ethnology* 38 (1939).

Lafrenz Samuels, Kathryn. "Trajectories of Development: International Heritage Management of Archaeology in the Middle East and North Africa." *Archaeologies* 5 (2009): 68–91.

La Marr, June, and G. Alan Marlatt. *Canoe Journey, Life's Journey: A Life Skills Manual for Native Adolescents*. Center City, MN: Hazelden Publishing and Educational Services, 2007.

Lane, Dakotah C., and John Simmons. "American Indian Youth Substance Abuse: Community Driven Interventions." *Mount Sinai Journal of Medicine* 78, no. 3 (2011): 362–72.

Lang, George. *Making Wawa: The Genesis of Chinook Jargon*. Vancouver: University of British Columbia Press, 2008.

Lang, William L. "The Chinookan Encounter with Euro-Americans in the Lower Columbia River Valley." In Boyd, Ames, and Johnson, *Chinookan Peoples of the Lower Columbia*, 250–71.

———. "Lewis and Clark on the Columbia River: The Power of Landscape in the Exploration Experience," *Pacific Northwest Quarterly* 87 (1996): 141–48.

Lassiter, Luke Eric. *The Chicago Guide to Collaborative Ethnography*. Chicago: University of Chicago Press, 2005.

Lawson, Michael L. *Aboriginal History/Research on Clark County and Findings by Michael L. Lawson, Ph.D., Senior Associate, Morgan Angel and Associates, Public Policy Consultants, Washington D.C.* Unpublished manuscript in possession of the author, n.d.

Lewis, David G., Eirik Thorsgard, and Chuck Williams. "Honoring Our Tilixam: Chinookan People of the Grand Ronde." In Boyd, Ames, and Johnson, *Chinookan Peoples of the Lower Columbia*, 307–25.

Lightfoot, Kent G. "Long-Term Developments in Complex Hunter-Gatherer Societies: Recent Perspectives from the Coast of North America." *Journal of Archaeological Research* 1 (1993): 167–200.

Lindquist, Wendi A. "Stealing from the Dead: Scientists, Settlers, and Indian Burial Sites in Early-Nineteenth-Century Oregon." *Oregon Historical Quarterly* 115, no. 3 (2014): 324–43.

Linenthal, Edward T. *The Unfinished Bombing: Oklahoma City in American Memory*. Oxford: Oxford University Press, 2001.

Lonczak, Heather S. V., Lisa Rey Thomas, Dennis Donovan, Lisette Austin, Robin L. W. Sigo,

Nigel Lawrence, and the Suquamish Tribe. "Navigating the Tide Together: Early Collaboration between Tribal and Academic Partners in a CBPR Study." *Pimatisiwin: A Journal of Aboriginal and Indigenous Community Health* 11, no. 3 (2013): 395–409.

Lowenthal, David. "Authenticities Past and Present." *CRM: The Journal of Heritage Stewardship* 6 (2009): 6–17.

Lurie, Nancy O. "The Indian Claims Commission Act." *Annals of the American Academy of Political and Social Science* 311 (1957): 56–70.

———. "The Indian Claims Commission Act." *Annals of the American Academy of Political and Social Science* 436 (1978): 97–110.

MacDonald, G.F. "The Epic of Nekt: The Archaeology of Metaphor." In *The Tsimshian: Images of the Past, Views of the Present*, edited by M. Seguin, 65–81. Vancouver: University of British Columbia Press, 1984.

Marshall, Yvonne. "Transformations of Nuu-chah-nulth Houses." In *Beyond Kinship: Social and Material Reproduction in House Societies*, edited by Rosemary A. Joyce and Susan D. Gillespie, 73–102. Philadelphia: University of Pennsylvania Press, 2000.

Matson, R. G., and Gary Coupland. *The Prehistory of the Northwest Coast*. San Diego: Academic Press, 1995.

McMillan, Alan D. *Since the Time of the Transformers: The Ancient Heritage of the Nuu-chah-nulth, Ditidaht, and Makah*. Vancouver: University of British Columbia Press, 1999.

McNiven, Ian J., and Lynette Russell. *Appropriated Pasts: Indigenous Peoples and the Colonial Culture of Archaeology*. Lanham, MD: AltaMira Press, 2005.

Meskell, Lynn. "Archaeological Ethnography: Conversations around Kruger National Park." *Archaeologies* 1, no. 1 (2005): 81–100.

———. "Archaeological Ethnography: Materiality, Heritage, and Hybrid Methodologies." In *Archaeology and Anthropology: Past, Present and Future*, edited by David Shankland, 133–44. London: Berg, 2012.

———. "Falling Walls and Mending Fences: Archaeological Ethnography in the Limpopo." *Journal of Southern African Studies* 33, no. 2 (2007): 383–400.

———. "The Nature of Culture in Kruger National Park." In *Cosmopolitan Archaeologies*, edited by Lynn Meskell, 89–112. Durham: Duke University Press, 2009.

———. *The Nature of Heritage: The New South Africa*. Oxford: Wiley-Blackwell, 2012.

Meskell, Lynn, and Peter Pels, eds. *Embedding Ethics*. Oxford: Berg, 2005.

Miller, Bruce Granville. *Invisible Indigenes: The Politics of Nonrecognition*. Lincoln: University of Nebraska Press, 2003.

Miller, Mark Edwin. *Forgotten Tribes: Unrecognized Indians and the Federal Acknowledgment Process*. Lincoln: University of Nebraska Press, 2004.

Miller, Robert L. *Native America, Discovered and Conquered: Thomas Jefferson, Lewis and Clark, and Manifest Destiny*. Lincoln, NE: Bison Books, 2008.

Minor, Rick, and Kathryn Anne Toepel. "Archaeological Investigations at 45CL4, Ridgefield National Wildlife Refuge, Clark County, Washington." *Heritage Research Associates Report* 37 (1985).

———. "The Search for the Cathlapotle Village: Archaeological Investigations at 45CL4 in the Lower Columbia Valley." *Archaeology in Washington* 5 (1993): 3–22.

Mitchell, Donald. "Predatory Warfare, Social Status, and the North Pacific Slave Trade." *Ethnology* 23 (1984): 39–48.

Monks, Gregory. "Prey as Bait: The Deep Bay Example." *Canadian Journal of Archaeology* 11 (1987): 119–42.

Moss, Madonna. "Shellfish, Gender, and Status on the Northwest Coast: Reconciling

Archaeological, Ethnographic, and Ethnohistorical Records of the Tlingit." *American Anthropologist* 95 (1993): 631–52.

Moulton, Gary E., ed. *The Definitive Journals of Lewis and Clark*, vol. 5. Lincoln: University of Nebraska Press, 1988.

———. *The Definitive Journals of Lewis and Clark*, vol. 6. Lincoln: University of Nebraska Press, 1990.

———. *The Definitive Journals of Lewis and Clark*, vol. 7. Lincoln: University of Nebraska Press, 1991.

———. *The Definitive Journals of Lewis and Clark*, vol. 10, *The Journal of Patrick Gass*. Lincoln: University of Nebraska Press, 1996.

Neel, David. "Bella Bella: The Rebirth of the Northwest Coast Canoe." *Native Peoples Magazine* 7, no. 2 (1994): 10–18.

———. *The Great Canoes: Reviving a Northwest Coast Tradition*. Vancouver, BC: Douglas & McIntyre, 1995.

Oliver, Emmett. "Reminiscences of a Canoe Puller." In *A Time of Gathering: Native Heritage in Washington State*, edited by Robin K. Wright, 248–53. Seattle: University of Washington Press, 1991.

Olson, Ronald L. "Adze, Canoe, and House Types of the Northwest Coast." *University of Washington Publications in Anthropology* 2, no. 1 (1927): 1–38.

Oregon Historical Society. *Proceedings of the Oregon Historical Society*. Salem: W. H. Leeds, 1900.

Parks, Virginia. "Discover Cathlapotle: Partnerships for the Past and Present, U.S. Fish & Wildlife Service." *CRM* 22, no. 3 (1999): 21–23.

Pettigrew, Richard M. *A Prehistoric Culture Sequence in the Portland Basin of the Lower Columbia Valley*. University of Oregon Anthropological Papers 22. Eugene: University of Oregon, Dept. of Anthropology, 1981.

Philbrick, Nathaniel. *Sea of Glory: America's Voyage of Discovery, the U.S. Exploring Expedition, 1838–1842*. London: Penguin Books, 2003.

Phillips, Kendall R., ed. *Framing Public Memory*. Tuscaloosa: University of Alabama Press, 2004.

Poirier, Claire. "Drawing Lines in the Museum: Plains Cree Ontology as Political Practice." *Anthropologica* 53, no. 2 (2011): 291–303.

Price, T. D. "Complexity in 'Non-complex' Societies." In *Archaeological Approaches to the Study of Complexity*, edited by S. E. van der Leuw, 55–99. Amsterdam: Universiteit van Amsterdam, 1981.

Price, T. D., and J. A. Brown, eds. *Prehistoric Hunter-Gatherers: The Emergence of Cultural Complexity*. San Diego: Academic Press, 1985.

Price, T. D., and G. M. Feinman, eds. *Foundations of Social Inequality*. New York: Plenum Press, 1995.

Pulling Together. Directed by James M. Fortier (with the Muckleshoot Indian Tribe). Turtle Island Productions, 2004. DVD.

Purser, Noel. "Bringing Back the Canoe: A Suquamish Story." In *Tribal Canoe Journeys*, 8–9. Suquamish Tribe, 2009.

Quimby, George I. "Japanese Wrecks, Iron Tools, and Prehistoric Indians of the Northwest Coast." *Arctic Anthropology* 22 (1985): 7–15.

Raibmon, Paige. *Authentic Indians: Episodes of Encounter from the Late-Nineteenth-Century Northwest Coast*. Durham: Duke University Press, 2005.

Ray, Verne. *Handbook of Cowlitz Indians*. Seattle: Northwest Copy, 1966.

———. "The Historical Position of the Lower Chinook in the Native Culture of the Northwest." *Pacific Northwest Quarterly* 28 (1937): 363–72.

Raymond, Anan. Interview by author. Sherwood, Oregon, January 9, 2006.

———. Interview by author. Sherwood, Oregon, March 6, 2007.

Reynolds, Nathan. *"More Dangerous Dead than Living": The Killing of Chief Umtuch*. Longview, WA: Cowlitz Indian Tribe, 2007.

Riding In, James. "Our Dead Are Never Forgotten: American Indian Struggles for Burial Rights and Protections." In *"They Made Us Many Promises": The American Indian Experience, 1524 to the Present*, edited by Philip Weeks, 291–323. Wheeling, IL: Harlan Davidson, 2002.

Robinson, Greg. "The Cathlapotle Plankhouse Project: A Bittersweet Victory." *Chinook Tillicums: The Voice of the Chinook Tribe*, Fall 2004, 1, 3.

Robinson, Sam. BirdFest presentation. Ridgefield, Washington, October 9, 2011.

———. Interview by author. Vancouver, Washington, August 27, 2008.

———. Interview by author. Vancouver, Washington, August 18, 2009.

———. Interview by author. Vancouver, Washington, July 25, 2010.

———. "Welcome Statement." Tenth anniversary celebration of the Cathlapotle Plankhouse, Ridgefield, Washington, March 29, 2015.

Ronda, James P. *Lewis and Clark among the Indians*. Lincoln: University of Nebraska Press, 1984.

Rose, Deborah Bird. "On History, Trees, and Ethical Proximity." *Postcolonial Studies* 11, no. 2 (2008): 157–67.

———. *Wild Dog Dreaming: Love and Extinction*. Charlottesville: University of Virginia Press, 2011.

Rosen, Lawrence. "The Anthropologist as Expert Witness." *American Anthropologist* 79, no. 3 (1977): 555–78.

Rosenthal, Harvey D. "Indian Claims and the American Conscience: A Brief History of the Indian Claims Commission." In *Irredeemable America: The Indians' Estate and Land Claims*, edited by Imre Sutton, 35–70. Albuquerque: University of New Mexico Press, 1985.

———. *Their Day in Court: A History of the Indian Claims Commission*. New York: Garland Publishing, 1990.

Roy, Susan. *These Mysterious People: Shaping History and Archaeology in a Northwest Coast Community*. Montreal: McGill-Queen's University Press, 2010.

Rubertone, Patricia, ed. *Archaeologies of Placemaking: Monuments, Memories, and Engagement in Native North America*. Walnut Creek, CA: Left Coast Press, 2008.

Ruby, Robert H., and John Brown, *The Chinook Indians: Traders of the Lower Columbia River*. Norman: University of Oklahoma Press, 1978.

Sarvis, Will. "Deeply Embedded: Canoes as an Enduring Manifestation of Spiritualism and Communalism among the Coast Salish." *Journal of the West* 42, no. 4 (2003): 74–80.

Schalk, R. F. "The Structure of an Anadromous Fish Resource." In *For Theory Building in Anthropology*, edited by Lewis Binford, 207–49. Orlando: Academic Press, 1977.

Shackel, Paul A., and Erve J. Chambers, eds. *Places in Mind: Public Archaeology as Applied Anthropology*. New York: Routledge, 2004.

Silberman, Neil. "Process Not Product: The ICOMOS Ename Charter (2008) and the Practice of Heritage Stewardship," *CRM: The Journal of Heritage Stewardship* 6, no. 2 (2009): 7–15.

Silverstein, Michael. "Chinookans of the Lower Columbia." In Suttles, *Handbook of North American Indians*, vol. 7, *Northwest Coast*, 533–46.

Smith, Laurajane. *Uses of Heritage*. London: Routledge, 2006.

Smith, Laurajane, and Natsuko Akagawa, eds. *Intangible Heritage*. London: Routledge, 2009.

Smith, Linda Tuhiwai. *Decolonizing Methodologies: Research and Indigenous Peoples*. 2nd ed. London: Zed Books, 2012.

Sobel, Elizabeth A., Kenneth M. Ames, and Robert J. Losey. "Environment and Archaeology of the Lower Columbia." In Boyd, Ames, and Johnson, *Chinookan Peoples of the Lower Columbia*, 23–41.

Sobel, Elizabeth A., D. Ann Trieu Gahr, and Kenneth M. Ames, eds. *Household Archaeology on the Northwest Coast*. Ann Arbor: International Monographs in Prehistory, 2006.

Spier, Leslie. *Tribal Distribution in Washington*. General Series in Anthropology 3. Menasha, WI: George Banta, 1936.

Stewart, Hilary. *Cedar: Tree of Life to the Northwest Coast Indians*. Vancouver, BC: Douglas & McIntyre, 1995.

———. *Indian Fishing: Early Methods on the Northwest Coast*. Vancouver, BC: Douglas & McIntyre, 1977.

Suttles, Wayne. "Coping with Abundance: Subsistence on the Northwest Coast." In *Man the Hunter*, edited by Richard B. Lee and Irven DeVore, 56–68. Chicago: Aldine Press, 1968.

———, ed. *Handbook of North American Indians*, vol. 7, *Northwest Coast*. Washington DC: Smithsonian Institution, 1990.

———. "The Shed-Roof House." In *A Time of Gathering*, edited by Robin K. Wright, 212–22. Seattle: University of Washington Press, 1991.

Swan, James G. *The Northwest Coast, or, Three Years Residence in Washington Territory*. Seattle: University of Washington Press, 1972.

Swanton, John R. *The Indian Tribes of North America*. Smithsonian Institution Bureau of American Ethnology Bulletin 145. Washington DC: Smithsonian Institution, 1952.

Swidler, Nina, Kurt E. Dongoske, Roger Anyon, and Alan S. Downer, eds. *Native Americans and Archaeologists: Stepping Stones to Common Ground*. Walnut Creek, CA: AltaMira Press, 1997.

Tanner, Helen Hornbeck. "In the Arena: An Expert Witness View of the Indian Claims Commission." In *Beyond Red Power: American Indian Politics and Activism since 1900*, edited by Daniel M. Cobb and Loretta Fowler, 178–200. Santa Fe: School for Advanced Research, 2007.

Taylor, Herbert C. *Coast Salish and Western Washington Indians III*. New York: Garland Publishing, 1974.

Thom, Brian. "The Paradox of Boundaries in Coast Salish Territories." *Cultural Geographies* 16 (2009): 179–205.

Thomas, Lisa R., Dennis M. Donovan, and Robin L. W. Sigo. "Identifying Community Needs and Resources in a Native Community: A Research Partnership in the Pacific Northwest." *International Journal of Mental Health and Addiction* 8, no. 2 (2010): 362–73.

Thomas, Lisa R., Dennis Donovan, Robin L. W. Sigo, Lisette Austin, G. Alan Marlatt, and the Suquamish Tribe. "The Community Pulling Together: A Tribal Community-University Partnership Project to Reduce Substance Abuse and Promote Good Health in a Reservation Tribal Community." *Journal of Ethnicity in Substance Abuse* 8, no. 3 (2009): 283–300.

Thomason, Sarah G. "Chinook Jargon in Areal and Historical Context." *Language* 59 (1983): 820–70.

Tribal Journeys Handbook and Study Guide. [Tacoma, WA]: Cedar Media, 2011.

Trieu Gahr, D. Ann. "From Architects to Ancestors: The Life Cycle of Plank Houses." In Sobel, Trieu Gahr, and Ames, *Household Archaeology on the Northwest Coast*, 57–79.

Trieu Gahr, D. Ann, Elizabeth A. Sobel, and Kenneth Ames. Introduction to Sobel, Trieu Gahr, and Ames, *Household Archaeology on the Northwest Coast*, 1–15.

Trigger, Bruce. "Alternative Archaeologies: Nationalist, Colonialist, Imperialist." *Man* [Royal Anthropological Institute of Great Britain and Ireland] 19, no. 3 (1984): 355–70.

Tully, James. *Strange Multiplicity: Constitutionalism in an Age of Diversity*. Cambridge: Cambridge University Press, 1995.

Tweedie, Ann M. *Drawing Back Culture: The Makah Struggle for Repatriation*. Seattle: University of Washington Press, 2002.

UNESCO. *Convention for the Safeguarding of the Intangible Cultural Heritage*. Paris: UNESCO, 2003.

———. *Operational Guidelines for the Implementation of the World Heritage Convention*. Paris: UNESCO, 2015.

US Fish and Wildlife Service. "Memorandum of Understanding between the US Fish and Wildlife Service and the Chinook Indian Tribe." n.d. Copy filed at the US Fish and Wildlife Service Cultural Resources Team Office, Sherwood, Oregon.

———. "Memorandum of Understanding between the US Fish and Wildlife Service and the Cowlitz Indian Tribe." n.d. Copy filed at the US Fish and Wildlife Service Cultural Resources Team Office, Sherwood, Oregon.

Vancouver, George. *A Voyage of Discovery to the North Pacific Ocean and Round the World, 1791–1795*. London: Hakluyt Society, 1984.

Walker, James V. "Henry S. Tanner and Cartographic Expression of American Expansionism in the 1820s." *Oregon Historical Quarterly* 111, no. 4 (2010): 416–43.

Walker, Richard. "Emmett Oliver, Founder of Paddle to Seattle, Walks on at 102." *Indian Country Today Media Network*, March 8, 2016. http://indiancountrymedianetwork.com/.

———. "Pullers Brave Rough Waters to Honor Warriors in Paddle to Quinault." *Indian Country Today Media Network*, August 5, 2013. http://indiancountrymedianetwork.com/.

Waterman, Thomas T., and Geraldine Coffin. *Types of Canoes on Puget Sound*. New York: Museum of the American Indian, Heye Foundation, 1920.

Watkins, Joe. "Native Americans, Western Science, and NAGPRA." *Society for American Archaeology Bulletin* 16, no. 5 (1998). www.saa.org/Portals/0/SAA/publications/SAA bulletin/16-5/SAA16.html.

Whaley, Gray H. "'Complete Liberty'? Gender, Sexuality, Race, and Social Change on the Lower Columbia River, 1805–1838," *Ethnohistory* 54 (2007): 669–95.

———. *Oregon and the Collapse of* Illahee: *U.S. Empire and the Transformation of an Indigenous World, 1792–1859*. Chapel Hill: The University of North Carolina Press, 2010.

Wilkinson, Charles. *The People Are Dancing Again: The History of the Siletz Tribe of Western Oregon*. Seattle: University of Washington Press, 2010.

Winichakul, Thongchai. *Siam Mapped: A History of the Geo-Body of a Nation*. Honolulu: University of Hawaii Press, 1994.

Wissler, F. Clark. *The American Indian: An Introduction to the Anthropology of the New World*. New York: McMurtrie, 1917.

———. "Material Cultures of the North American Indians." *American Anthropologist* 16 (1914): 447–505.

Wuerch, William. "History of the Middle Chinooks to the Reservation Era." Master's thesis, University of Oregon, 1979.

Wylie, Alison. "The Promise and Perils of an Ethic of Stewardship." In Meskell and Pels, *Embedding Ethics*, 47–68.

Zenk, Henry B. and Tony A. Johnson. "Chinook Wawa and its Roots in Chinookan." In Boyd, Ames, and Johnson, *Chinookan Peoples of the Lower Columbia*, 272–87.

———. "A Northwest Language of Contact, Diplomacy, and Identity: Chinuk Wawa/Chinook Jargon." *Oregon Historical Quarterly* 111 (2010): 444–61.

INDEX

Page numbers in italic refer to illustrations.